Naming Properties

卯
觀
子笠
前
行
年
七
十
歲

Bashō Sitting. By Ogawa Haritsu (1663–1747), painter and poet of the Bashō
school. Regarded as one of the more authentic depictions of Bashō. (Courtesy of Professor Konishi Jin'ichi and the Ichiō Museum.)

Naming Properties

Nominal Reference in Travel Writings
by Bashō and Sora, Johnson and Boswell

EARL MINER

Ann Arbor
THE UNIVERSITY OF MICHIGAN PRESS

Publication of this book was generously supported by a grant
from the Japan Foundation.
Published in the United States of America by
The University of Michigan Press
Manufactured in the United States of America
∞ Printed on acid-free paper

1999   1998   1997   1996   4   3   2   1

A CIP catalog record for this book is available from the British Library.

Library of Congress Cataloging-in-Publication Data

Miner, Earl Roy.
    Naming properties : nominal reference in travel writings by Bashō
and Sora, Johnson and Boswell / Earl Miner.
        p.   cm.
    Includes bibliographical references and index.
    ISBN 0-472-10699-6 (alk. paper)
    1. Names in literature.   2. Literature, Comparative—English and
Japanese.   3. Literature, Comparative—Japanese and English.
4. Travel writing.   I. Title.
PN56.N16M56   1996
820.9'355—dc20   96-8830
                                                                      CIP

In Gratitude to
The Japanese Comparative Literature Association
for the Success of the Thirteenth Congress
of the International Comparative Literature Association
and
the American Society for Eighteenth-Century Studies
for having entrusted me with office

Contents

Preface

The four travel accounts considered here are chosen for their intrinsic interest and their comparability. Given their origins, study of them necessarily involves a degree of sustained intercultural comparison that is new, to the best of my knowledge. To provide further grounds of comparison and to elucidate major literary issues, the accounts of journeys are considered in terms of naming. An ancient and perennial subject in literary studies, naming is also a subject of recent excitement among philosophers. For all their insights and examples, philosophers have their difficulties in applying their theories to literature. Because travel accounts necessarily feature names of persons, places, and even of times, they provide—in more than one sense—grounds for studying the properties of names. The voyage on which this study embarks is, then, a new one in its object of discovery and old in its use of literary sails and philosophical oars.

If we seek valid literary generalizations and principles, intercultural evidence is essential. That is simply—or not so simply—because names are used and defined differently relative to various linguistic cultures. Given the nature and the complexity of the variables involved, it has been necessary for me to be as explicit as possible about what is being undertaken. I begin with some characterizing of the individual writings. The next step involves initial comments on naming. As the discussion advances, a set of subjects should be clarified: naming, travel writing, the travel accounts used as examples, and the act of literary comparison itself.

The mere act of recalling a name gives us satisfaction heightened by a sense of authority. The pleasure is yet greater when we find that we are able to supply a name others cannot, or when we devise an intimate name for someone loved. We reach the ordinary limits of our naming authority in choosing, as the philosophers say, a "baptismal name," a denomination of that which had no name before. That is typically a child. But it may be a place. It may be a new variety of flower, a hitherto unknown and therefore unidentified, unnamed comet. Such is the satisfaction, that the discoverer may decide that only a version of her mother's name will serve or that only one's own surname will fit. Human speech is largely represented by two areas of our brain, Broca's and Wernike's. The two discoverers of the functions of those areas no doubt took pride in baptizing those areas with their own names. But how much satisfaction would physicians like Down and Parkinson derive from knowing diseases were named after them?

The duties of secretaries and of police naturally lead to the use of many names. For others of us, the experience richest in names is travel, with a host of new people, a cartography of place-names, and even names of times (Mardi Gras, Saturnalia, St. Bibbia's Day, Tanabata). The more names we encounter in the more places, the greater are the variations we perceive in usages and assumptions. A New Zealander of English extraction traveling in far-off England is not apt to have many surprises or difficulties, but there are sure to be both in a journey through more proximate India or China—nearer in distance but not in culture.

Whether familiar or strange, names are means of identifying what we know. For daily life, the names of those things near to hand are most pressing. Yet to understand the nature, range, and significance of naming, evidence ranging beyond our immediate purviews is so important as to be truly essential. Not all women are named Mary or Marie, Maria or Miriam. Evidence from other ages and places—Nausicaa, Nayantara, and Noriko—increases the adequacy of our understanding. It follows that intercultural evidence is more revealing than intracultural for understanding what it is that people assume when they name, what they imply, and even what they think less important or ignore.

Such matters have been among the motives for undertaking this study. The examples chosen are accounts of two journeys to northern, remote areas of island countries: in 1689 by the Japanese poets Matsuo Bashō (1644–94) and Iwanami (later, Kawai) Sora (1649–1710), and in 1773 by the British writers Samuel Johnson (1709–84) and James Boswell (1740–95). Precious little has been written to guide us in making well-founded, just comparisons of works of such diverse origins.

A long-standing concern with issues of comparability, especially with grounds for such intercultural comparison, has led me to a series of studies culminating in *Comparative Poetics* (1990). Whatever contribution to literary and especially comparative understanding those studies have provided, they have had a deficiency that I seek to remedy here. In my previous work, individual literary examples have been only that: examples. Some of these matters are set forth in the introduction. But the principles and methods making individual writings integral to the study are presented more at length in the first chapter, along with consideration of Western and Asian loci classici of naming and attention to recent philosophical discussions of onomastics, the study of names. The Greeks did indeed have a name for names, *onoma,* whence not only *onomastics* is devised but also Latin *nomen,* from which we have derived our English words *names* and *nouns.* The usual Japanese word for nouns is *meishi,* or "name words." The many Japanese personal nouns used (when they so infrequently are used) instead of our pronouns, the verbs for "to name," and actual practices of employing those various linguistic resources differ considerably from what European languages have to offer.

Two books cited in the bibliography have assisted comparison between the two members of each pair of travelers. Pat Rogers (Rogers 1993) has paired the accounts of Johnson and Boswell, more or less on facing pages. It is a puzzle whether to praise more the freshness of the conception or the handsomeness of the result. Because Johnson's account is so much briefer than Boswell's, Professor Rogers has had the happy idea of adding to Johnson's account letters he sent to Mrs. Thrale in London. Adorned as it is by fine typography, numerous illustrations, and pertinent marginalia, the book is a pleasure to contemplate and read. The editor and I disagree on only one head. He has chosen Boswell's printed version, considerably cut, to pair with Johnson's account, whereas I have preferred Boswell's unrevised—one might better say unbowdlerized or un-maloneized—*Tour,* for reasons that will be noted on occasion. The counterpart, Sugiura Shoichirō's Iwanami Bunko edition (Sugiura 1968), is by no means as attractive a book, but it does print Sora's diary along with Bashō's *Narrow Road through the Provinces* (*Oku no Hosomichi*). In fact, although seldom mentioned by critics, it is an unusually important edition. Both books enable a reader to become, as it were, a third party on the Scottish and Japanese journeys alike.

By a similarly easy metaphor, this book offers to readers one person's service as guide on a journey in intercultural comparative study at once of naming and of four examples of it. It will be the choice of my readers to decide whether the aim of this intellectual travel is the typical Western one of discovery of the unknown or the typical Japanese one of confirmation of the known. Perhaps we can learn from such study both to discover and confirm things about ourselves.

Acknowledgments

Professional and legal requirements must be satisfied first. For use of pictures and calligraphy from Yosa Buson's *Oku no Hosomichi Emaki*, I am grateful to Itsuō Bijitsukan and Yutaka Shobō. I must thank Professor Konishi Jin'ichi for securing the permission, as also for making available Ogawa Haritsu's portrait of Bashō used as the frontispiece. I am happy to acknowledge the aid and permission of the Princeton University Libraries, including the Gest Oriental Library and the Department of Rare Books. The latter was the source of illustrations from the following: Charles Cordimer, *Antiquities and Scenery of the North of Scotland*, 1780; Cordimer, *Remarkable Ruins and Romantic Prospects of North Britain*, 1788; Francis Grose, *The Antiquities of Scotland*, 1797; Thomas Pennant, *A Tour in Scotland and Voyage to the Hebrides*, 1774; and Thomas Rowlandson, *The Picturesque Beauties of Boswell*, 1786. The Department also did the photographic work for Buson's *Emaki*.

It is a forlorn hope to acknowledge all the assistance received in the lengthy period of study and writing period required for this book. A few names will have to stand for many, with the bibliography a kind of intellectual index. If it includes, as it does, a number of titles of my own, that is for more than one reason. It enables me to acknowledge the publishers and journal editors who have helped me identify subjects, devise principles, and improve methods. It also gives access to further evidence than is often appropriate here: some studies have appeared in less than obvious places. Otherwise, the bibliography is confined to the most pertinent work by others, and an unadorned citation often signals a great intellectual indebtedness. Those works cited so frequently as to justify abbreviated references have obviously been indispensable.

The University of Michigan Press engaged a scholar of Japanese literature whose comments I deeply appreciate and whose anonymity I honor, little appropriate though it is for this study that I cannot give the name. Although the Press did not require it, a reader well acquainted with Johnson and Boswell was, I knew, essential. And here I can name an old and respected friend, Jean H. Hagstrum, who read every word. I am deeply grateful for the assistance of his learning, for his identification of especially Japanese matters requiring elaboration or clarification, and for his numerous suggestions. It was his last scholarly act before illness led to death on 2 November 1995.

Readers acquainted with my work in Japanese will know that I have debts of many years to Konishi Jin'ichi (unless otherwise noted, the Japanese order of names is used). Those debts began in 1957 and, for this book, ended with the final revisions in 1995. His generous friendship is itself a major blessing for what is now nearly four decades. It will be less obvious that Jin'ichi and my sometimes coauthor Odagiri Hiroko have assisted my radical reassessment of features of Bashō's *Narrow Road through the Provinces*. Although I have never met the poet and Bashō critic Andō Tsuguo, over the years his criticism has stimulated my ideas of the design of Bashō's art.

Others I wish to thank include Kawamoto Kōji, Bruce Redford, Greg Clingham, Jonathan Arac, Eleanor Kerkham, J. T. Rimer, and, with Western name order, Makoto Ueda and Hiroaki Sato. Jonathan Lamb read the whole, making numerous observations in a letter that became a study in itself. I have no doubt omitted the names of many other people who have mattered, and apologize to them for my neglect.

My three greatest authorial pleasures in writing this book have been: first, learning to appreciate—beyond an already lively sense of the matter—the sheer complexity of Bashō's *Narrow Road;* next, discovering Boswell's difficulties in understanding himself; and lastly, rolling up my sleeves in the effort to wrestle with Plato's *Cratylus* and philosophical studies in its wake. But I have deeply enjoyed hearing again the Johnsonian music in both his own deep baritone version and Boswell's lively tenor. Also, in learning how difficult it is to ascertain details about Bashō's *Oku no Hosomichi,* I have come to appreciate even Sora's *Nikki*—a degree of understanding that I hesitate to measure.

The assistance of my good friends Nakanishi Susumu and Haga Tōru provided me with an invaluable visiting professorship for six months at the International Research Center for Japanese Studies in Kyoto. I thank them wholeheartedly for an exciting and fruitful period, aided by the hospitality of the academic and professional staff. From the latter, Usui Sachiko eased and enhanced our visit before, during, and after our stay in Kyoto. Other visitors to the Center from around the world brought excitement and unusual compression of time to our visit. We enjoyed the use of an apartment and other benefits from Otemae College. For that we wish to thank Fukui Hideka. And to her generosity we must add the kindness of Mori Michiko, a fellow Miltonist, along with Fujii Haruhiko and Fusako. It is difficult to believe that he and Michiko were students of mine in 1960–61 or that Fusako preceded us to Princeton when she studied at the Westminster Choir College. Before moving to the Otemae apartment we had the privilege of using the Higashiyama-Sanjō, Kyoto apartment of Kamachi Mitsuru (whose washing machine bears the trade name Shizuka Gozen, and one of whose pillowcases the Heart Sutra). The arrangements for that and other good things were made by Murakata Akiko, with whom we are related by the connection between her father and my wife's parents. But to enter further into Kansai and Hokkaido friendships would require another book.

The period at the Center was part of a year of leave also supported by Princeton University. I am very grateful for that as also for a visiting professorship at Stanford University in the spring quarter term of 1994. That was made possible by my friend Makoto Ueda, whose kindness is proverbial. I can say all too feelingly that I must thank the staff of the Stanford Hospital for easing the first painful period of a seriously broken back. I would also thank my Princeton physicians if they had not forbidden me to drink wine because of that crazy spine.

There are two published versions of lectures that ought to be mentioned, because both contain much that is important conceptually to this study and some matter that could not be treated here. Before the thirteenth congress of the International Comparative Literature Association in Tokyo (August 1991) Kansai Gaidai University invited me to give a talk half in Japanese and half in English and asked to publish an essay of mine on the topic. To the latter end, I extended considerably a previous lecture in English given at the International Research Center for Japanese Studies at the invitation of Nakanishi Susumu. This became "Boswell and Johnson in the Footsteps of Bashō: *Oku no Hosomichi* and the Tour of the Hebrides," *Journal of Intercultural Studies* 19 (1992): 22–53. After the congress a smaller conference was held in Yamagata at the invitation of Haga Tōru, and a talk there was later published: "*Oku no Hosomichi* ni Okeru 'Mono no Na,'" *Dentō Bungaku to Sono Fusensei— Bashō, Mokichi, Miyazawa Kenji* (Yamagata: Yamagata Prefecture Life-long Learning Center, 1993), pp. 1–5. A subsequent tour of part of the route traversed by Bashō and Sora was among the many things to make that occasion memorable. I am grateful to both institutions for the invitations to speak and for providing me with steps toward this book. Princeton University also assisted my tour of certain parts of Scotland traversed by Johnson and Boswell but new to me. One or two photographs reproduced as figures derive from that investigation.

I am grateful as well for important assistance in readying this study for the printer. Hosea Hirata prepared the copy for the itinerary of Bashō and Sora, which accompanies a map drawn originally by Mary Potter of the School of Geography at Oxford for my *Japanese Poetic Diaries*. And Joann Boscarino of the Department of Photographs and Slides of the Marquand Art Library at Princeton has made the map for Johnson and Boswell's Scottish tour.

There is another person whom it is unnecessary to name and whose role these forty-five years has been greater than even she knows. To her, to those others named or categorized, to those in the dedication, and to those a faulty memory has overlooked I offer my gratitude.

However much assisted, authors do not actually make books. They rely on the professional talents of others to translate words into bound pages. It is with great pleasure that I close these acknowledgments with the names of people at the University of Michigan Press. They are Kevin Rennells, the copyediting coordinator; Jillian Downey, the production coordinator; and Lisa Langhoff, the jacket designer. From her first quick response to my inquiry Susan B. Whitlock has won my gratitude, satisfaction, and peace of mind. I wish other authors the services I have enjoyed from my copyeditor, Richard Isomaki. At a number of publishers, many of Richard's predecessors have edited books for me, to my considerable advantage, but none with his uncanny ability to distinguish what was important from what was indifferent, to enter into the spirit of the book with such vicarious understanding. In thanking them, I must not add the error of thinking that they have saved me from leaving errors uncorrected. But there is some satisfaction to an author, this one, even in knowing that the errors that have eluded detection are his own. Let the credit be theirs.

Illustrations

Figures

Abbreviations

The following are abbreviations for works frequently cited.

Diaries Bashō. *Oku no Hosomichi*. In *Japanese Poetic Diaries*, ed. and trans. Earl Miner. Berkeley and Los Angeles: University of California Press, 1969.

Journey Samuel Johnson. *A Journey to the Western Islands of Scotland*. Ed. J. D. Fleeman. Oxford: Clarendon, 1985.

Nikki Sora. *Sora Oku no Hosomichi Zuikō Nikki.* . . . Ed. Yamamoto Yasusaburō. Ogawa Shobo, 1943.

Taisei *Teihon Bashō Taisei*. Ed. Ogata Tsutomu et al. Sanshōdō, 1962.

Tour James Boswell. *The Journal of a Tour to the Hebrides with Samuel Johnson, LL.D.* Ed. Frederick A. Pottle and Charles H. Bennett. New Haven: Yale University Press, 1936.

Zenkō Matsuo Bashō. *Oku no Hosomichi Zenkō*. Ed. Matsuo Yasuaki. Chūdōkan, 1974.

Introduction

"Must a name mean something?" Alice asked doubtfully.
 —Carroll, *Through the Looking-Glass*

they also spend their days in travel and
make their home in wayfaring.

 —Bashō

"The knowledge of names is a great part of knowledge," Plato said in his *Cratylus*.[1] Each of us knows the satisfaction, even the feeling of authority, that comes with the mere act of recalling a name. We reach the ordinary limits of our authority in choosing that "baptismal name" of the philosopher's usage—a denomination for that which had no name before. That is typically a child, but it may be a place, a gadget, or a theorem. The importance of naming to our lives has ensured its place in myth and sacred writings as well as its study by literary critics, philosophers, geographers, and others. In some eyes the study loses no appeal when garbed in the Hellenic dignity of "onomastics."

We need only consider what literature (or the rest of life) would be like if there were no names. But of course we know that there *are* names. Yes, but what does "names" mean in the phrases, "if there were no names" and "there are names"? What are the properties necessary for a word (or phrase) to be a name? For all the effort devoted to the subject, it seems to have had little attention involving, at the same time, those general issues and literary practice. This book addresses the issues in comparative terms, attending closely to four examples of English and Japanese travel literature. Those are examined with attention to ancient lore and to recent philosophical studies.

---

1. Jowett 1892, 1:323. See the bibliography for full citations. The remark is made by Socrates in his first speech and is never gainsaid, so being one of the few certainties in the dialogue.

Few important subjects were lost on Milton, who begins the eighth book of *Paradise Lost* by invoking a Muse:

> Descend from Heav'n *Urania,* by that name
> If rightly thou art call'd, whose Voice divine
> Following, above th' Olympian Hill I soar,
> Above the flight of *Pegasean* wing.
> The meaning, not the Name I call: for thou
> Not of the Muses nine, nor on the top
> Of old *Olympus* dwell'st, but Heav'nly born,
> Before the Hills appear'd, or Fountain flow'd,
> Thou with Eternal Wisdom didst converse,
> Wisdom thy Sister, and with her didst play
> In presence of th' Almighty Father, pleas'd
> With thy Celestial Song.

Milton seems to be saying that by Urania, the Greek Muse of astronomy and of Christianized celestial knowledge, he means the Holy Spirit. Since he uses or drops no few names, he must truly be interested in their meanings if he calls for them rather than for names in themselves.

Two trials held in Milton's century suitably offer other evidence of the varied properties of people's names. In the better known of the two, the defendant, one Faithful, is arraigned before the judge, Lord Hategood, whose last declaration to the jury is that the defendant deserves to die the death. The jurors who file out are the foreman, Mr. Blind-man, followed by Mr. No-good, Mr. Malice, Mr. Love-lust, and so on to Mr. Implacable. This trial in Vanity Fair is one of the unforgettable moments in Bunyan's *Pilgrim's Progress,* and most readers today assume the names to be purely artificial and allegorical. But at a trial in Sussex in 1609, the jury did in fact include Kill Sin Pimple, Fly Debate Roberts, More Fruit Fowler, God Reward Smart, Be Faithful Joiner, and Fight the Good Fight of Faith White. During the national commotions between the two trials, it is sweet and decorous that a man named Richard Lovelace was a Cavalier and that another, John Wildman, was a Roundhead. Goldsmith observed similarly that little poetry could have been expected from a Restoration versifier called Elkanah Settle. The twentieth century has been enlarged in some sense by William Faulkner's gift of memorable names such as Montgomery Ward Snopes and Wall Street Panic Snopes. To these fictional denominations our fellow citizens have devised names for figures other than Milton's celestial sisters. Like the other names mentioned, Ima and Eura Hogg or the businessman Armand Hammer testify to our sense of the meaningfulness and the inscrutability as well of human ingenuity as of Providence divine.

We mere mortals may have difficulty with names, meanings, and their properties. How many of us know what we term the real names of Joseph Stalin, Marilyn Monroe, and Mishima Yukio? Do not countries change in name frequently? Do not standard and daylight saving (summer) time differ, and are there not on this earth more than twenty-four "times" at any given instant? (Some countries like India set but half an hour difference in adjoining areas.) What differences exist between fictional and real names, between names in the news: of people and of corporations?

It will be evident that the first crucial issue is not that question raised by Shakespeare's Juliet, "What's in a name?" It is rather what *is* a name? The answers are various, complex, and by no means consistent. Some answers, the three in Plato's *Cratylus* for example, seem to assume that a name is any, or almost any, word. Some answers (Plato's own in that dialogue, for example) are so—so profound?—that is sometimes difficult to agree with oneself as to what it all means.

Our bafflement clearly does not occur without reason. A major problem with naming is what has been already questioned: what does the word include, and what indeed does it exclude? When we posit, with some confidence, the importance of one category, we find it difficult to exclude the next similar one. Everyone seems to agree that a single proper noun is a name. Then what of plural proper nouns? What of singular common nouns? Or plural?

Most philosophers are willing to consider certain predicates to be equivalent to names, as of James Madison, *fourth president of the United States of America,* for example. What, then, of *President Madison?* Then there are surnames: Charlemagne, Karl der Grosse; Ethelred the Unready, "good Queen Anne." Japanese has personal nouns where English has pronouns: is there an onomastic difference, or is the difference only, as we say, nominal? Since *noun* as well as *name* derives from Latin *nomen* (from Greek *onoma*), should we include all nouns—and noun phrases ("fourth president of the United States of America" again)? And if the noun, *red,* why not the adjective, a form of predication like that for Madison? And if any predicates at all, why exclude verbs?

If one can imagine consensus among philosophers, they seem (when pressed) to include all parts of speech except articles or particles (this book is concerned with Japanese, too), and connectives like *of, also,* and their kin. The reasons for the exclusion are not wholly clear to me, but it is very, very evident that philosophers wish to talk about singular proper nouns as much as possible.

On his Scottish journey, Samuel Johnson found that even so close to home naming practices might differ from those familiar south of the Tweed (*Journey,* 127–28):

> Where races are thus numerous, and thus combined, none but the Chief of a clan is addressed by his name. The Laird of *Dunvegan* is called *Macleod,* but other gentlemen of the same family are denominated by the places where they reside, as *Raasay,* or *Talisker.* The distinction of the meaner people is made by their Christian names. . . .
>
> Our afternoon journey was through a country of such gloomy desolation, that Mr. *Boswell* thought no part of the Highlands equally terrifick, yet we came without any difficulty, at evening, to *Lochbuy,* where we found a true Highland Laird, rough and haughty, and tenacious of his dignity; who, hearing my name, inquired whether I was of the *Johnstons* of *Glencoe,* or of *Ardnamurchan.*

Since this study deals with journeys, it will be confined almost entirely to a restricted range of names, those with which philosophers are most comfortable. The concern is with three kinds of proper names (or words like such names): those for people (mostly who travel); for places (mostly visited); and for times. For our January, the most common name in classical Japanese was Mutsuki, but there were over forty other names. The twelve months of thirty days had sometimes multiple names for a given day (such as the last), but no weeks with their repeated days were distinguished until modern times. We can settle for First Month and last day, or use I.30 for shorthand. A day had twelve hours (of double the minutes of ours), and we can get by with rough equivalents to our twenty-four.

These details suggest what is manifestly the case: consideration of the meaning of names in literature is not a matter of one language or culture. Only comparative study can explain the different properties borne by names in different literatures. To give the properties some differential range, comparison should be intercultural—ideally encompassing the full range of variety. This study does not meet that ideal, considering as it does mostly Japanese and English evidence. There is more than one reason for that. It is not necessary to dwell on the spacious gaps in my knowledge. There is also the difficult matter of the right amount of data. Too little sends us, like students of antiquity, to coins, inscriptions, and guesswork. Too much thwarts us, like students of modernity, from locating in the huge piles of data those that constitute grounds for evidence.

The first chapter deals with those matters by identifying the four travelers and their journeys—Bashō and Sora in 1689, Boswell and Johnson in 1773—and by reviewing the grounds of principled comparison. It continues by setting the specific names involved in two contexts: one context being the "classical places" of Eastern and Western antiquity and the other the ideas of our contemporary philosophers. The literary, logical, and cognitive issues are reviewed, and some conclusions stated, in the last chapter. One issue from these more general discussions of naming, that just referred to as "the grounds of principled comparison," is held off for its initial discussion as the last problem in this introduction.

Each of the two journeys saw its pair of travelers through remote areas of island countries. In the spring of 1689 Bashō and his younger disciple Sora left Edo (now Tokyo), heading at first toward the northeast. (For their route, see fig. 1.) It is hard to imagine a more factual or unappealing record of that departure than what Sora recorded.

> On III.20 depart Fukagawa Depart by boat. Reach Senju before
>   11 A.M.
> —27th   Spend the night at Kasugae More than 35 km from Edo
> —28th   Spend the night at Mamata About 35 km from Kasugae
>   From night before rain falls Stops by 8 A.M. (*Nikki*, 3)

Many days later, near the northern end of the main island of Japan, they crossed west over the mountains to the Sea of Japan side. From there they turned southwest along the coast. In reaching Kanazawa, where they turned southeast to recross the island, the road now lay out of what were perceived of as the remote provinces. The season had now turned to the fall of the year, and Bashō last reports taking a boat for the

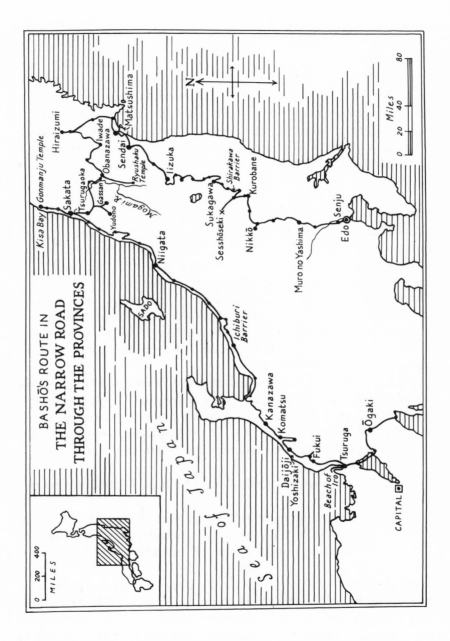

Fig. 1. Map and principal places of the *Oku no Hosomichi* journey. With Japanese for major place-names. (From Miner 1969.)

The Narrow Road Through the Provinces
奥の細道

Months	Days	Places (See Appendix I)	
III.	20.	Edo, Sampū's Cottage	杉風の別宅
	27.	Senju	千住
	29.	Muro no Yashima	室の八島
IV.	1.	Nikkō	日光
	3.	Kurobane	黒羽
	19.	Sesshōseki	殺生石
	22.	Sukagawa	須賀川
V.	3.	Iizuka	飯塚
	4.	Sendai	仙台
	9.	Matsushima	松島
	12.	Hiraizumi	平泉
	14.	Iwade, Shitomae no Seki	岩出、尿前の関
	17.	Obanazawa	尾花沢
	27.	Ryūshakuji	立石寺
VI.	1.	Gassan, Yudono	月山、湯殿
	10.	Tsurugaoka, Sakata	鶴が丘、酒田
	15.	Kisagata	象潟
VII.	2.	Niigata	新潟
	12.	Ichiburi no Seki	市振の関
	15.	Kanazawa	金沢
	24.	Komatsu	小松
VIII.	?8.	Daishōji, Zenshōji	大聖寺、全昌寺
	?13.	Fukui	福井
	14.	Tsuruga	敦賀
	16.	Beach Iro no Hama	種の浜
IX.	?3.	Ōgaki	大垣

grand shrines at Ise. He would not return to Edo for two more years
(Sora did, however). His account in *The Narrow Road through the Provinces (Oku no Hosomichi)* involved numerous side-excursions, pauses,
and omissions from his narrative. But it can be visualized more or less
as a counterclockwise movement of a leftward tilting and bent clock
from approximately three up to twelve and back down to six.

The journey made by Johnson and Boswell is remarkably similar in
its counterclockwise movement upward from Edinburgh, across the
Highlands, from isle to isle of the Hebrides, back to the main island, and
then to Edinburgh again. (See fig. 2.) One hundred days passed from
Johnson's arrival in that Lowlands city to his departure. He strikingly
omits it and Glasgow from his account. Boswell makes a great deal of
Johnson's two periods in Edinburgh, no doubt thinking rightly that his
triumph in getting the great British lion to Scotland would be most
appreciated there.

The chief places and dates mentioned in the accounts of the two
journeys are set forth in appendix 1.

Chapters 2 to 4 deal with the accounts made by the four travelers.
The second chapter provides initiation in several senses: initiation in
the kinds of names that dominate, both in the journeys and in the
differing accounts of those journeys. Sora and Boswell hold to the daily-
record form of diaries, although there is no little retrospection and
preview in Boswell's account. Sora took as his responsibility recording
his poetic master's journey with a solemn self-denial concealing certain
genuine merits. Johnson's method is, with one major exception, narration of the journey by short chapters given place-names as titles. The
exception involves an excursus or essay of considerable length worked
into the entry for "Ostig in Sky[e]." Bashō emphasizes places, although
his account is continuous, not disparted. He gives dates only infrequently (and then not always accurately), but the sense of time's passage is sustained by means of setting his account radically apart from
the other three: the inclusion of poetry largely accounting for progress
from that spring to that fall. The poems, passages, and allusions are
very numerous indeed, including Chinese as well as Japanese, poems in
the waka form inherited from antiquity, and—most significantly—fifty
of his own hokku. (Hokku or "opening stanzas" are those that initiate,
or are written as if to initiate, a renga or haikai linked sequence; the
haiku form developed in later times from hokku.)

The brevity of this second chapter yields to much increased length

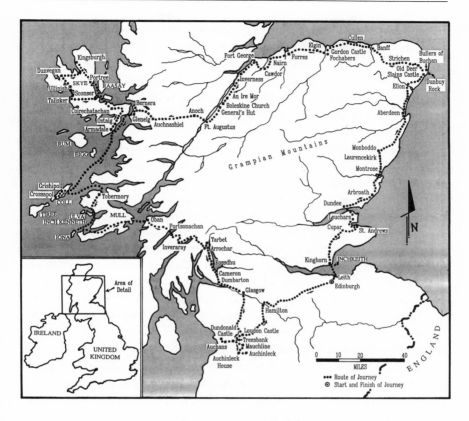

Fig. 2. Map of the Scottish journey.

in the next two. The third chapter deals with that crucial stage of travel narratives, the stage when the journey and its account have begun but when the conception of the journey and the method of narrating it must be fully worked out. Sora shows no change from the boniness of his opening: the date and time, weather, place of departure, distances between places—then the next place, time of arrival, persons met, any happenings (e.g., temple visit, verse composition); then again the date and time, weather . . . Johnson's account adds a physiology to Sora's anatomy. He remarks on the sparsely populated areas just out of Edinburgh, the ruins of old ecclesiastical buildings, and what he thinks is the total absence of trees older than himself. It is a grim landscape, and some grand ancient artifacts have suffered from what Johnson not altogether cooly attributes to the barbarous behavior of Knox and the Scottish Reformation. When he names individual Scots, however, he is consistently lavish with gratitude for good treatment and omits much that Boswell shows annoyed him. This mixture is delivered in a style remarkable for its compromise of Caesar-like clarity and Cicero-like balance. Those features are directed by a conceptual generalizing that can be prized in his phrase as the "grandeur of generality" or as what is simply a powerful, selective intelligence.

Boswell's account of their getting under way also traces the route from Edinburgh up to and across the Highlands and onward to the verge of a boat to the Hebrides. Boswell is also clear, but in a different way and about significantly different things. His clarity is partly the product of a far lengthier account kept from garrulousness and tedium by a sense of human interactions. As with Austen in one of her most prized styles, Boswell combines situation and action with dialogue in a way featuring distinct tones and accents. Whether words are actually spoken or not, Boswell's own style bears the air of conversation, and his narration is dramatically scenic. His exertion of the closest possible attention to others has a motivation that gradually becomes clear: if he can only successfully show what others are like, he will discover the key to the most interesting mystery of all, himself.

Bashō's record of getting under way sees him to the two points that his opening had named as his particular interests. These are the relics of the Shirakawa Barrier point (Shirakawa no Seki) and the moon at one of the three places thought most beautiful in Japan, Matsushima. By long tradition, the Shirakawa Barrier represented the gate to the remote northern and eastern provinces. From numerous earlier poems, the barrier had become a special site, one of the places of name (nadokoro) of great price in Japanese literature. We shall observe later the significance of 1689 being half a millennium after the deaths of two figures important to Bashō. People of the past seem to hover, and people of the present to disappear, at this stage of Bashō's art. (By contrast Sora's account is well populated by names.) Between the two famous places Bashō leaves us a sense of drifting through a summer landscape marked by place-names and his complex, brooding mind. His account reaches a climax and crisis at Matsushima. The many islands making up the place are personified to a degree probably not paralleled in Japanese literature. As place seems to replace people, Bashō the deeply reflective poet narrates in eloquent prose the personal crisis of his *not* writing in verse about Matsushima. Puzzling over these matters makes the reader acutely aware that Bashō is not only the most complex of the four travelers but also the most varied. To an extent probably unreproducible in another language, he often writes passages that begin with the aura of Chinese prose and then shift decisively to correction by either the purity of classical Japanese or the mixed style of Japanese cum Sinified diction that is the basis of the language today. His tone or attitude is often mixed, straining the understanding of careful readers. Appropriately but mystifying enough, the crisis Bashō faces at Matsushima causes a crisis in our own understanding. Attention to his literary traditions and his conception of the whole is necessary for us to convince ourselves that he and we have understood the nature of the problem and solved it.

Bashō's crisis suggests a general problem for travel writing. This can be viewed in terms of the relation between the wayfarer's sensibility and the numerous people and places that are its objects. The problem turns on the traveler's capacity to give meaning to the names of those people and places: to do so requires both that they have discoverable meanings and that the discoverer can devise new names or use old ones significantly. These problems are but part of a larger one of the ends of the journey—what is sought and how to find it. Only Boswell can be said to have in mind an Odyssean nostos, and even for him that is far too simple. Parting from Johnson in Edinburgh was hardly the end he sought. No doubt all narrative involves not merely sequence but continuum to some telos, an end often realized in the sequential process itself. In older theological terms, that end is the anagogy or quo tendit of the work.

The lengthiest chapter in this study, the fourth, seeks to deal with these matters in all four travel accounts. In one sense, each of the four is examined in turn for the same thing, for what revolves on the axis of the individual's ideology. By ideology is meant, not the distorted thinking by others, but that complex of ideas, motives, ideals, and interests functioning in everyone's thought and action, sometimes in contradictory but more often in mutually reinforcing ways. Approached in these terms, even Sora acquires a degree of independent interest. Johnson's qualified mercantilism and nationalism make Scotland more interesting to him than he had expected.

Boswell's urgent need to understand himself, and the socially interactive means by which he sought to satisfy it, are manifested in many ways. Johnson is certainly the object of his attention. But nobody else in his account holds for us, or for him, the interest and mystery he does to himself. Yet he does not like to be alone. As a result, he is steadily more successful in understanding others than in understanding himself. As if he were a handful of quicksilver, he finds himself slipping through his own grasp. He requires other people, Johnson in particular, to fix his sense of himself. Fortunately, their very names bring them into focus and thereby provide his means of steadying his own vertiginous sense of himself. Readers of his *Life* of Johnson will recall his wife's dislike of the gross, corpulent, awkward genius of the day. Readers of his *London Journal* will recall his basically sordid infidelities. Readers of his journal of this Hebrideian tour will find that he does not name his wife or their daughter. It is as though the mark left by Scottish Calvinism on him was not the cry of Bunyan's Christian ("What shall I do to be sav'd?") but "What does the name *Jemmy Boswell* mean?" On days of good fortune, he knew the answer, which he did not so much lose as require anew on another day.

The extraordinary skill exhibited in the prose and the unwonted inability to write poetry at Matsushima testify to Bashō's sustained intensity in devising means to combine ever-shifting nuances of high and low, fact and fiction, comedy and tragedy, repose and exertion, silence and sound: to make his journey into art. In one fashion or another that effort is basic to the achievement of the other three as well, and indeed of any artist. In Bashō's case, however, making his journey into art was (in a metaphor he famously literalized) the second step. The prior step was to conceive of his haikai art as a journey. For as he said, the initial stanza (hokku) of a linked poetry sequence was his journey's first step, from which there was no thought of turning back.

On this understanding, the leg of the journey leading to the Shirakawa Barrier site and on to Matsushima reveals some matters we had partially understood and others that we had not suspected to exist. The strikingly unusual attention to places and their names while ignoring people and their names adapts to his haikai art centuries of aesthetic practice. Not only is he concerned with places long known to poets as places of name (nadokoro) but also with lowlier places that his haikai art can make into new places of old name, as it were.[2] The reasons or

---

2. Although Bashō is still sometimes called a poet of haiku, the word was not in use in his day. And although he wrote what he termed opening stanzas, hokku (which are formally the simulacrum and historically the origin of haiku), his pride was his haikai art of linked-poetry sequences (*Taisei*, 652). On linked poetry, see appendix 2.

evidence for that are chiefly two things. One is that by contrast to the Western understanding of travel—as voyage into or discovery of the unknown—Japanese travel is poetically understood as confirmation of what had been poetically known, although it lay on hitherto untraveled ways.

This is underscored by the definition of travel as something away from the capital or between two other points; to go to the capital was to "return" from poetic places of name. For another thing, Bashō emphasizes the significance of places of name by understanding many of his place-names literally. Not only does Ryūshakuji mean "temple of rocks standing on rocks," but visiting it shows that it is so. The Sinified name Gassan is translated to poetically pure Japanese Tsuki no Yama for a hokku in which it does become "mountain in moonlight." He presented himself in verse and prose alike as a traveler (tabibito), defining both his life and art as travel.

Bashō's naming may be said to itinerize art as a prior step to aestheticizing travel. That order of stages is attested to in his recorded conversations and, as recent criticism in Japan has made clear, has taken on a third dimension in the modeling of *The Narrow Road through the Provinces* upon a haikai sequence. This is a matter too complex for explanation at this stage, but one illustration (with or without a look at appendix 2) can serve. Unlike the heads of the two schools of haikai in rivalry with his own, he insisted on the importance of the agitation introduced by love (usually erotic yearning for what is absent or lost) to the lengthy middle of the three parts of a linked poetry sequence. A hokku by Sora on waterfowl as a conjugal emblem is traditional, and the next by Bashō on the eve of the Seventh Night Festival anticipates the celestial Herd Boy's single annual tryst with his beloved Weaver Girl. Those are followed by an encounter with two prostitutes—revealed by Sora's *Nikki* to be a fictional event—a very haikai treatment of love. The final love "stanza" is the episode at Fukui, in which echoes of *The Tale of Genji* turn a shabbily dressed old woman into a comic version of Genji's first great love, Yūgao, and Bashō himself into a yet more comic version of Radiant Genji.

The evidence of such famous names of literature being applied with such good humor to a woman as old and humbly dressed as he is himself proves the extent to which he recovers after Matsushima. Significantly enough, these adapted love-episodes and shifts into comedy often involve veiled political criticism or a pessimism needing all the relief that can be envisioned. The metaphysical basis of these matters must await fuller discussion.

For now it suffices to predict confidently what readers will discover: that by a just fusion of travel and art, and by a just naming of their joint constituents, Bashō provides not only the most beautiful but also the most profound account among these four, and indeed a masterpiece that in one sense is longer as well as greater than the others. Boswell possesses greater fascination in his excited failure to understand what Bashō understood all too well as the tragic journey and comic travail of haikai art. A second or third reading is also required for a reader to appreciate Johnson's mental clarity. He offers a remarkable fusion of the general with the particular, using even omissions to promote moral cognition. Sora: his virtues are lesser, often in fact negligible but sometimes essential.

The final chapter returns, with knowledge of the now much examined four accounts, to philosophical considerations of naming. These include possible differences between fictional and factual naming, a distinction that these four dominantly factual accounts show to be too stark. But the philosophers who have attended seriously to naming emphasize certain conditions that are timely reminders to an age in which too many critics have been jesting Pilates or unavailing nominalists. (Yet it is as hard to make good a claim to be Plato's Cratylus as his Hermogenes.) The act of naming is irrefutably intentional and referential. It may be silly, as were the pious seventeenth-century parents who named their son Fight the Good Fight of Faith. And it may be mistaken, as all of us have discovered because of, and to, our confusion at various times. But it is a common human act of reference, a way of identifying and making sense of things in an existing world. Plato's Cratylus no doubt exaggerated the connections between words and things, but it was a mistake about and in a real world.

Some of these issues are illustrated by the fact that Japanese has two verbs, "to name." One, *nazukeru,* is nothing other than what those philosophers termed baptismal naming, "giving a name" to that which had none (e.g., a newborn child), whereas the other, *nazasu,* is what we usually mean by naming, "using a name" that designates something. Plato's conventionalist Hermogenes was right to argue that "to give a name" (nazukeru) is an arbitrary, convention-making act. But he was wrong to presume that therefore "to use a name" (nazasu) is arbitrary, since *not* to use the conventionally established name is the willful, arbitrary act. As poets certainly know, names (words) undergo change or may be meaningfully altered. But to exceed the license of using rather than being used by convention is social as well as intellectual solecism. One is in trouble by thinking seriously that Fuji is Japanese for "fudge." There are good reasons for learning the periodic table of the elements and for keeping out of the reach of children medicines whose labels they cannot understand. Each of our four writers of travel records puts such things differently, but each also shows that naming is intentional, that it refers to something presumed real, and that the three most important coordinates of that reality are designated by the names of people, places, and times.

Bashō and Sora, Boswell and Johnson show their understandings of these matters in their individual ways, just as we can understand their ways by our individual own. This is one of that very large number of things that would go without saying if we could readily say what going *with* implies. The things said to this point obviously deal with understandings of journeys by two pairs of often foot-weary travelers who had no knowledge of each other and with the very different understandings of travel in the two cultures. It has been presumed all along that it is possible to assume principled comparison between them. It remains a scandal that we self-styled comparatists have shown such indifference to what may be called the canons of comparability. What *is* the nature and what *are* the means of just comparative study (of literature)?

In an earlier book (Miner 1990) I sought to provide a first account of poetics—theories of literature—conceived by intercultural comparison. That book grew directly from an earlier long essay on the genesis of systematic theories of literature (1978–79), from a study of mimetic and alternative views of art (1983), and from a study of the nature and implications of various kinds of literary collections (1985). In yet another essay (1987), I tried to suggest canons for literary (and other) comparison. In none of these studies was there any extended uniting of the problem of comparing with consideration of actual literary examples, a serious omission that this study is intended to repair.

Just comparison is governed by two easily understood constraints. We cannot logically compare something with itself, since the supposed two elements are not dual but one, identical. At the other extreme, we cannot justly compare things that are too different, because we then no longer are comparing the (sufficiently) same things. In practice, there is little danger that we shall attempt to compare something to itself and considerable danger that the things compared will be insufficiently alike. This problem is especially acute precisely in that realm which holds greatest promise, intercultural comparisons. It would be an egregious error to think that a common date of circa 1000 C.E. was a sufficient basis of comparable identity for Ælfric's hagiographies and Murasaki Shikibu's complex narrative, *The Tale of Genji*.

We need to seek out the nearest approach to identity possible in the matters to be compared. "Matters" may be widely various: conceptions of titles, designations of authorship, specific issues of orality, functions of panegyric, and so on. All too often we (or our readers) discover that the examples of a given matter agree insufficiently in common category. No doubt it will remain true for as long as I have a chance to observe these things (and rather longer, one might guess) that genuine intelligence can make more interesting, valuable work of a flawed comparison than routine correctness can ever achieve. But since we can more easily correct our methods than increase our intelligence, it is clear where the task lies.

In my attempt to understand, through an intercultural comparison, the matter of naming in literature, I have acted on the belief that the topic alone was insufficient for assurance of just comparison. That obviously explains my choices of what to compare: two journeys to the remote northern (and other) parts of island countries in days before canals, trains, or airplanes could be used for travel. And it explains why my choice of journeys features pairs of travelers, each of whom kept an account that survives. A much earlier Japanese poet wrote of the sorrows that travel brings, and Western writers often use travel as a metaphor for life. There are also joyous journeys and routine travel. And for a common topic, there is travel with its names and their properties.

Much depends on whether we think a journey is a nice little trope for life or whether we believe our travel may define the rest of the travail of our lives. Let our example be Bashō. He has a hokku in which he hears somebody call out to him, "O traveler!" It is that cry that we may use as a common name for each of the four authors studied here and, in Bashō's spirit, for ourselves.

Chapter 1

Naming Properties

the man . . . who first assigned a name to everything, an achievement
which Pythagoras thought one of supreme wisdom.

—Cicero

His very name . . .

—Murasaki Shikibu

The poet's eye . . . gives to airy nothing
A local habitation and a name.

—Shakespeare

Four Travelers on Two Journeys

Accounts of two journeys, each involving a pair of travelers, to remote
reaches of island countries provide the literature on which this study is
chiefly founded. The chief Japanese example is a classic, *Oku no
Hosomichi* (*The Narrow Road through the Provinces;* pub. 1702) by Matsuo
Bashō, who

> taking with him Iwanami Sora, departed from Fukagawa [in Edo,
> now Tokyo] on the twenty-seventh of the Third Month, 1689, and
> assembled in a concise style an account of a great journey . . . to
> Ōgaki [in Mino, present Gifu] and extending over about 1,500
> miles and seven months—the exemplary account of travel writing
> [kikō bungaku] in Japanese literature.[1]

---

1. Itō et al. 1968, 1702; cited here as a standard account. The exact dates of Bashō's
departure from Edo and of his arrival in Ōgaki are unclear: see figure 1 for the route and
some dates; see appendix 1 for additional information.

His companion, Iwanami (later Kawai) Sora, kept a careful if prosaic diary whose chief interest derives from the light it sheds on Bashō's classic in prose and verse.

The English example is of a journey taken by the English lexicographer and man of letters, Samuel Johnson, with his younger Scottish friend and later his biographer, James Boswell. Their aim was the remote parts of Scotland, particularly the Highlands and the isles of the Hebrides.[2] Edinburgh, in the southeast Lowlands, was their point of departure on 18 August 1773 and their point of return on 10 November. Their journey took under three months, but they enjoyed each other's company in Edinburgh some days before and after the journey, so spending a hundred days together in all. (See fig. 2 for their route around Scotland.)

The courses of the two journeys were surprisingly alike, and not only in their sharing, as we have seen, a counterclockwise direction. Also, in traversing remote areas, they shared hardships unfamiliar to travelers today. Johnson's *Journey* and Boswell's much more expansive *Tour* give remarkably different human versions of their travel. It will be no secret that I think their accounts more interesting than Sora's, Boswell's than Johnson's, and Bashō's than Boswell's. My opinion is not solely personal. For although I doubt that many of us have read all four, Bashō's at least is well known to readers of European languages, more of whom are likely to have read his *Narrow Road* in translation than have read Boswell or Johnson's accounts in English or other tongues.

In this brief survey of my subject, to make sense of basic matters, it has been necessary to use names. The names are those of four people, of two countries traversed in successive directions implying a variety of places by land and sea, and of a few times. What does such naming imply? What kind of human act, what human knowledge, is involved? What relation does it have to the persons, places, and times named? Does naming differ in Japanese from English practice? The rest of this chapter will be concerned with questions like these, although full answers will be reached, if they are reached at all, only by the conclusion of this journey of another kind through various problems and practices.

---

2. They were accompanied at various times by Scottish hosts, servants, and local people varying in number. These people were all highly important to the journey but, except for Boswell's servant, Joseph Ritter, not to accounts of it. Bashō and Sora made their way more often on foot, but they had company on more of the way than Bashō implies.

Comparatively Speaking

The importance of names to literature has long been obvious, and even matters of emphasis have seemed important. We expect a list of the dramatis personae with a play, and summaries of narratives are chiefly accounts featuring names of characters acting in their named places and times. Lyrics that seem to treat as if anonymous their people, places, and times wager all on two often shadowy entities: the person (or thing) most worthy of an apostrophe or address; and always to be sure, whether explicitly or implicitly, that name above other human names, "I."

But is that last not "error and upon me prov'd?" Bashō and Sora seldom use *any* of the first-person nouns available to them. In addition to his two surnames, Sora changed the Chinese characters for *Sora* to religious ones before setting forth. Bashō is not so named by himself or by Sora, whose diary refers to him as Bashō himself often did in these years, as *Okina*, the Old Man, which is less a lament than a boast, a claim to status, the *Lao* of Lao-tzu or the respectful Lao Du (J. Rōto) for the great Tang poet memorably quoted by Bashō, Du Fu. On the other hand, the Old Man does not deny that he is Bashō, speaking obliquely (toward the beginning) of his Banana Plant Hut, his Bashō An. In fact "Bashō" (a pen name derived from that hut or hermitage) signed himself so variously that place-names sometimes seem more fixed to him. He and Sora give a sense of time in differing ways. Sora tirelessly ticks off the months, days, and hours. Bashō's temporality is chiefly seasonal as recounted in his verse and prose. They specified years (when they did at all) by those of regnal eras or by place in a sixty-year cycle combining the twelve signs of the Asian zodiac with the five elements.

There is a certain number of ways to accommodate diversity, whether with the Chaucerian recognition that "In sondry londes sondry ben uságes," whether with insistence on one's own parochial customs, or whether with trials ending in Scotch verdicts. None of us disputes, in principle, that it is wiser to make claims that account for the evidence available rather than to deny existing evidence to fit habitual claims. Acquiring knowledge of differences in naming practices should assure augmented interest. And not just interest. Our confidence in our generalizations grows as our evidence is drawn from wider ranges— from additional languages, from numerous periods.

Such taking is usually called comparative and, where the examples are literary, comparative literature. On oath, I cannot swear that the ruling passion of self-styled comparatists has typically extended much beyond the past two centuries, beyond the ample prose stretches of the novel, or to the terra incognita that is not Europe and North America. But times change, and even the learned profession with them. Many years' acquaintance with the International Comparative Literature Association have shown that there is genuine and growing "comparative" curiosity about the "uságes" beyond the broad road and about what may be found by exploring other roads, which lately seem less and less narrow. In fact there is more than curiosity. There is genuine conviction that an increase in sources makes a difference for the better, affording us greater security in our judgments. That is altogether evident as a principle, but where can we turn for a logical account?

In certain kinds of logic there exists a term or category that is believed to sustain or, in its absence to invalidate, a comparison between two other terms. This *tertium comparationis* holds value for comparative literature solely as a reminder that comparisons, whatever their scope, hold or fail to hold depending on the extent of the likeness of the integers and the congruence of categories compared.

To introduce as simple an example as possible, it is evident that when people possess more than one name, full designation requires that one be given before the other and that usage varies between priority to given names (e.g., most European languages) and priority given to surnames (e.g., East Asian languages, Hungarian). Given that the logical term is a Latin one, one could seek a *tertium comparationis* in Roman usage. What one discovers of course is a usual combination of praenomen, nomen, and cognomen along with other possibilities. No *tertius quis* there.

If we appeal to Japanese literature for our *tertium comparationis*, we discover: that in both heroic drama and narrative, clan or family names, given names, titles of office, pen names, and other denominations may be given (or not be used), and that royalty lacks family names. The hero of *The Tale of Genji* is royally born but made a noble commoner of the Minamoto clan or family (Genji). He is known to Japanese as Hikaru Genji, which is a genuine name if not of a kind we are accustomed to.[3]

---

3. The author herself, Murasaki Shikibu, derives her "Murasaki" from her principal heroine and her "Shikibu" from some male relative with an appointment in the Bureau of Rites. We have no idea what her given name was, but she came from a lesser branch of the Fujiwara family and would have been known at court as Tō Shikibu ("Tō" being the

What was sought for as a *tertium comparationis* turns out to be an augmentation—additional data that may or may not be made usable as evidence.

So much for the utility of a *tertium comparationis*. What, however, of the comparatist's supposed business, comparison? It is one of our commonest mental acts, and yet it has been scarcely considered by philosophers, psychologists, social scientists. In fact, the subject—the grounds, canons, methods of sound comparison—has been almost entirely ignored by those who claim to practice comparative study of literature.[4] It is an intellectual scandal. And the scandal becomes absurdity when we observe that much of what goes on in departments of comparative literature is not truly comparative at all, for the simple reason that it involves no comparison. If, like a misery, an absurdity loves company, this one has it, since what is true of "comparative" study of literature holds as well for "comparative" study in the social sciences.[5] It is necessary to rehearse some fundamental matters if the writings dealt with in this study are to be shown to be justly compared.

It seems that a major difficulty with comparison is that, although the mental act is simple, even common or customary, it is also the case that its general principles are difficult to develop and its practice is easily got wrong. One readily understands that the two central features, the necessary elements, of comparison are likeness and difference. The seeming contradiction involved surely is a major cause of our difficulties. We know that when we reach one critical point, identity, likeness becomes sameness and comparison is impossible. And we know very well how easy it is to reach the opposite point, one hard to locate and hard to avoid. With too great a difference yielding insufficient likeness, we slide into uselessly weak analogy, into the far-fetched or strained, and even into logical solecism. There are also the familiar critical dangers of the vasty deep and of the altitudinously trivial.

The usual problem, insufficient likeness, makes especially difficult for us the otherwise most valuable kind, intercultural comparison. The virtues of method sought must include clarity, distinguishability among kinds of comparison, availability of evidence, and hence justifiability or

---

Sinified reading of the character for "Fuji-," as "Gen" is for "Minamoto").

4. There are intelligent remarks by intelligent people: Brodsky-Lacour 1995; Culler 1995; Melas 1995. But they are irrelvant to the principles of making justified comparisons.

5. See Zelditch 1971. What follows here is a simplified version of earlier discussions: Miner 1987; 1990, chap. 1.

rejectability. The central feature of my ventures has been identification of topics that allow for two or more parallel exemplars. Because they exemplify a common topic, the exemplars possess an initial or presumptive sameness, ensuring that the comparison is principled, sound. Because the exemplars derive from diverse sources, the comparison yields differentiation within the bounds of that common topic or category. To put the matter somewhat differently, this method requires identification, as it were, of a species within which the subspecies exemplars bear a common relation to the larger category. There is difference because the exemplars are by definition not identical, and the differences are within bounds because the topic (species, category, etc.) governs the exemplars equally.

This method has been tested by use with two subjects: the emergence of poetic systems and the practice of making literary collections. The former is of great importance to understanding theories of literature as well as features of literary history. The latter is reassuringly smaller in scale and rich in historical evidence.[6]

What is involved in the specifically intercultural features, and what further may be sought, can be suggested by identifying the relations of what I have been terming category to exemplar, of exemplar to category, and of exemplar to exemplar.

Over the centuries a stock comparison has been of more or less contemporary writers: dramatists like Shakespeare and Marlowe, lyric poets like Du Fu and Bo (or Bai) Juyi, novelists like Tolstoy and Dostoyevsky. We feel security in the comparisons because each pair writes in the same verse (or prose)—but also at least equally so because they are contemporaries writing in the same languages, the same literary traditions, and the same genres.

An immediate, striking result of that kind of comparison is the initial conviction of difference between contemporaries writing in the same language. How different are Bo (or Bai) Juyi from Du Fu, Fujiwara Teika from Monk Saigyō, Shelley from Keats, Goethe from Schiller! But how different in other terms things seem after a second step, a comparison of pairs of these pairs. No longer confined to the most restricted (a single language and age), but still retaining the examples begun with in adding another pair, we discover that we have moved up a step in

---

6. The references are to Miner 1978–79 supplemented by 1991 and chap. 1 in Miner 1985. My dissatisfaction with some social postulations in the latter has been one motive to consider further methodological possibilities.

categories from the most limited in our examples. And, lo! how different are the Japanese from the Chinese, and the German from the English. But, behold! now how alike the two Chinese or the two in another pair seem. Surely it is evident that the likeness of poets within a given pair when contrasted with a pair from another literature derives from a genuine comparability confirming, and confirmed by, the original grounds of comparison: contemporaries writing in like kinds in the same languages-literatures.

Moreover, we can go on in similar fashion to devise further stages of larger comparison with similar results. The two pairs of Chinese and Japanese poets, who seemed so different when solely poised with each other, become comparable—more alike—when compared with pairs of European poets. In fact, one can draw a kind of calculus of pairs, leading from the initial sense of difference between just two members, to likeness of those members when an alternative pair is introduced—and so on in a series whose each step imparts likeness to "predecessors" who seem unlike when only they are involved: as long as "the topic (species, category, etc.) governs the exemplars equally." An illustrative column can do no harm, given the paucity of concern with these matters.

a) Chinese lyric poets who are contemporaries.
b) Japanese as in a.
c) French as in a.
d) French (or other) dramatists (or novelists).
e) French historical novelists.
f) French historians who are contemporaries.
g) Political economists as in f.
h) Statisticians as in f.

The principle of alteration at a given point might also be a shift from the criterion of the examples being contemporaries, from standard French to Caribbean or Algerian, and so on. It is obviously crucial that each shift involve our awareness of both the shift itself and of its purposiveness in the choice of successive examples.

The awareness will warn that without care even such small moves—and enlarged comparisons all the more—lose a degree of control or likeness that requires vigilance. The absence of contemporaneity between our Chinese and Japanese exemplars and the further lack of a language common to them and the European examples are overlooked at methodological peril. But presuming such care and appropriate measures, we may proceed with intercultural comparison.

The same principles establish a foundation for two other kinds of comparison. One need only be mentioned, since it is the usual kind, the intracultural: German and French, Spanish and English, and the like. It need only be mentioned, but with the warning that application requires thought. For example, Renaissance lyricism can scarcely involve contemporaneous events in Italy and in England: Petrarch lived in Chaucer's, not Wyatt's or Sidney's generations. Or again, it is sometimes suggested that there is a culture based on use of Chinese characters as a learned language. This is an attractive possibility when we recall, for example, that some 85 percent of extant premodern Korean literature is so written. And it gives hopes that Southeast Asian literatures may be joined to the family. But the very great difference between the one learned language and the many vernaculars should signal caution. Those Asian vernacular languages do not have a common origin in the same linguistic family, as is the case with the European languages (with exceptions like Basque) and the learned tongue, Latin.

Strange to say, there is another kind of literary comparison that is usually not admitted to belong to the halls of comparative literature (which would be holy halls if there, too, rage was unknown). This kind is comparison within a single literature, and its dismissal is for no good reason that I can discover. We all do it, and the only serious issue must be the same as for the larger intracultural kinds and for the intercultural varieties. Do we do it well: in principled, disciplined fashion? The only reasonable caveats worth adding apply to all other kinds of literary comparison (and other study) as well. It should be interesting but not merely fashionable. It should be of heft but not ponderous.

Our subject is, however, intercultural comparison. It is not difficult to suggest other subjects that could be examined profitably with the method described. Surely we could find meaningful comparison in the comparison of prefaces to works, collections, or editions. Studies of the emergence and use of prefaces would reveal much about the social roles of authors and literatures. It is also wholly likely that distinctions would need to be drawn: for example, between authorial and nonauthorial prefaces; between those contemporary with first publication and those added later like Henry James's famous ones to the New York edition; between pretendedly or genuinely authorial or nonauthorial; between dedicatory with a patron as at least nominal addressee; and between other kinds. Properly ordered and well handled, this topic seems to me a potentially rich mine for understanding many features of literature that can be defined in relation to authors, publishers, and readers.

Whatever the merits of the comparative methods described, they have possessed a serious limitation in my practice. That is, their only relation to individual poems, plays, or novels has been to use them as illustrations rather than as proper ends of study in themselves. The methods have not allowed for examination, analysis, practical criticism, reading—whatever term one prefers. Some innovation, some further refinement, or some redirection is clearly necessary.

The change exemplified by this study involves alteration of the fixed category-exemplars model. The new model can be described in rather negative terms as an unfixing of the constituent units, the category and exemplars. To put matters positively, the new approach is based on entities that are reciprocal, at least in the sense that each may be a "category" and each an "exemplar" of the other. To characterize the entities generally, they are naming practices and travel accounts. As we shall be seeing in the remainder of this and in some of the final chapter, naming is a very large and very meaningful category. But insistence is necessary: that meaningfulness requires a disciplined ground of comparison. The ground chosen here is travel literature, within which naming is especially prominent. The main concern of most of the book is, however, understanding by comparison specific features of individual examples of travel writing, using nominal reference (giving and using names) as the disciplined basis for comparison. Naming practices and travel writings are equally feasible as topics and as examples, and this reciprocity ensures disciplined comparison. Beyond that, moreover, it involves discussion of the individual examples, whether of naming practices or travel writings, as the earlier methods did not.

It will not be amiss at this point to recall *The Pilgrim's Progress,* since John Bunyan is such a master of literary names and such an attender to ways of going wrong or not far enough—as well as means of arriving where one wishes to. One way of going forth might be to define the examples of travel writings as those featuring two men traveling mostly as a pair. The choices of Johnson and Boswell to set beside Bashō and Sora in each case joins an older with a younger man and authors with different ideas of the kind of thing most important to be recorded. There are other Japanese and European accounts of traveling pairs, for example, Jippensha Ikku's *Hizakurige (Shank's Mare,* or *Footing It from Edo to Kyoto)* and Cervantes's *Don Quijote.* I do not deny altogether the possibility of using them or other possible examples. But it does appear to me that a first attempt along these lines should have more of Bunyan's discipline than does his Pliable. The stories by Ikku and Cervantes do not fully fit with either the Japanese or English examples chosen. For one thing, both *Don Quijote* and *Hizakurige* are dominantly fictional, whereas our accounts are dominantly factual. More importantly, these others going in pairs, whether the Knight of the Sorrowful Countenance or Sancho Panza, whether Yajirōbe or Kitahachi, are fictional creations: characters, not authors. With such mismatchings (and other difficulties could be mentioned), the very method might be put at hazard. In any event, our choices must be considered choices, as can be shown by examining a Strong Assertion against comparative study.[7]

In his *Picture Theory,* W. J. T. Mitchell (1994) seeks, among other things, to go "Beyond Comparison" (chap. 3). He justly finds fault with "the comparative method" when it deals with "the field of representation and discourse with a single master code (mimesis, semiosis, communication, etc.)" (84). Clearly, it is one faulty thing to object to a single explanation applied in and out of season. But is it not another faulty thing to argue the case from the single Western perspective (representation, mimesis)? The criticism of narrow bounds is itself narrowly bounded.

There is something of a concession:

> At its best, the comparative method can offer a kind of intellectual housekeeping, sorting out the differences and similarities not only between various kinds of cultural objects but also between the critical languages that are brought to bear on them. (86–87)

In its ordinary versions, it is deplorable.

His opposition to comparison is not explicitly to the literary version but to comparison among the arts. Apparently Aristotle and Horace deserve a spanking, or would have, if Mitchell had remembered

---

7. In my jargon, a Strong Assertion is one that is useful for propounding an argument forcefully and clearly, with none of your uncertain terms. Even if one chooses to reject it, the assertion is useful for dispersing the usual fog. It must, however, have some freshness so that it is not just a loud claim and enough intelligence to be worth considering.

them. So would Murasaki Shikibu and Chikamatsu Monzaemon, if he had prized and considered them.[8] His dudgeon is difficult to account for. Comparison of the arts, literary and otherwise, may have been abused, but so has every kind of study. If we compare literary with other aesthetic kinds, we quickly understand what is otherwise often not understood: one of the features of the aesthetic, its virtual status, need not be fictional. In fact literature is the only kind that *can* be fictional, because a fiction requires language. A vase, a dance, a sculpture are neither fictional nor factual.[9]

In particular, our anticomparatist wishes to reject as "ideologemes" (an example of giving a dog a bad name to hang it?) certain things in comparative method, things that may usefully be set down on the page somewhat graphically:

> tropes of differentiation
> > between verbal and visual representation
> > > (time and space,
> > > convention and nature,
> > > the ear and the eye). (88)

The pairs or doublets (note the difference between "and" in the quotation and "or" earlier in this sentence) would do Petrus Ramus credit. They also look for all the world like the comparative method being rejected.

By the end of his book, our author has indeed gone "Beyond Comparison" as that is usually conceived. At least a political agenda becomes clear. Walter Benjamin on fascism as the aestheticizing of politics is defrosted again, and all right-thinking people are urged to guard against incipient fascism in the United States by opposing the aestheticizing of politics (421–25). On the other hand, anaesthesia, the politicizing of aesthetics, appears devoutly to be wished.

The penultimate sentence of the book seems to be earnestly meant:

---

8. See Murasaki Shikibu: *The Tale of Genji (Genji Monogatari)*, "The Broom Tree" ("Hahakigi") and "The Picture Composition" ("Eawase") chapters. I quote Chikamatsu in chap. 5.

9. The all-too-brief argument here does not suggest that literature is necessarily fictional (a common Western assumption) or factual (a common east Asian assumption). Nor am I suggesting that it is impossible to substitute other statuses for the aesthetic. It is all too possible. (See chap. 5 for lengthier discussion.)

"In short, though we probably cannot change the world, we can continue to describe it critically and interpret it accurately" (425). It is difficult to imagine justification of uncritical description or inaccurate interpretation. What seems so particularly familiar to one reader of that sentence and book is the utter lack of definition of what constitutes not only comparison but also of description and interpretation. This is an instance of a hard case when an enemy of comparison is no more helpful than its friends.

The attention to *Picture Theory* shows that our caveats and injunctions apply to any choice of method one might make. The warnings apply to the choice of subject as well. There is nothing sacred about accounts of travel. Travel does, however, have special virtues for a study concerned with naming. Since it is by definition a kind of movement through a spatial sequence, names of places emerge as a natural topic.[10] Since spatial movement is not instantaneous, times must be designated "from time to time" at least. In the hands of a gifted author, even the daily entries of a rigorously preserved journal form can seem aesthetically necessary and inevitable. The most important names of all, those of people, appear equally naturally in travel literature. Anticipation or recollection can summon, by some name, to a traveler's present thought a person presently in another place or from another time. There may be a crucial tension in travel journals and diaries between the overwhelming presence of the seldom self-named diarist and the often briefly known but necessarily named persons met. So it may be, but so on occasion it may not be. We shall observe in due course. But after closing this section with justification of the examples chosen, we shall need to turn to features of naming, to traditional features of naming, and then to philosophers on names.

Multiple accounts make comparison possible, certainly enticing, for both the Japanese and English journeys. There are also problems of authorial selectivity and of text, for which Bashō may serve as immediate example. His journey, recorded from spring to fall 1689, actually continued for about two years more before he returned to Edo. There are difficulties in putting together an account of the complete venture: we would need to consult various other writings by him in prose, in verse and, like *The Narrow Road*, in mixed prose and verse. Yet there are

---

10. The issues of referentiality will arise later in this chapter and in the last chapter when philosophers' discussions of naming are considered.

problems in confining attention, as here, to *The Narrow Road*. What may well be termed its leg of the journey was over in 1689. Bashō lived until 1694, and it is clear that he revised his account, although how often or how extensively it is no longer possible to judge (except for some of the verse). In addition, the work was not published until 1702, eight years after his death. Since none of the existing texts is in his hand, we cannot deny some degree of intervention by others, if only (but who knows?) in choice and usage of Chinese characters or in addition of punctuation, paragraphing, and distinguishing of units. (All these differentiate modern texts of *The Narrow Road* from the early ones.)

Bashō's traveling companion, Iwanami Sora, exercised great diligence in gathering information that has never been accorded literary excellence, although it is of very great importance in understanding Bashō's far richer account. Sora kept prose and verse apart, prose in a kind of artless diary form, and poetry more ambitiously. One of Bashō's principal if unacknowledged aims in travel was to propagate his school of poetry. Sora therefore kept a (separate) record not only of individual beginning stanzas, or hokku, but the sequences that they were so often used to initiate.[11] More will be said of his notations later.

It is easier to understand the textual details of the accounts by Johnson and Boswell—once one has their pattern in mind. For both there were, as might be expected, stages preparatory to writing out. Johnson had his book of remarks, his letters to Mrs. Thrale being saved for his return, perhaps some notes, and certainly (as we shall be seeing) a remarkable memory. Boswell's preparation was more scribal. It consisted of a kind of diary: he complains to himself when he has let his "journal" fall a few days behind, or congratulates himself on saving some Johnsoniana for a barren time ahead. Since Johnson had only to read once to remember, and because he read many parts of Boswell's "journal," that must be counted a further source for him.

The published versions began in 1774 with Johnson's account, *A Journey to the Western Isles of Scotland* (corrected version in 1775). This version (in J. D. Fleeman's standard 1985 Oxford edition) is that used here and is referred to as his *Journey*. Johnson died in December 1784, and in the following March, Boswell set about in his usual undirected fashion to revise for publication a version he had put together in almost

---

11. Sora notes when individual hokku ("ku" in his *Nikki*) or haikai sequences ("hai") were composed, especially by Bashō. He collected the actual poetry in his *Register*. See bibliography, Sora 1943.

Fig. 3. The cover of Sora's diary. "Sora's Diary Accompanying Bashō on the Narrow Road through the Provinces. With a Diary of 1691."

complete form in 1780–82, a version that Johnson saw in whatever degree of completeness it suited Boswell to show and him to read. We shall return to this manuscript journal. When, during his 1785 visit to London, Boswell revised and completed a fresh version for publication, his work was greatly speeded when he was aided and directed by the important editor of Shakespeare and Dryden, Edmond Malone. Unfortunately, Malone had a more squeamish notion of propriety than did Boswell. As a result, the version his contemporaries knew, *A Tour to the Hebrides* (1785), is salt that has lost its savor. That eighteenth-century published version is not used here. Fortunately, the manuscript version was included in the famous "Boswell papers" acquired by Yale. That version was first published in 1936 as *Boswell's Journal of a Tour to the Hebrides*. This Yale edition edited by Frederick A. Pottle and Charles H. Bennett is so superior in interest that it is the one used throughout this study for quotations and references. To be complete or fussy in the matter, their edition consists of three units: Boswell's manuscript journal from its "Introduction" and 14 August through 26 October 1773 (1–359); an addition or completion running from 27 October to 22 November (359–404); and a conclusion consisting of an annex of letters (394–403). Malone must have played some role in the second and third of these units, but they are treated here as Pottle and Bennett treat them, parts integral to the journal. In short, for textual purposes, *"Journey"* refers to Fleeman's 1985 edition of *A Journey to the Western Islands of Scotland*. Similarly, *"Tour"* refers to Pottle and Bennett's 1936 edition of the uncut manuscript (with final additions).[12]

In spite of things we cannot know with any assurance, there are some matters as clear as one would wish, perhaps because of the multiplicity of versions. Bashō's *Narrow Road* is a classic of its literature known to every Japanese with pretense to education. Sora's records are known only to specialists, who use them as means of interpreting Bashō's account. It is not literary judged by any familiar criteria, including Japanese, which grant literary status to a large number of factual writings. Although Johnson read Boswell's *"Tour,"* his *Journey* is a separately considered creation. Both English versions are commonly taken as literary to a kind of cadet degree. This brief comparison may conclude with observance of the high degree of factuality of all four "rec-

---

12. See the list in Abbreviations for a reminder at any time.

ords."[13] The two versions closest to the facts of actual events are Sora's and Boswell's. As has been said, the former has no literary importance, whereas Boswell's is more attractive than Johnson's, for all its merits, to most readers, including myself.

Such preferences apart (if they ever can be wholly held apart), the details of likeness and difference seem sufficiently clear to show what we most require showing. That is, the qualities and properties identified justify the intercultural comparison and allow hope for reaping its advantages. Both the justice of the comparison and the benefits accruable should grow with the identification of that central focus of our approach—the onomastic, the calling of names. Sometimes, however, we create mazes for ourselves.

Cultural Essentialism and Relativism:
The Comparatist's Caveat

As is well known to the citizens of the United States (alias Americans), they are idealistic and moral to a fault, as the French know they are sentimental to a fault, and the Chinese that they are individualistic to a fault. These are the positive versions of the mote-and-beam problem identified by Jesus (Matt. 7:3–5):

> why beholdest thou the mote that is in thy brother's eye, but considerest not the beam that is in thine own eye? Or how wilt thou say to thy brother, Let me pull out the mote out of thine eye; and, behold, a beam is in thine own eye? Thou hypocrite, first cast out the beam out of thine own eye; and then shalt thou see clearly to cast out the mote out of thy brother's eye.

But of course Sunday school is for others, particularly in an age when hypocrites have been succeeded by hypercrites.

This problem of presuming to know exactly what others are essentially like has a counterpart in the too easy gesture of throwing up the hands, declaring that everything differs, and that one thing cannot possibly be better than another. Everything is relative to its time and place and, when in Rome, you know what to do.

---

13. Modern critics assign *The Narrow Road* to the class of *kikō bungaku:* recorded travel literature. Fact and fiction are discussed in chap. 5.

It is not altogether clear why dilemmas have horns, but we have here the comparatist's dilemma of the error of presuming that only one or three things go for the Japanese or the English or, to the contrary, that anything goes. Fortunately, the dilemma is more apparent in intercultural study. Unfortunately, it becomes even harder to deal with. We have an instance with a self-appointed authority writing about what I should certainly agree is the unusual importance of collections in Japanese literature and certain related cultural practices. That commentator is kind enough to apply the lessons learned from the collective and the individual in certain literary phenomena to the culture at large:

> there must be implications [of these literary practices and assumptions] for a wider range of phenomena in Japanese life. Those should include assumptions governing social organization, ideas of the family, the organization of political parties, and the nature of various other groups like the literary establishment (bundan) or a farmers' cooperative. . . . Japanese have presumed a kind of relation between the individual and the collective that is distinct, different in its emphasis from that presumed in other highly developed societies.

Jerome K. Bruner somewhere defines intelligence as "going beyond the information given." One can see what he means. One can see as well that the phrase describes error as well as intelligence. There are always data easily impressed into evidence by a pet theory like that we have just seen on the individual and the collective. I regret that the quotation is self-quotation.[14]

Truly, it is unfortunate that it is difficult to say what can be learned from such a mistake. Comparatists pay little attention to the principles of comparison. They pay no more heed to problems of relativism than do the historians. Reviewers of my *Comparative Poetics* all but uniformly ignored the first chapter (on comparison) and the last (on relativism), so missing the opportunity to set me right (little enough in the scale of things) and to lead to genuine increase in our understanding of truly central issues.

---

14. Miner 1985, 57. Pleading for mercy, I shall mention that the clause first quoted is preceded by a conditional and the second remark is preceded by a warning. Recognizing justice, I concede that the damage has been done nonetheless.

Having tried before in vain to emphasize the difficulty and importance of these issues—the sharpness of those horns I do not really
understand—it seems out of place to dwell on such matters in this
book. But three observations will not be amiss.

First, then, for (intercultural) comparison to be just, it is necessary
that there be a credible assumption of sameness in the two sides. Second, it must be assumed that the differences observed do not disqualify
the "credible assumption" but are revealing and important. Third, there
must be a standing caveat that neither the samenesses nor the
differences violate the integrity of those observed. In the fine print of
this third, there is also a clause against violating our own sense of
ourselves, but that is not our besetting sin. Entering this standing caveat
does not guarantee its being honored in the ensuing pages. But I promise to try, and if it becomes necessary to name others at fault, I shall at
least offer as examples people who are admired by others as well as
myself.

Caveat lector. Caveat comparator. And so to another start.

Naming Rights: The Classical Places

"In the beginning God created the heaven and the earth." So the familiar opening of the Bible. And, for God, creation is simple, following the
divine Word: "'Let there be light'; and there was light." Since this occurs "In the beginning," although God preexists the beginning, there
had been no created light before God used the word. *After* divine naming, the thing exists with its name, and by using the name, God's human
creatures refer to what God had brought into meaning by speaking the
name.

It is a long travail, and certainly not at the speed of light, from
Genesis to issues debated in contemporary philosophy and in literary
study. Since the use of names is a basis for the intercultural comparison
of this study, it will not be amiss to specify some of the issues wearing
the onomastic guise. After naming the names, as it were, we can trace
some of the concerns traditional in discussions of names.

Some issues concern boundaries and all involve distinctions of one
kind, of one degree, or another. Not only English *name* derives from
Latin *nomen,* itself derived from Greek *onoma.* The same is true of English *noun.* Is the discussion limitable only to names, or even only
proper names, or proper singular names? Are all nouns admissible, or

are only those allowed which come accompanied by definite rather than indefinite articles? Since English has, and some languages do not have, articles; or since some usages of definite articles may be only signs of noun substantives—shall we inspect nominal passports for demonstrative visas? Or why exclude verbs and adjectives, crucial as they are to predications about, say, a single proper noun? What are the proper distinctions to be drawn between names literal, metaphorical, and fictional? What are the bounds between, what the coexistent elements of statement, reference, and truth value? Since we are not God, what imparts meaning to our words? Or, are words after all arbitrary things, conventional things? If so, does "arbitrary" mean the same thing as "conventional"? Whose will arbitrates? What society convenes? Do words exist without a world to which they refer? If so, where in the world can they exist?

Easier questions than these produce differing answers. Some of the differences will emerge from this first attention to examples of naming; others will come only at the close. Let our first example be from another story of a divinity, one with assumptions about naming very different from those in Genesis. It is no familiar thing, a divinity in sore straits, drowning. The source is the first work written (after a fashion) in Japanese, the *Kojiki*. The episode concerns the minor Shinto spirit, the Divinity Sarutabiko (Sarutabiko no Kami):

> When Sarutabiko no Kami was in Azaka, he went fishing; he got his hand caught in the shell of a pirabu and sank into the sea. When he had sunk to the bottom, his name was Sokudoku Mitama ["bottom-touching spirit"]; when the frothy bubbles appeared on the surface of the sea, his name was Tubutatu Mitama ["frothy-bubbles-appear spirit"]; when the foam gushed forth, his name was Awasaku Mitama ["foam-forming spirit"].[15]

The divinity has three names (apart from that by which he is introduced), each of which designates not so much a different individual as a single one showing progressive symptoms of drowning.

Contrary inferences may be drawn from this example. Some might

---

15. Philippi 1968, 142 (chap. 40), orthography and other details modified. I owe the example to Konishi Jin'ichi, who mentioned others from the *Kojiki* with the general opinion that the "mentality" of such naming lasted into the seventh century and perhaps later.

well hold that a name (and what names those are!) is unstable to the point of changing to reflect each important stage of just one event, the death, in the life of a spirit. If names properly designate "things"—in this case an unfortunate spirit—then the name first given should be retained. The multiple names designate not differing individuals but purely convenient, temporary locutions. Others might well hold, on the contrary, that Sarutabiko no Kami remains the same and that the alternatives designate nicknames, noms du fleuve, that reflect reality in its changes and making sense of the changes. We shall return to the issue and to Shintoism.

The possibilities are played with in a characteristic poem by John Donne (1573–1631), "A Valediction of My Name, in the Window." The title refers to the practice of scratching with a diamond one's name on the glass of a window. The male speaker inscribes his name as he bids his lover good-bye, taking comfort in the fact that the glass will be as honest (transparent) as he and yet reflect her eye as she gazes on it, that the glass will withstand wind and rain, and so on. Then, in a characteristic shift, Donne's speaker laments that his lover will fling open her window for another man, and the mere sounds of a name are "No meanes our firme substantial love to keep" (62).

The Western locus classicus for the philosophical issues of naming is Plato's *Cratylus* dialogue. Hermogenes the Sophist argues that names are merely customary, just conventional signs, whereas Cratylus argues to the contrary: names truly designate realities. The philosophical issues are considerable, complex, and far from trivial—or clear, as has been suggested. It is not simply whether Hermogenes is, as his name suggests, descended from Hermes (the interpreter), but whether any name—any Greek onoma or Latin nomen or English name/noun or Japanese meishi—truly designates, and if they can or do truly designate, not only whether truth is possible but also reference. And if reference is possible, whether the existence of an actual world must be accepted. From that, we are led to fictions and possible worlds. And from those, to admixtures of fact and fiction. We have then moved far beyond the bounds of singular proper nouns to language at large, escaping the much laundered doubts of nominalism for the dusty raiments of realism. Of course, neither part nor all of this offers immunity from error. Quite the contrary: presuming these things entails presuming the reality rather than the mere illusion of possible error. It cannot be said that Socrates—or Plato—eases matters any.

Plato has both Hermogenes the nominalist and Cratylus the realist appeal to Socrates, who—to the mystification of students of the dialogue—agrees with neither of them. The fact that Socrates spends twice as long arguing against Hermogenes as against Cratylus might mean more if so much of that argument were not taken up with word derivations so fanciful as to make the seriousness dubious.[16] Socrates is presented asking—with many names, a large thesaurus of words, and a seeming junk heap of fancifully meaningful sounds or parts of words— whether some individuals, in reality, are wise and some foolish, some good and some bad, matters of some importance to us as well as the Academy. "He words me," as Cleopatra observed on another occasion.

Whatever one's philosophical position, it will be evident that the ability to name, in the wide sense we have arrived at, gives the namer great power. That point is evident from the other Western locus classicus, Adam's naming of the beasts. As is widely known, the book of Genesis gives differing accounts of the creation of Adam and Eve. In the first (commonly called Priestly), God says, following the Authorized Version,

> Let us make man in our image, after our likeness: and let them have dominion over the fish of the sea, and over the fowl of the air, and over the cattle, and over all the earth, and over every creeping thing that creepeth upon the earth. (1:26)

The second account (commonly called Yahwist) adds:

> And out of the ground the Lord God formed every beast of the field, and every fowl of the air; and brought them unto Adam to see what he would call them; and whatsoever Adam called every living creature, that was the name thereof. (2:19)[17]

---

16. See *Cratylus* in Jowett 1892, 1: 323–73 for Hermogenes and Socrates and 373–89 for Cratylus and Socrates. Jowett's analysis and introduction appear on pp. 253–321. See also Baxter 1992.

17. The Genesis 1 Priestly and historically later account conceives of man as plural, inclusive of "male and female"; the Genesis 2 Yahwist account treats Eve as made from Adam's rib and so subordinate to him. For other details, see the next note. There is actually a third biblical account, uniformly ignored by literary critics, in Genesis 5; it concurs with that in Genesis 1.

Well aware of the differences in the two accounts, Milton sought to harmonize them. In *Paradise Lost* Raphael tells Adam that, in creating the world, God says in part,

> Let us make now Man in our image, Man
> In our similitude, and let them rule
> Over the Fish and Fowle of Sea and Aire,
> Beast of the Field, and over all the Earth,
> And every creeping thing that creeps the ground.
> This said, he form'd thee, *Adam*, thee O Man
> Dust of the ground. . . .
> Male he created thee, but thy consort
> Female for Race; then bless'd Mankinde, and said,
> Be fruitful, multiplie, and fill the Earth,
> Subdue it, and throughout Dominion hold.
>
>   (7:519–32)

And later God declares,

>   all the Earth
> To thee and to thy Race I give; as Lords
> Possess it, and all things that therein live,
> Or live in Sea, or Aire, Beast, Fish, and Fowle.
> In signe whereof each Bird and Beast behold
> After thir kindes; I bring them to receave
> From thee thir Names, and pay thee fealtie
> With low subjection.
>
>   (8:338–45)[18]

The traditional interpretation of God's creation of "man" in "our" likeness is that the human creature is rational and free. Before the Fall the reason was wisdom, and wisdom gave power to name, as naming gave "dominion." Truly to be the "first [who] assigned a name to everything" would be "an achievement of supreme wisdom"—and power, as philosopher-king (Cicero 1971, 1, 25). To be sure, Adam's is a special case. And not only was his naming day before Babel but, according to parascriptural authority, as originally created, "man" also knew the

---

18. These two passages have attracted significant attention. See Fisch 1967; Evans 1968; Jacobs 1969; Leonard 1990.

language of beasts. The combination of wisdom and power united images of two divine attributes, omniscience and omnipotence. The Ciceronian epigraph at the head of this chapter shows that this primal naming was a sign of wisdom and power to pagan antiquity as well as to Judeo-Christian thought. But what if wisdom degenerated and power was disputed?

Those disasters befell the race in two stages, according to Genesis: the Fall from paradise (Gen. 3) and the result of punished pride in building the tower of Babel (11). We observe that although in both episodes the fault is not in false naming but in sins centered on pride, the punishment of those sins deprives human creatures of the dominion they hold by true language.

Degeneration from pristine, true language need not be couched in religious terms, however. There is an important passage in Thucydides (3:82) on civil strife:

> The meaning of words had no longer the same relation to things, but was changed by them [of both parties] as they thought proper. . . . For the leaders on either side used specious names, the one party professing to uphold the constitutional equality of the many, the other the wisdom of an aristocracy, while they made the public interests, to which in name they were devoted, in reality their prize. Striving in every way to overcome each other, they committed the most monstrous crimes.
> (Jowett 1900, 1:242, 243)

Of course if evil results from the imposition of false names (calling evils good, goods evil, etc.), then it is conceivable that right naming might bring evil to good. Such is the hope suggested in Asian thought by one of the major Confucian classics, the *Analects* (Ch. *Lunyu*, J. *Rongo*). When asked about his first act if the prince of Wei were to ask him to administer his country, Confucius replies:

> It would certainly be to correct names. . . . If language is incorrect, then what is said does not accord with what is meant; and if what is said does not concord with what was meant, what is to be done cannot be effected. If what is to be done cannot be effected, then rites and music will not flourish. If rites and music do not flourish, then mutilations and lesser punishments will go astray. And if

mutilations and lesser punishments go astray, then the people have nowhere to put hand or foot.[19]

The correcting of language (Ch. zhengming; J. seimei) is usually rendered "the rectification" of words or names. Whatever the translation, the passage well accords in spirit with that from Thucydides.[20]

If there is a problem, it is rather that Japanese poets (in the wide sense of Dichter) have not often been enthusiastic about Confucian assumptions or other practices of neat, symmetrical order.[21] It takes no special insight to recognize the very Chinese and very un-Japanese character of the insistently repetitious, parallel syntax in the passage just given. To Japanese, particularly to literary Japanese, the primacy held by Confucianism in China is held instead by Buddhism, especially as Buddhism was adapted to Shinto and was selected from for congenial conceptions.

In philosophical and particularly metaphysical terms, Buddhism is antirealist: the doctrine of emptiness (kū) implies that words are no more than a convenience or expedient (hōben) and are fundamentally illusory. For that matter so are things; so is time in its order of past, present, and future.[22] In terms every Buddhist would understand, concepts of time, place, and person are also expedients, devices of convenience to assist our clouded minds in understanding the teachings of

---

19. Waley 1949, 171–72 (13:3). See also 2:19 and 12:22 on the crooked and the straight as also 22:4 on weights and measures.

20. Yang 1991, 347–75 observes that in China the decline in belief in a deity, and the concomitant rise of humanism, occurred far earlier than in Europe. His evidence comes from both Confucian and Daoist sources. Buddhism was less influential there than in Japan, and the still widespread Chinese popular belief in spirits lacks the articulated animism of Japanese conceptions, although the less erudite forms of Daoism have provided a fertile complement to the Han rationalism to be found most purely in Confucianism.

21. The Japanese counterpart for zhengming (the rectification of names), seimei, is not even to be found in the standard dictionary, Kōjien. With too little humor one may suggest that the fact testifies to lack of Japanese rectification. At least I know of no other language whose graphs for personal and place-names are so difficult to read that every bookshop serving students or educated adults carries dictionaries for "difficult to read" (nandoku) names of those two kinds. Many a name graph is written by every Japanese with no idea how it is pronounced; and some combinations whose meanings are clear have no known pronunciation.

22. For example, time: see the very clear statement by Nakamura 1972: s.v. "sanze." He says that Buddhism does not consider time to be actual or to have real existence; distinctions of past, etc. are merely expedient. This way of thought will concern us again in the final chapter.

the Buddha, who uses all possible means to bring us to enlightenment.[23] The expedients resemble the parables in the *Lotus Sutra* (*Hokkekyō*) in being fictions that ordinary people may find useful for seeking enlightenment but that, strictly speaking, are not substantial.

Buddhist metaphysical ideas are really much more subtle, and its practice more variable than that. A few examples will suggest a variety or even inconsistency as recognizably human as the Stoic philosopher in Johnson's *Rasselas*, whose composed mind could contemplate misfortune with equanimity—until he lost his daughter. The annual observances (nenjūgyōji) of the Japanese court included three days beginning XII.19 devoted to "depictions of the Buddhas' names" (butsumyōe). All in all, the names of 11,093 Buddhas and bodhisattvas were set forth: from the past, present, and future (Nakamura 1962, s.v. "butsumyōe"). Similarly, the concept of the last, degenerate phase of the Law, the idea of mappō, obviously depends on a premise of real time to make any sense. These are complex matters, but in many versions the Buddhist ideas are philosophically realist rather than nominalist. Similar realism and reliance on the truth of names are implied by versions of the nenbutsu (recitation or address using the name of the Buddha). Somewhat resembling a "Hail Mary" in its simplest and most familiar form, "Namu Amida Butsu," it makes sense only if the Amida Buddha is presumed to exist, and the words truly to address a real Buddha. To render simple what is so various and complex, we may say that strict Mahayana Buddhist philosophy uses words to put the significance of words in doubt and to convey by negative means an extremely complex metaphysics; whereas to the wider, ordinary Japanese view, time, place, and persons are real things, and, moreover, words for time, place, and things realistically designate those things.[24]

Even if we hold that Buddhism is consistently antirealist or nominalist, there are other kinds of thinking that are no less Japanese and that presume a doubly realist view: not only is the world real in time and place but also human words describing it do so rightly. For those

---

23. Robert E. Morrell, my American docent in Buddhist matters, has strongly stressed in correspondence that, properly speaking, Buddhism philosophy could recognize words and names as no more than expedients, and he is obviously right.

24. Legends about Murasaki Shikibu illustrate one range of complexity: either she was doomed to suffer in hell for her lies or she was an avatar of Kannon Bosatsu. It is appropriate that Genji's decisive justification of monogatari in the chapter "Fireflies" should involve Buddhist proof or analogy but that the exact nature of the Buddhist argument should be a matter of some dispute.

assumptions it was not necessary for Japan to await the more formal realism of Neoconfucianism. The assumptions were present in Shinto thought all along. The drowning spirit with whom this discussion began, Sarutabiko no Kami, is taken to have real existence, and his three other names as he drowns are changes of words signifying changes in reality.

These usages show that, as they say, language is arbitrary in the sense that in every language certain sounds are assigned meanings that could be wholly different. But *arbitrary* itself is a word that can be used arbitrarily. There are two other senses in which language is not arbitrary. For one thing, the phonology—not to mention morphology, grammar, and (variously) syntax—must be systematic, logical or, more exactly, conventional. For the second, once a language is arbitrarily established in the first sense, it becomes arbitrary not to abide by conventional system and logic. Negatives serve as example. That they may serve many purposes and develop, natural languages are loose, flexible systems, and a word (a word devilishly difficult to define for all languages) may designate different things. Japanese *yama* means, as one learns, "mountain," but unlike *mountain* may also designate "hill," "temple," "parade float," and so on. *Mount* may designate a mountain, a rise in the hand scrutinized by a palmist, or a horse. The Latin word behind the English, *mons,* may of course mean "mountain" but also proverbially a large promise little fulfilled, as by a mouse ("ex monte mus"), or in *mons Veneris* a real, erotic part of the body. Of course, this flexibility has limits: what one can get variously right one can also get variously wrong. But without a sense of right there can be none of wrong, even innocently, as when one mishears "yami" ("darkness") for *yama* or "count" for "*mount* your horses."

Or, again, "words" may designate, as they say, "things." For English *things,* Japanese has two words, *mono* and *koto,* the former designating more physical "things" (but see *mononoke,* a possessing spirit) and the latter more conceptual or abstract "things." Obviously the words may carry religious meanings. In contrast to Western views (and also to Chinese?), it is striking that in Japanese thought the order of existence is not a decline from the human or spiritual, but a scale beginning with nonhuman things, including what we consider inanimate. This is not the place to explore the many meanings of *mono* (nineteen current as in *Kōjien*) and *koto* (fifteen) or to speculate on the reasons why the former, which is more concrete in many usages, should yet be part of "*mono*noke." But the ancientness of the outlook should and can be exemplified: by passages from the *Kojiki* and *Nihon Shoki* (or *Nihongi*). In the latter we read of Japan: "That Land in the Midst of the Reed Plains has long lain desolate. All its creatures, down to the very rocks and plants, are fierce and wild." Not only that: "in that land there are many gods who sparkle like fireflies, as well as wicked gods, noisy as a swarm of summer flies. And even the grasses and trees have the power of speech" (see Konishi 1984, 100–101). The meaningfulness of the passages should not be underestimated. Both rest on the concept that divinity exists in things (once again, mono, koto) and on the concept that the word spirit or kotodama may evoke the divinity in things. The utterance of a kotodama speech act was termed a *kotoage*, and the first quotation just given from the *Nihon Shoki* is preceded by this: "Then [Ōkuninushi] uttered this kotoage." In a world where plants and trees may speak and rocks be wild, human and divine speech may have magical effect.

As many have seen, the concept of kotodama and kotoage influenced Japanese conceptions of Buddhism. There is that peculiar Japanese enlargement, to the point of heterodoxy, of the idea of the Buddha's Original Vow to make enlightenment available to all sentient beings.[25] So much was widely held. Japanese went to unusual lengths—to Shinto lengths, one may say—in defining sentient things. The relevant pronouncement or slogan (best known from its first and last words) is: "sōmoku kokudo shikkai jōbutsu" ("The plants, the trees, and the earth itself will all attain Buddhahood"). The phrase has scriptural origin (in the *Nirvana Sutra*, *Daihatsunehangyō*), but no other people has made of it what Japanese have. Although a Chinese clause, it sounds like a kotoage, and it agrees in temper with pronouncements of more evident literary and Shinto character.

From Lore to Learning

There is, then, no difficulty in showing the very special importance accorded naming from earliest times. We have revisited some of the principal classical places, have reviewed loci classici of naming. Now, so long after the beginning of the heavens and the earth, so long after the confusion of tongues at Babel, the excitement and the problems of names remain. The issues are rediscovered again and again in various

25. See Nakamura 1962, under "hongan" for more detail.

guises. What shall we call our baby? What shall we name this new building? The questions arise on two occasions: the philosophers' "baptism" or first naming, and what all of us remember well, the easy art of forgetting names already given. Issues of naming keep all our social groups occupied, showing up anywhere—in a legislature, a university, or a factory. Because there is no single place for naming, its problems and its lore are at once local in identity and ubiquitous in occurrence.

Learned attention to the subject is analogously extensive in predication and local in emphasis. Search in an American university library shows that in the West today, naming is one of the sciences claimed by philosophers in their logical dress. Ideas and decisions vary, but the issues and approaches are few enough for focus, and therefore summary, to be feasible.

Naming derives its importance from its centrality to our understanding of ourselves, and others, in our times and places. If we leave out people, "We rely," as one philosopher puts it, "very largely for our orientation on the use of place-names and of dates, but," as he adds, "their reference is not self-explanatory. We have to be able to identify the places and times which they denote" (Ayer 1964, 152). Although the statement brings home the importance of what we mean by *names,* its simplicity hardly suggests the differences of opinions as to what logically constitutes a name.[26]

Personal names are of first importance to individuals and their societies. Many varying practices can be discussed from age to age, language to language, and culture to culture. We never learn the supposed full real name of the eponymous hero of *The Tale of Genji.* But by the end of the first chapter the still youthful hero has been taken from princely status and been adopted into the Minamoto family or clan (what "Genji" means). And from his charisma of light he is called "hikaru" or rather "Hikaru Genji," "Shining or Radiant Genji." The name is almost inauspiciously auspicious, and gossip enters its subtractions, as the author emphasizes by beginning her second chapter with, "The very name . . ." or "The name alone . . ." ("Na nomi . . ."). Most philosophers hold that other proper nouns go along with personal names, although some feel that one can speak strictly only about singu-

---

26. The alternatives, or range designated, in what follows draws not only, or even principally, on Ayer but on: Schwartz 1977; Schwarz 1979; Kripke 1980; Carroll 1985; and Nelson 1992. It is a "range" in the sense that the first few kinds are included in almost all discussions and the last in but few.

lar proper nouns. Others are comfortable with plurals and with common nouns. Personal nouns (as in Japanese, not names and not pronouns) come next, followed hard after by pronouns. Since in a sentence such as "George Washington was the first American president" the common noun *president* is only part of the predicate of the sentence, verbs are also included as names in many discussions. Some generous philosophers also include adjectives, demonstratives, and articles. Only a few words seem to be barred admission from these discussions, words that join and direct: *also, but, not,* and so on. And there must be a discussion somewhere that includes them as well.

Differences in choice and emphasis derive not solely from the complexity of the matter but also from the interests of the inquirers and certain inherent ambiguities in the language used. These matters can be best introduced by a comment in which concession yields to admonition:

> You can walk without knowing leg anatomy and you can talk grammatically without knowing a thing about grammar; moreover, you can use semantical terms, including meaning without having a theory of semantics. But do not confuse habit and theory. (Nelson 1992, 5)

Of course there is not only habit and theory. There are habits and theories. Among people interested in literature there will be differences (and not solely of habits and theories) between a classicist (Baxter 1992) and a critic concerned with metaphor (Brooke-Rose, 1958, 41–48, 212–18). There are dyers' hands among anthropologists and ethnologists (Lévi-Strauss 1966; Tooker 1984; Alford 1988).

Western philosophers turn to certain major (Western) figures as totems of logic. They seem not to have heard of anyone before John Locke, and the chances today are that any initial review will discuss John Stuart Mill on proper names, Gottlob Frege on names as descriptions, and Saul Kripke on causal chains and rigid designations (Nelson 1992, chap. 2; Carroll 1985, chap. 8; Kripke 1980; Donnellan 1977).

Although here spoken of earlier, only relatively recently (see especially Kripke 1980) have distinctions been drawn, or resolutions been made, in the ambiguity inherent in the use, in most languages, of the verb *name,* whether to bestow a name on that which has none or using a name that has been given. There is a further distinction, one I have not seen discussed but surely dealt with somewhere. That may be termed renaming or rebaptism, for which there are familiar scriptural examples: Jacob becomes Israel and Saul becomes Paul the apostle. (We may recall again the name-changing divinity Sarutabiko.)

The question these inquiries seem designed to answer concerns the difference names make, what they do or mean. Putting things in such terms, our understanding advances to certain sets of subissues that are far from easy or light. The issues may be cast semantically: what meaning or truth do names possess? And of course answers vary, from none to a great deal. (See Chisholm 1981; Carroll 1985; Nelson 1992.) But the much deeper cut comes with dropping the metaphor of names as actors and asking what we (subjects, actors) who use names mean or do and whether we consider the implications of our acts truthful: that is, corresponsive to, or designative of, the way things are. So considered, issues of meaning and truth are—or rather, *also* are—matters of intention (actions mental or physical) and reference (to objects in the wide sense of knowables). It is a major step to combine intention and reference in a single clause: "What is to be learned . . . is that reference is indeed intentional . . . either reference is unanalyzably object directed (as are beliefs, hopes etc.) or there can be no semantics and, in general, no psychology" (Nelson 1992, 35). The repudiation is only, but wholly, one of language or semiotics as an actor in favor of the user of words and signs. The repudiation is hardly likely to be consistent with certain kinds of literary sophistication, especially that adapting semiotics of usual (non-Peircean) kinds.

There are sure to be those who reject as naive the idea that names involve intentional reference by human subjects dealing with objects (including other subjects in addition to "the wide sense" mentioned above). But those who reject the idea must be firmly told that they subject themselves to a version of the reflexive principle: what is postulated about human roles applies, since they are human, to them as much as to others. If I hold that signs have agency whereas human agency and subjecthood is illusory, I logically must apply that to myself: I am a subjectless, agentless entity whereas signs are subjects—at least agents—and can act. One need not be a utilitarian to invoke the utility of thinking we human subjects use words and names rather than the reverse. And one need not be a philosopher to appreciate the philosophical views current (i.e., among philosophers if not literary critics).

The issues come to a head over the reference or referentiality of our use of *names*. Since there is considerable latitude in what may be reasonably meant by *names*, and not a little by referentiality as well, different things are implied by various discussions of reference. Great as those may be or seem, the use of names to refer is generally accepted by contemporary philosophers. Here is a little roll call from but a dozen or so years: Ayer 1964; Schwartz 1977 (a collection of studies); Schwarz 1979; Kripke 1980; and particularly Nelson 1992, *Naming and Referring*, and chap. 10, "Direct Reference."[27] The importance of the issue can scarcely be exaggerated, especially given the widespread agreement that we are discussing that central complex of human experience of ordinarily communicable kinds: the nexus of cognition or thought, of names or language, and of person or thing. It is no less than the possibility of naming by a given human subject in a given real situation. These matters have been expressed with great concision: "meaning arises in the reference relation, not from (gratuitously!) pinning a semantical interpretation on a mental representation" (Nelson 1992, 212). It appears that the only realistic position to assume is the realistic one.

As a botanical example will show, however, the altogether realistic assumptions that plants exist and may be named does not answer all the questions that may be posed. As examples, we can use a variety of plant names in natural English sentences.

1. Wild carrot is an inedible weed.
2. Queen Anne's lace is a summer-blooming wild flower.
3. Daucus carota is a tap-rooted, self-seeding European biennial now naturalized in the United States, where it is typically found in meadows and by the roadside.

Wild carrot, Queen Anne's lace, and Daucus carota are of course names for the same plant, and the predicates given for their names could therefore be exchanged without botanical error. But "an inedible weed" best suits "wild carrot," as "summer-blooming wild flower" best suits "Queen Anne's lace," and as "tap-rooted, self-seeding European biennial" best suits "Daucus carota." Surely we feel that the three names for "the same thing" are three names for three affectively differing if not

27. Philosophers make such numerous distinctions that few generalizations are clear out of context. Chisholm 1981 may be used as an example. In discussing referentiality, he distinguishes: meaning, reference, attribution, object, sense, designation, propositions, and attributions.

botanically different things when accompanied by differing predications. And the affective differences are sufficient to govern to no small
degree our conceptions. To phrase that differently, the reason for their
being three names is that somewhat different semantic and experiential
meanings are involved. The difference is not as great as that between
them and other plants with white flowers. But as we have seen, differing names for the same thing elicit different features and therefore
different responses. Anyone wishing to pursue this example may consider whether any of the three names (e.g., Queen Anne's lace) is a
proper name.

It should be evident that the necessary realist assumption requires
a degree of skepsis or dubiety, and not only because of our repeated
demonstration of capacity to get things wrong. Yet to start from any
ground other than philosophical realism seems impossible: not only
must there be something postulated to exist before its limits can be
logically discussed, but also a man who denies existence of the real has
no basis for assuming his own actual existence. One who denies that
names for persons, places, and times do designate persons, places, and
times must explain how a denier can exist, anywhere, any time.

Given the "linguistic turn" familiar in some literary discussions,
certain distinctions can be clarified by considering a logical counterpart
of the linguistic concept of marking. The unmarked form is the generic,
holistic, primal. The marked form is the specific, the included, the secondary. Unmarked forms include the singular, the positive, and the
declarative (or indicative). Inflection, addition—some modification,
and hence marking—is required to alter the singular into the plural, the
positive into the negative, the declarative into subjunctive or interroga-
tive and, for adjectives, the positive into comparative or superlative.
(That is simply a sample: in inflected Japanese, adjectives may be conju-
gated; in uninflected Chinese, additional characters must be added for
marking.) Realism is so far the logically unmarked that we often hear of
"naive realism." In the quarrel between realists and skeptics, the burden of proof lies on the skeptic who would "mark" realism. Again, the
reflexive principle requires that skeptical doubt about the real pertains
first of all to the reality of the doubter.

That this is so has implications, I believe, for the realist position as
well: the realist no more than the skeptic has access to another order of
logic or being that precedes the unmarked. To live and act, we are
realists and assume that we possess valid knowledge of a real world.

We cannot know whether what we know to be real is real in the senses we know it. Such knowledge is divine rather than human. We can and do know, as we are enabled—and constrained—to know: "We assume, making some adjustment here and there for miscuing and bad intention, that the evidence is in, and we are not totally in the dark as to what refers or applies to what. Our mission is to explain what everyone knows" (Nelson 1992, 201).

We name our names and speak our sentences with the premise that our references are assured. Human usage implies motivation, purpose, intention. Apart from special cases like God's infinite, and Edenic prelapsarian, capacities, naming can be conceded to be arbitrary in some sense. But conventional seems a better description, since *arbitrary* is not easily grasped: whose will, whose purpose, whose decree? *Conventional* is far more easily understood as matters of tacit agreement among users of a given language. There is no sempiternal reason why we should use the sounds "cat" (J. "neko") to mean cat or "star" ("hoshi") to mean star. But "language competence" means learning, knowing, and using such "conventions." Once we have learned the conventional or so-called arbitrary meanings signified by "cat" and "star," we will not attempt to feed a star or navigate by a neko. Once an actual linguistic system (i.e., "conventions") is in use, a "real" (i.e., rules-bound) relation obtains between thing and words for it. Since none of us (or anybody we can name) was alive when the organization (rules) of a language was set, our linguistic competence entails the premise of philosophical realism at least to the extent that, as language is used, denial of the premise requires assumption of its validity. Without assuming that competent praxis, we have no basis for human thought of any kind including, it must be said, the very comparison that is the basis of this study.

So brief a résumé of the lore and learning of *names* (especially presuming a reading of the works referred to) would show that the matters so quickly reviewed here point to the major issues of philosophers and others who have been concerned with names. There are also some matters of lesser importance that have been treated with such solemnity as to have some comedy in them. One of these might be termed, after one of its avatars, the French Academy rule. That is the belief that right naming cannot be left to ordinary citizens: under the influence of the Academy, there is a French legal list restricting what may indeed be termed the baptismal names that may be given to children.

There are other matters that might be pursued but that seldom emerge in philosophical discussions of onomastics. One is suggested by the distinction between artificial and natural languages. Mathematicians and logicians are among those who have devised artificial languages to achieve an exactitude not found in natural languages, an exactitude purchased at the cost of potential for growth and of connotative wealth. Another concerns what Western rhetoricians have technically termed "abuse" of words—usage in other than normal ways. Writers are among those who use ("abuse") language cunningly to achieve various ends, among them the resources of figures, whether of words (tropes) or syntax (schemes). Some of these matters are explored in Brooke-Rose 1958 and in Ferry 1988. They are not, however, central to the ends of this study.

A third consideration is important, however: fictions. It has been shown that a fiction—one kind of nonfactual statement—may allow for true propositions about what is, after all, nonexistent and therefore not true—*providing* the proposition is made with the right intention (Donnellan 1977, 218–19). Whether or not Donnellan is aware of it, he has made a distinction that has escaped certain didactic minds: the difference between fiction and a lie.[28] The liar pretends the truth of certain declarations that are not true. The dramatist makes no such pretense in setting a play in antique Thebes or present Brazil. The distinction is so easily made and grasped that the difficulty is in understanding how it can be missed. Another involves classes of fictions about things that do exist, albeit on terms different from those fictionally attributed to them. Here the conspicuous example is the legal fiction: for example, that a corporation is a person who may sue or be sued in court. Our very word, *fiction,* derives from the *fictio* used in Roman law for such purposes.[29] Since this subject will emerge naturally in the discussion of travel accounts, conclusive philosophical views of the issues may be deferred to the last chapter.

This rapid survey of philosophical concerns will serve, I hope, to

---

28. Donnellan's very interesting discussion will be examined in the final chapter, when the relation between fact and fiction is at issue.

29. Donnellan is closely associated with Kripke because what Donnellan terms "the historical explanation theory" of reference is philosophically very close to Kripke's "causal theory" of "rigid" designation by certain classes of "names." Since this is no secret, I mention it to discourage the assumption that Kripke's discussion of possible worlds is the same as Donnellan's "discourse about fiction": see Kripke 1980, 15–20.

provide an understandable initial microcosm of the larger world of problems and implications of naming. The small and the large ones alike show that some of the implications of the problems are at once important and difficult. But acquaintance with these issues as they are currently perceived would show that I have chosen to examine classes of names widely agreed to be most obviously central and secure to concerns with reference. The names considered are mostly singular, proper, and assigned to one of three groups: names of people, names of places, and names of times. Not only that: the names are also almost wholly factual, actual names, not fictions. Of these three groups, only that of the names of times is apt to pose any difficulty. A review of names of times may therefore be of use as a close to this part.

The calendar and calculations for time units were for Johnson and Boswell substantially the same as ours. So, too, were the names. The East Asian calendar and terminology differed in certain major respects. A year consisted of twelve months of thirty days each, so obviously necessitating occasional intercalary adjustments and readjustments (as we shall have occasion to see in the next chapter). The concept of weeks and their days did not exist until contact with the West in the late nineteenth century.[30]

Other details will be mentioned in Japanese usage, which may or may not be shared with China and Korea. Years were identified in two ways: most commonly as the initial or subsequently numbered years of a given regnal era of a given reign; but also among the learned as years in a sixty-year cycle based on combination of signs or names of the five elements with the twelve signs or names of the zodiac. Days of the month were named after versions of their number in the thirty—except for the special names for the first and final days. The year was punctuated as well by naming days in other fashion, essentially by their place in whatever pattern of annual observances (nenjūgyōji) was followed by the period and social class of the follower. Doubled days (first of the first month, etc.) were held to be special for various reasons. Over time, each month had many names. The four seasons were held with special respect, particularly in poetry, where they constituted most highly es-

---

30. Japan and Korea made up weeks beginning with days named like the first two in English, etc.: Sun-Day and Moon-Day, followed by counterparts of Tuesday through Saturday named after the five East Asian elements: Fire, Water, Wood, Metal, and Earth. The Chinese designated Monday through Saturday as First through Sixth Star-Days, and Sunday as Sun-Day.

teemed categories or topics. There was close correlation, of a coded or conventional kind, between natural phenomena (fauna, flora, diurnal stages, etc.), as in the seven autumn (or spring) plants, haze as emblem of spring and moon as emblem of autumn, although in actuality both appear in all four seasons. Certain times of the day were associated with seasons: dawn with spring, evening with autumn, and so forth.[31] Plants deemed important became identified with a given season or month, and many a day was distinguished by this or that customary human activity.

None of these matters is completely different from Western practices, and none is identical with them. But it still holds true that selection of names for people, places, and times is much the most conservative and assured in accounts of reference. And further reason for these choices will be evident as soon as it is recalled that the issue of names is raised to provide additional focus for comparison of accounts of travel. It is high time for us to join our four travelers, carrying with us as intellectual luggage the nature and problems of names—for persons, places, and times—reviewed in this initial discussion.

31. The locus classicus is the opening of *The Pillow Book* (*Makura no Sōshi*) of Sei Shōnagon (b. ca. 996). Her formulation is so central that departure from it required special measures.

Chapter 2

First Steps

One has no thought of retracing a single footprint.

—Bashō

On the eighteenth of August we left Edinburgh.

—Johnson

Names of Record

Although travel and hazardous exertion—travail—have long been synonymous and although travel has its dangers even today, it has held no small claim in Western literature. From the *Odyssey* in antiquity to the picaresque origins of the novel to imagined space or time travel today, such purposeful human motion has stood for the directions we take in our lives and in fact for life itself. It is one of the complex "universals" that may assist in imparting order and meaning, especially to narrative literature. It is therefore somewhat surprising to learn that Bashō uses his art—his kasen version of linked poetry—as a metaphor for travel rather than travel as a metaphor for life.

> The Master said, "A kasen is to be thought of as thirty-six steps. In taking the first step [writing the hokku], one has no thought of retracing a single footprint. The making new by devotion to travel derives solely from the desire to continue going."[1]

A kasen is a thirty-six stanza sequence (see app. 2). Bashō emphasizes the literal meaning of *hokku*, beginning stanza, presuming others follow: we must put anachronistic thoughts of haiku from our minds.

---

1. *Taisei*, 628. The source is the *Sanzōshi* (*Three Books*) of Hattori Dohō (1657–1730), quoted from in the first chapter. It and the *Kyorai Shō* (*Kyorai's Notes*) of Mukai Kyorai (1651–1704), also in *Taisei*, are accepted as authentic records of Bashō's remarks and are used extensively in what follows.

Bashō describes travel with three ends unfamiliar to most of us: to recognize and honor places poetically familiar, to compose poetry in sittings (za) with others met on the journey, and to set out as if death may be expected. Other distinguished linked-poetry masters typically composed solo sequences. Not Bashō, a fact emphasizing that not only companionship led him to travel accompanied.[2] Each companion would provide him with at least one reliable composer of sequences (haikai) composed in places and among other people however unfamiliar. When no other personal names appear in *The Narrow Road*, those of Bashō and his companion poet are implied. Although classed by Bashō himself as "a diary of the road" (michi no nikki), he seldom dates his entries. The names for times are implied, rather, by the seasonal imagery and topics necessarily celebrated in the various hokku written on the road. Place-names are another matter, as we shall have special reason to consider in chapter 3. And as we shall be seeing here in this account of first steps, each of our four travelers treats names of these three kinds in distinct ways.

No brief journey lay ahead for Bashō. (See fig. 1 and app. 1.) It will be recalled that he spent about seven months in 1689 traveling by boat, horse, and mostly on foot some fifteen hundred miles on his *Narrow Road*—and then another two years of less strenuous movement before returning to Edo. His companion, Sora, seems content to be Bashō's shadow. Fortuitously enough, *waki* designates both the second stanza in a sequence and the secondary role in nō, and Sora seems to have thought of himself so, with Bashō as hokku or the principal role, shite, in nō. Awed by being chosen companion, he seems to wish to conceal his every emotion and personal reflection. He bears the burden of duty to the leader and other members of the Bashō school. Here he is on setting out from Edo toward the narrow road.

On III.20 depart Fukagawa Depart by boat Reach Senju before
    11 A.M.
27th   Spend the night at Kasugae More than 35 km from Edo

---

2. Dates, fellow traveler, and titles include: 1684–85, Chiri for *Nozarashi Kikō* (*The Moor-Exposed Skeleton Journey*) or *Kasshi Ginkō* (*Journey of Haikai Composition in 1685*); 1687, Tokoku for *Oi no Kobumi* (*A Traveler's Book Satchel*); 1688, Etsujin for *Sarashina Kikō* (*A Journey to Sarashina*); 1689, Sora for *The Narrow Road* and again in 1691 for *Saga Nikki* (*The Saga Diary*). Others were frequently involved. Tokoku was the most gifted poet of the four.

28th   Spend the night at Mamata About 35 km from Kasugae
From night before rain falls Stops by 8 A.M.

(*Nikki,* 3)[3]

Reliable? No doubt whatsoever, if what one finds is what one wishes to rely on.

The anticipations and fears we experience in beginning a long journey are not to be found in Sora's account. No reader would accuse him of guile or literary excitement. To rouse myself from his unarousing opening, I have picked off the shelf another account of setting forth, the opening of Apollonius of Rhodes's *Argonautica* (Rieu translation), finding it slier than ever. In a parody of Homer's catalogue of the ships (*Iliad* 2), which is the sole instance in which he is more interesting than Homer, he manages to assemble the best if unlikeliest crew (including Orpheus and Herakles!), and get the moping Jason elected leader. The haruspical Idmon foretells that only he will die on the trip, but be famous for having made it. When many travel, there is always someone who urges the rest to get going; here that rousing, "awe-inspiring call" comes from no less a source than "Pelian *Argo* herself." With a speaking ship to urge and Achilles (though still a babe in arms—this story predates Homer, you see) to see his Dad Peleus off, the *Argo* quickly sails past this place and that place until becalmed at "Lemnos th' Aegean Isle" (so Milton's epithet), where "in the previous year, the women had run riot and slaughtered every male inhabitant" (Apollonius 1959, 44–53). Sora would be more at ease with telegrams than the Penguin classics.

The Caledonian Way

Samuel Johnson's *Journey* with his younger friend, James Boswell, required only about half the time needed by the two Japanese. Boswell records that his friend arrived in Edinburgh on "Saturday the fourteenth of August, 1773, late in the evening" and that on 9 November they returned there "this night . . . after an absence of eighty-three days." (See fig. 2 and app. 1.) On 22 November Boswell records that

---

3. Many scholars treat Sora's date of departure, the twentieth, as a mistake for the 27th (omitting the character for 7), but some say he would have corrected a mistake in the opening and that the implication is that he and Bashō spent six or seven nights in Kasugae. If so, then *that* requires explanation. See appendix 1. Sora measures distances here by *ri.* One such "league" equals 3.93 km or 2.44 miles.

"We breakfasted together, and then the coach came and took him up" for Newcastle and London (*Tour*, 11, 377, 393). One of Johnson's editors manages a quasi-eighteenth-century cadence in her summary:

> The narrative framework of the *Journey* can be indicated in a few lines. The first four and the last ten of its hundred days were spent in Edinburgh: the earlier spell gave Boswell the opportunity to exhibit his friend; the latter allowed Johnson to consolidate his ideas. The interim, during which these ideas had been gathered, was occupied by a journey, interspersed with visits, when and where hospitality and the weather detained the travellers. They traversed in its course regions of Scotland remarkably various: making their way northwards up the east coast to the Moray Firth; westward by the shore of Loch Ness and Fort Augustus; [thence to the Hebrides] visiting Skye (twice), Raasay, Col [or Coll] (unintentionally), Mull, Ulva, Inchkenneth, Iona; and [from the islands] making an irregular circuit of the south-west, to include Auchinleck [Boswell's father's seat]. (Lascelles 1971, xiv–xv)

Johnson's own version is sparing of words, complimentary, and authentic.

> I had desired to visit the *Hebrides*, or Western Islands of Scotland, so long, that I scarcely remember how the wish was originally excited; and was in the autumn of the year 1773 induced to undertake the journey, by finding in Mr. Boswell a companion, whose acuteness would help my inquiry, and whose gaiety of conversation and civility of manners are sufficient to counteract the inconveniences of travel, in countries less hospitable than we have passed.
> On the eighteenth of August we left Edinburgh. (*Journey*, 1)

This is honest eighteenth-century prose, although those unfamiliar with Johnson and Boswell might so far miss some of the things implied here as to wish to hear the *Argo* call out again. One observation must suffice for now: Johnson's account strikingly combines a supervising, knowing observer with places that are matters of fact, in principle always and in practice normally. What that observer does not report held no interest at the time, or if it did (as we learn from Boswell), his omission implies a standard of decorum or interest differing from his companion's.

Johnson's first word, "I," quickly yields to a "we" only formally inclusive of Boswell, whose no less "acute" first-person singular often attended to what Johnson bypassed and saw different things in beholding the same.

Johnson's method has a celerity of mind that is not the first impression taken of his style. After his initial paragraph, Johnson mentions Edinburgh, only to dismiss it with the trope of being "too well known to admit description" (1). "Inch Keith, a small island" admits enough description to tell its emptiness; then, after almost unadorned naming of "*Kinghorn, Kirkaldy,* and *Cowpar*" (2), we discover that Johnson's "we" have arrived—by the bottom of the second page—at St. Andrews. Thereafter, observation with extensive or curtailed view surveys all it chooses to survey in units to which places give the title. In formal terms, Johnson's labeled *Journey* is divided into a succession of what "we" observed by units coded with place-names.

Boswell's itinerary was only cartographically the same as Johnson's. One cannot say that his account is more detailed than Sora's, since detail is Sora's only staple. It certainly is fuller, however, than those of the other three. His opening resembles Johnson's in some features of polite style.

> Dr. Johnson had for many years given me hopes that we should go together and visit the Hebrides. Martin's Account of those islands had impressed us with a notion that we might there contemplate a system of life almost totally different from what we had been accustomed to see; and to find simplicity and wildness, and all the circumstances of remote time or place, so near to our native great island, was an object within the reach of reasonable curiosity.[4]

Three sentences later:

> When I was at Ferney in 1764, I mentioned our design to Voltaire. He looked at me as if I had talked of going to the North Pole, and said, "You do not insist on my accompanying you?" "No, sir." "Then I am very willing you should go." (3–4)

---

4. *Tour*, 3. Boswell refers to Martin Martin's *Description of the Western Islands of Scotland* (1703), which, as a boy, Johnson had received from his father and which they carried on their journey. Among his many helpful comments, Jean H. Hagstrum has reminded me that Boswell's "simplicity and wildness" with remoteness effectively introduce a major eighteenth-century topic, the sublime.

The paragraph continues through two lengthy sentences expressing Boswell's doubts that Johnson would be willing (whether or not he knew of the *nihil obstat* of the author of *Candide*) to make the trip.

The next paragraph announces Johnson's agreeing to do so in 1773. Boswell seems to have failed to inform Voltaire, but the reader is soon given the names of the worthies whose aid Boswell quickly solicited: Mrs. Thrale in London, the clan heads of Macdonald and MacLeod, "Lord Ellibank, Dr. William Robertson, and Dr. Beattie," and he generously quotes his letters to the last two, along with Beattie's reply. The strategic maneuvers of Boswell the impresario are continued for the reader's admiration, along with an apology that almost requires its own apology:

> My lord Ellibank did not answer my letter to his lordship for some time. The reason will appear when we come to the Isle of Skye. I shall then insert my letter, with letters from his lordship both to myself and Mr. Johnson. I beg it may be understood that I insert my own letters, as I relate my own sayings, rather as keys to what is valuable belonging to others than for their own sake.[5]

We shall see, sooner rather than later.

Although Boswell is in Edinburgh as a narrator (when not in Ferney with Voltaire), he still has not got Johnson to the heart of the Midlothian. He decides to introduce Dr. Johnson, LL.D., with the due fanfare of his "character—religious, moral, political, and literary" (6). It is well-measured praise, praise measured the more easily perhaps by the fact that it is published after Johnson's death, and indeed praise wholly harmonious with that in his *Life*. Portions from its beginning and ending will suffice.

> Dr. Samuel Johnson's character . . . nay, his figure and manner, are, I believe, more generally known than those of almost any man, yet it may not be superfluous here to attempt a sketch of him. Let my readers then remember that he was a sincere and zealous Christian, of high-Church-of-England and monarchical principles,

---

5. *Tour*, 6. In Boswell's revised version, published in 1785, he failed to include his own letter but did the others promised. That edited, published version is lively enough (almost getting Boswell involved in a duel) but much less animated after Edmond Malone's washing and starching.

> which he would not tamely suffer to be questioned. . . . He was
> voraciously fond of good eating, and he had a great deal of that
> quality called *humour,* which gives an oiliness and a gloss to every
> other quality.
>
> I am, I flatter myself, completely a citizen of the world. In my
> travels through Holland, Germany, Switzerland, Italy, Corsica,
> France, I never felt myself [away] from home.[6]

It is fruitless to inquire whether Boswell was the mere key to other
people's locks or they keys to him.

Another page (11) and it is that 14 August 1773 in Edinburgh when
Boswell welcomed his friend to Scotland and sauntered "arm-in-arm"
through the uncertain "dusky night" streets of Edinburgh to his house.
Ensuing pages show our narrator basking in the role of arranger for the
great Englishman—and crossing his fingers that there be no explosion.
The entry for four days later (Wednesday, 18 August) sees them on their
way. "On this day we set out from Edinburgh. . . . I have given a sketch
of Dr. Johnson; my readers may wish to know a little of his fellow-
traveller."

> Think, then, of a gentleman of ancient blood, the pride of which
> was his predominant passion. He was then in his thirty-third year,
> and had been about four years happily married. His inclination
> was to be a soldier, but his father, a respectable judge, had pressed
> him into the profession of the Law. He had travelled a good deal
> and seen many varieties of human life. He had thought more than
> anybody supposed, and had a pretty good stock of general learn-
> ing. He had all Dr. Johnson's principles, with some degree of relax-
> ation. (*Tour,* 32–33)

The mention of Dr. Johnson here is delicious in itself and for the warrant
Boswell seems to find it gives him to end his stint before his mirror by
quoting the last half of the first sentence-paragraph of Johnson's opening (quoted in the preceding) with its praise of James Boswell, Esq.

Another way of putting this initial comparison of initial things
involves two matters. First, in thirty-three pages Boswell reaches the
point Johnson does in one paragraph, the number of pages by which

---

6. *Tour,* 6–10. It seems that Boswell was acquainted with the proverb, "The wise are
at home in all countries."

Sora is almost half finished with his reports of people, places, times, lodging, and the weather on the entire journey. Also, in thirty-three pages Boswell gets the subject of Johnson in Scotland so inextricably tangled with that of himself that they never do get unraveled. None of this alters our sense of their differences or our conviction that Boswell's account is more interesting by far than Sora's or even Johnson's.

Wayfarers of the Centuries

How far would Boswell's thirty-three pages take us on Bashō's narrow road? The answer is not easily given. In the closely printed, three-column text of the authoritative one-volume edition of Bashō (*Taisei*), the entire *Narrow Road* is crowded into eleven pages. My annotated translation (in *Diaries*) requires about forty pages. The very fully anno-tated edition I use for amplest accounting (*Zenkō*) runs to almost five hundred pages. One moral inferable is that your Bashō neat is a power-ful elixir.

In fact, as Sora is the most remarkable for monotonous homoge-neity of style, Bashō is much the most various. (For samples of Sora's *Nikki* see figs. 20 and 21.) Like the thirty-six "steps" of a haikai kasen design, the successive episodes of *The Narrow Road* vary remarkably in style. Even the famous opening is complexly orchestrated, as not even my translation can obscure.

> The months and days are the wayfarers of the centuries, and, as yet another year comes around, it, too, turns traveler; sailors whose lives float away as they labor on boats, and horsemen who use the bit to guide their mounts, are turners to old age, spending their days in travel and making their home in wayfaring; many of old also have met death on the way. I, too, although I do not know what year it began, have long yielded to the wind like a loosened cloud and, unable to give up my desires to wander, have taken my way along the coast, so that finding last autumn, as I cleaned the old cobwebs from my dilapidated house by the river, that the year had suddenly drawn to a close, I imagined going beyond the Shirakawa Barrier, sufficiently possessed by some peripatetic urge that I thought I had a personal invitation from the god of travelers, and becoming unable to settle down to anything, I mended my underpants, then took three doses of moxa cautery and, unable to

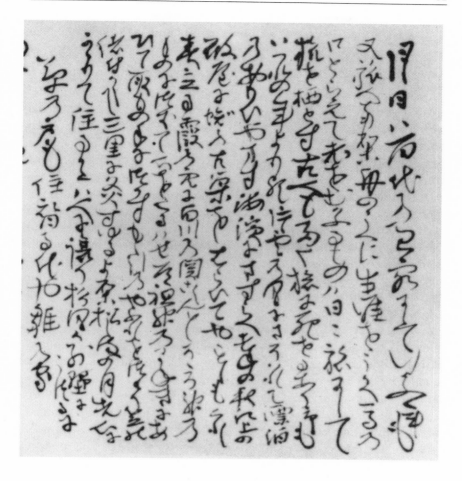

Fig. 4. The opening of *Oku no Hosomichi*. Buson's calligraphy. Note the lack of punctuation; the sole indentation is for Bashō's first hokku, not a paragraph. (From Buson 1973.)

put from my mind how lovely the moon must be at Matsushima, moved to Sampū's cottage, leaving behind and affixed to a pillar of my hut—

This thatched hut also
yields to the change of generations
now a Doll Festival house

—and the other seven stanzas opening a hundred-stanza sequence.[7]

Something of a prose poem, this famous opening describes the human condition in terms of travel, and given the association Bashō made between travel and a haikai sequence, it is appropriate that on leaving his hut he should post a hokku, which he quotes, and the rest of the eight on the front side of a sequence of one hundred stanzas. (One hundred stanzas would be written down on the fronts and backs of four folded sheets.) Underlying the travel and motion of life and art is the successive passage of time as a universal of human experience. This is stressed in various ways. The mention of "last autumn" refers to Bashō's return to Edo from travel to Suma and Sarashina in the early fall of 1688, as his subsequent tidying of his hut tells of his residing there for some months—till "the sky of the new year [of 1689] filled with the haze of spring." The hokku dates as III.3 the time of his leaving the hut to a family brightened by a daughter or daughters celebrating the girls' Doll Festival.

Time and travel are also joined in Bashō's allusions. Just how many there are depends on distinguishing as allusion what may be formulaic. But Japanese critics agree that Bashō does allude in the first clause to a preface by the Tang poet Li Bo (or Bai); and in the reference to spring's advent and travel to the Shirakawa Barrier perhaps to a verse by Li Bo, perhaps to the Taoist *Shuangjie (Sōshi)*, more likely to a waka by Mibu no Tadamine, and certainly to a poem by the eleventh-century waka poet and literary traveler, the monk Nōin (*Zenkō*, 55–57).

Poised with poets unnamed but alluded to from a valued past are two places from the Edo present—Bashō's hut and the elegant retreat of his poetic follower and a financial sponsor, the merchant Sugiyama, with the pen name Sampū. Two place-names suggest the travel ahead. The Shirakawa Barrier was famous from many poems, particularly Nōin's, and was taken as the gateway to the back country of northeastern Japan. Matsushima was a place famous in poetry and lore as one of the three principal beautiful sites of Japan. This beginning leads us to expect again evocative prose—and verse—at those locations.

---

7. This and other passages translating Bashō's *Oku no Hosomichi* are taken from *Diaries*, often revised, here especially the syntax, to take it closer to Bashō's continuing flow. For Buson's calligraphic version of the opening, see figure 4 and note the lack of punctuation. Indentations downward are not for paragraphs but to set off hokku and other poems.

The poising of two places in Edo and two places of name (nadokoro), as linked-poetry critics classified them, has a Chinese balance unlike the usual Japanese preference for asymmetry. There is also a stylistic matter usually missed by Bashō's readers (although not by all; see *Zenkō*, 57, 60). That is the Chinese-style parallel syntax of the very opening: two pairs of parallel clauses followed by another parallel pair that introduces further parallel subclauses that are just enough out of kilter (two subclauses here, one there) to flow into the more natural Japanese syntax that follows. Diagramming the clauses will show what is involved. First, in translation:

A   The months and days are the wayfarers of the centuries, and,
A' as yet another year comes around, it too turns traveler;
B   sailors whose lives float away as they labor on boats,
B' and horsemen who use the bit to guide their mounts,
C   are turners to old age,
    (1) spending their days in travel and
    (2) making their home in wayfaring;
C' many of old also
    (1) have met death on the way.

And now in transliteration:

A   Tsukihi wa hyakutai no kakaku ni shite
A' yukikō toshi mo mata tabibito nari
B   fune no ue ni shōgai o ukabe
B' uma no kuchi toraete
C   oi o mukōru mono wa
    (1) hibi tabi ni shite
    (2) tabi o sumika to su
C' kojin mo ōku
    (1) tabi no shiseru ari.

In a rhythm repeated often in *Oku no Hosomichi*, the Chinese element is then displaced by a Japanese, here a flowing syntax recalling Heian literature and its legacy. In fact, the entirety of the rest of the opening is one sentence or expression: from "I, too, although I do not know what year it began" ("Yo mo izure no toshi yori ka") to the hokku and the added clause, "stanzas opening a hundred-stanza sequence" ("omote hakku o iori no hashira ni kakeoku"). That opening clause of the long run seems, like one or two others, to have the very different—and Japanese—source, *The Tale of Genji*. That classic begins, "Izure no ōontoki ni ka." If so, Bashō stresses that he is embarking on a revised, more personally appropriate beginning, one involving Japan, Radiant Genji, and himself.

The personal relevance certainly is stressed by Bashō's use of a first-person noun (yo), something as attention-calling here as in the rest of classical Japanese literature. It has been well observed (*Zenkō*, 56–57) that this gesture associates him with the earlier mentioned "many of old" who died in travel: not only Li Bo (d. 762) and Du Fu (d. 770), but also in Japan Bashō's favorite waka poet, Monk Saigyō (d. 1190) and his most admired renga poet, Sōgi (d. 1502).[8] It is remarkable that this recollection should come just as Bashō is shifting from Chinese to more natural Japanese syntax. But the beginning with a Chinese march and the shifting to a Japanese dance is a stylistic shift he often finds suits his purposes.

The hokku that climaxes the opening passage is almost too well known to quote: "Kusa no to mo / sumikawaru yo zo / hina no ie." But we must not fail to notice Bashō's art in his delicate yet strong repetition that joins the conclusions of the "Chinese" prose opening, of the Japanese prose opening, and of the Japanese hokku:

Kojin *mo* . . .
Yo *mo* . . .
Kusa no to *mo* . . .

The repetition is quite unusual for a haikai poet and so joins the great writers of the past with our poet, led to travel yet again. The mention of another family ("Kusa no to mo . . .) at the Bashō An in Edo, at once completes and breaks the parallelism, leading to a Japanese asymmetry. This allows us to add a second interpretation to "many of old also" ("kojin mo"), now as referring to "the man of old" ("mukashi no hito") in *The Tales of Ise* (*Ise Monogatari*), the classic model of elegant Japanese prose leading to verse. And that man of old is presumed to be founded on an earlier waka poet-traveler, Ariwara Narihira. Bashō's point is of course that the man of old and himself at present are equally poets traveling to old age. They also share a name. After a certain point in *The*

8. Saigyō is the waka poet most often quoted in *The Narrow Road* (sometimes from poems wrongly attributed), with Monk Nōin next.

Tales of Ise the Narihira figure is called "okina" or "old man"—as in these years Bashō insisted on his followers naming him. (Sora of course follows the rule with his usual fidelity.)

As was said earlier, some of these likenesses may not entail deliberate allusion so much as evocation of certain matters by formulas with many exemplars. Bashō's use of them testifies to his ambitions. Dismissed though they were by the arbiters of taste in his time, haikai verse and prose alike were, he knew, his claim on posterity. But being Asian, he also knew that a claim of the present on the future could be established only by justification from the past. The claim and the necessity can be clarified from two passages in a brief account of a journey completed about a year before that in *The Narrow Road* began: *A Traveler's Book Satchel* (*Oi no Kobumi*).

For the first we must bear in mind the movement we have seen from "many of old also" to "I also." It is one of his most famous pronouncements: "In the waka of Saigyō, in the renga of Sōgi, in the pictures of Sesshū, in the tea of Rikyū true art is single in nature" (*Taisei*, 301). Who can doubt but that he implies addition of "and in the haikai of Bashō"? Later in the same account (*Taisei*, 302), he again names names. Ki No Tsurayuki, author of *The Tosa Diary*; Kamo no Chōmei, author of the *Kaidōki* (*Records of a Journey by the Sea*) and of *Ise Ki* (*Records of a Journey to Ise*); and Nun Abutsu, author of the *Isayoi Nikki* (*Diary of the Waning Moon*) are all, he says, authors of "diaries of the road" or travel accounts that he labels "bun," or true literature. That they are like his own in nature is clear enough from his adding, with that first-person noun, "yo," a comment including, "I have traversed the contours of them all." His claim was denied by his age. But there can be no doubt that he made it, and no doubt but that it has since been increasingly honored.

This is not to say that one sees into his mind or even that making up our own minds is always simple. (In the next chapter we shall find the contrary to be true.) But we can seek to identify a range of possible poetic and other connections. Each of the associations suggested is distinctly possible. Their aggregate and their presence elsewhere in his work makes a general claim far stronger than an insistence on any one example.

The ambition and seriousness of his claims must, however, not blind us to the fact that his haibun (prose associated with haikai) is tinted with the very special comedy of haikai change (haikaika). The

first three instances come almost hand in hand in the opening passage
we have been considering, as he prepares for the arduous journey. The
first example involves the deflation from the loftiness of what precedes
to the quotidian and material: his underwear, his old hat, and the pro-
phylaxis of burning moxa at certain spots of the body. The next change
occurs with the hokku, itself a poem about change in time and change
of generations of residents. From an old man's dusty quiet there will
emerge a girl's happy laughter and bright sleeves—the joke is no doubt
on both of them in this sorry world.

Aspects of the third haikai change seem to have gone unre-
marked.[9] Bashō's hokku is, he says, pasted or otherwise attached to an
inner post of his hut—a Japanese and even more a Chinese custom.
That hokku is the first of eight stanzas, the omote hakku or front of the
first sheet. This is the opening of a hundred-stanza (hyakuin) sequence
in renga and haikai; its stanzas make up an initial introduction (jo) for
the introduction-development-rapid close (jo-ha-kyū) movement of all
linked-poetry sequences. (See app. 2.) That Bashō should have composed a solo (dokugin) sequence of a hundred stanzas is one of the less
likely claims made in 1689. For one thing, he only suggests a whole
sequence. For another, he rarely and one might almost say never will-
ingly composed anything but thirty-six-stanza sequences. For yet another, he never wrote a solo sequence apart from the minimal hokku-
waki (two-stanza) piece. For a final thing, the other seven stanzas do not
exist.

We are meant to smile in recognition of the disparity between
things as they might be and things as they are. We are meant to smile
rather more over the drop from Chinese formal seriousness and Japanese high verities to the poet's mending underpants and imagining a
girl's pleasure in displaying her dolls. We are meant to smile also with
little amusement in recognition that in all this alteration, real and imagined alike, there is a world left behind to others and a new road ahead
for the poet. Through these shadings of mood, our indulgence of a shift
impelled by thoughts of time yields to the assuaging surmise of fictionalized place. The moment of fiction (and all the stanzas following
the hokku are fictional in haikai) casts a dreamlike, spring haze–like
aura over the whole opening. Nothing in the openings of the other three
accounts remotely resembles the artistry here.

---

9. Very important although noncomic significance has been shown by Andō 1974,
179–85.

The contrafactual (or seeming) claim to have written a solo hyakuin assists Bashō in establishing his self-definition. He is not a person cut off from human companionship. The reference to Sampū ensures that. So does his subsequent mentioning (without a Homeric or Apollonian catalogue of the ships) of the group of people who saw him off, and soon after that, Sora, "who accompanied me on the journey." All the same, he maintains an air of distance from others, a sense of detachment from the present world and society. Or rather the details and the contingencies of that social world are set at a distance from him. He seems to wish to stress the isolation a traveler feels in setting out upon unknown ways, and to define by that isolation his existential and even metaphysical common ground with others on the basis of the interrelation of travel, poetry, the great figures of the past, his own sweat on dusty paths, and a sense of the mystery that colors even the certainties of nature and death.

The features of Bashō's initial self-definition and the art sustaining them will require our continuous attention. What he chooses to stress naturally implies lesser emphasis on other matters, or, to put it comparatively, understanding more fully his self-definition requires attention to the openings of the other three accounts. Sora's modesty and devotion to detail is so safe as to make us aware that Bashō runs genuine risks with his soaring—and his descents. The openings of Johnson's and Boswell's accounts, in each of which the other is an important presence, suggest a deeper immersion than Bashō's in present human society. The conspicuous names in each of their openings are those of their companion and of Scotland distinct from England. To Bashō, the important names are those of named evocative places and poets of a valued past evoked by allusion.

Johnson and Boswell will modify their initial stance. Johnson will become more and more the authoritative observer, seeing and knowing all, over the heads of others. Boswell will intensify his engagement with others, giving many, many people their names with our sense that their hearts beat. That continues to the end, even after our discovery that the aim of taking the pulse and blood pressure of others is his way of trying to assure himself that his own blood courses. By a kind irony not of his making and from which Boswell is never able to extricate himself, his realization of that very assurance is assured by its never fully succeeding or failing. In this, Boswell is the polar opposite to that model of self-effacement, Sora. So different are they that it seems unlikely that even that self-styled citizen of the world, Boswell of ready words, or that lexicographer of people as well as words, Johnson, could find them to describe Sora. On the other hand, although there is scant profit in doing so, we easily enough imagine what Sora might write about them if he had encountered them on his way:

15th Sky clear later clouds Crossed the Morikawa by ferry Two foreigners on boat, one named Johnson, one Boswell Stayed night at Kawaguchi with Zenkichi Two sets of hai[kai]

We may be grateful to Sora for his modesty and devotion to Bashō and for his showing so incontrovertibly that, although art may conceal art, artlessness cannot conceal itself. As for Johnson, he shows that exceptional intelligence and distinctive personality will not fail to sustain interest. But the least attentive reader would fully understand that his account lacks the appeal of the travel records by Bashō and Boswell. Their minds and their art invest interest in that which may seem doubtful or devoid of appeal, even to them. Minds and arts of their differing kinds are equally born and made.

Journeys and Journals

As our travelers start out, it will not be amiss to bear in mind the differing means or approaches they took for their narratives. Japanese distinguish diaries, or nikki from diary literature, or nikki bungaku. (We are revisiting *A Traveler's Book Satchel:* those "diaries of the road" were considered literary.) The distinction emerged in the tenth century when a new kind of nikki emerged as a rival to an older. The older was and continued as the province of men, who kept their daily records in what may, with courtesy, be termed Chinese: a succession of Chinese written characters that educated Japanese could understand but not pronounce in Chinese and that educated Chinese could pronounce but often not understand. Around 930 or 935, Ki no Tsurayuki—whose originality was most conspicuous in the genius displayed in devising the model for a poetic collection (i.e., the *Kokinshū*, the first of the twenty-one compiled by royal edict)—extended his province of wit by inventing a diary written in a Japanese that not only could be pronounced as well as understood but that, being in pure Japanese, was open to reading and subsequently to writing by women. That is the point of the opening of his *Tosa Diary* (*Tosa Nikki*): "It is said that diaries are kept by men, but I shall see if a woman too cannot keep one" (Miner 1969, 59). It is assumed that Tsurayuki wrote his *Tosa Diary* from notes (perhaps an actual diary) and poems that he obviously assembled during the return from his governorship of Tosa (southern central Shikoku) late in 934 and early in 935. As that first sentence shows, Tsurayuki chose a fictional woman as his diarist-narrator, and real women as well as men followed his example.

Like *diary* and *journal*, *nikki* means *daily* records. Among the many diarists of travel, Tsurayuki and Sora maintain the presentation of events by daily entries. So does Boswell, although his nervous, restive spirit often flits to the past or jumps ahead. Johnson chooses a radical formal difference in organizing his account by place-names. His result is somewhat more of an itinerary than a diary, but time is not ignored in the succession of places. Neither place nor time is finally as important, however, as the sense that this is what was seen by and mattered to me, Samuel Johnson—as universal truths and convictions of the heart—and this is what you, reader, should consider as I have.

Bashō is hardest to deal with. As we shall be seeing, he occasionally (eleven times in all) mentions dates. The fifty hokku by him and those by others must refer, as by rule, to phenomena that indicate which season and which stage of the season it is among the spring, summer, and autumn of those seven months or so of 1689. That is, the hokku are factual, whereas those that follow in the sequence are fictional. What is true of a haikai sequence is true also of *The Narrow Road*: time as season defined by poetic codes matters more than any calendar. Yet, for reasons that will emerge in the next part, place matters more than time, or rather is inclusive of time. So far is that the case that editions commonly designate parts of *The Narrow Road* by divisions according to locality. That is, unlike the other three, Bashō presents a series, a continuous sequence not in accord with any single principle, whereas his editors' dominant method of commentary involves division of the text into parts based largely (but not solely) on place. Since this differs from practices in annotated editions familiar to me in other literatures, it is worth pointing to.

For example, we can consider Matsuo Yasuaki's edition, *Oku no Hosomichi Zenkō* (*Zenkō*). It divides Bashō's account into sixty-six units: sixty-five numbered and an unnumbered postscript. Most of the sixty-six are designated by one or more place-names, with three places being divided into two: 13–14, the Temple Unganji; 18–19, Sukagawa; 45–46,

Gassan. One place is divided into three parts: 488–50, Kisagata. The sections not labeled by place-name are 1, Introduction; the borderline 2, "Sampū's Cottage"; 3, "Departure"; 22, "Relics of Vice Governor Satō's Family"; 58, "Sora's Departure"; and the unnumbered final postscript. Minute, systematic commentary of various kinds is provided for each of these sections.

To specify: the "Introduction" is taken to be what is presented as the first seven lines plus one word in the translation of the opening given above: seven clauses in all, and just over four lines of the "original" in the largest size of type used in the edition. Below it is a translation into modern Japanese given in the smaller but medium-sized type of most of the rest of the material for each episode. There follow two lines of textual annotation, this in a third, the smallest type used. The bulk of the ensuing commentary follows in four parts set in the mid-sized type. The first section consists of twenty-seven lines of commentary that explains words and phrases in the original in ways related to the translation into modern Japanese. Next there are twelve lines on features of the figurative language. That is followed by eleven lines of the editor's commentary. The final section is much the longest, a forty-three line digest of commentary selected from earlier scholarship and criticism.

From this it should be evident why the dozen pages or less in the *Taisei* could, with commentary and all, stretch to nearly five hundred in this edition (*Zenkō*). Such scale justifies two other inferences. *The Narrow Road* enjoys special status as a classic. In addition, this classic is deemed so rich and, yes, so difficult that no lesser measures would be adequate. We do not seriously misrepresent *Oku no Hosomichi* by terming it a very complex poem. It is not surprising, especially given Bashō's perfectionism, that he should not have completed it to his entire satisfaction during the remaining five years of his life. It is less easy to understand why eight more years would pass after 1694 before it was published.

Our rereading of any except Sora's account will almost certainly find them less transparent than greater familiarity allows. In fact it is quite normal that even the first time our progress from the beginning both clarifies and complicates understanding; once knowledge of the whole is acquired, subsequent readings differ from the first. As a matter of fact, simple Sora is only a seeming exception. In the end we shall discover that he, too, repays critical faith, the willing suspension of our superiority.

The likenesses of the sense of openings assure us that the differences we perceive are real. All are genuine beginnings, and each beginning is validated by the other member of its linguistic and historical pair. Nothing in any of the beginnings invalidates the thesis that the beginning concerns a start to back country that the author has read about, but into which he has never before set foot. Nothing invalidates the thesis that it is just such sameness that enables us to compare, to draw securely the lines of difference between each account and the others.

The setting forth of our travelers does not end with the beginnings just considered. Each place (emphasized formally by Johnson), each day (emphasized by Sora), and each fusion in an episode of the place and day (stressed by Bashō and Boswell) yields another beginning. But, as we know from our own travels, none of the later beginnings matches in anticipation—in mixed hope and dread—the excitement of the first beginning. In what follows here a further presumption will be made as to the principal stages that follow the beginning. The second stage (chap. 3) will be treated as one of hitting stride, of developing the emphases that determine the basic features of the journey, and particularly of the ways of telling those features. The third stage (chap. 4) will be taken as one of harvest, of reaping the benefits of earlier planning and care. And the final stage (involving aspects of this and the next two chapters) will deal with the ends we discover with the travelers, the teleology, the biblical interpreters' anagogy, the understanding arrived at. I believe there will be curiosities and perhaps occasional surprises along the way but that we shall not have cause to abandon our initial sense of each of the four travelers. We shall certainly not confuse one with another. And in reflecting for a moment on ourselves as readers, we recognize that we have taken with them the initial steps on their narrow roads. With that recognition, we are readied to continue with them on conjoined ways.

Chapter 3

Under Way

in medias res.

—Horace

diaries of the road.

—Bashō

How seldom descriptions correspond with realities.

—Johnson

I cannot express the ideas which went across my imagination.

—Boswell

Bearing Names

Our travelers have taken their first steps. Neither in actual travels nor in accounts of them does a beginning end or does a middle begin so decisively as the Aristotelian view of beginning, middle, and end suggests. We should not expect such lowerings and raisings of stage curtains. Yet there are often moments when, without fanfare, the recording traveler and the attending reader recognize that the journey is fully under way. Such a moment can be discerned in Boswell's *Tour* two days out of Edinburgh, as is shown by all of one brief paragraph and the first sentences of the next two.

> I have not preserved in my Journal any of the conversation which passed between Dr. Johnson and Professor Shaw, but I recollect Dr. Johnson said to me afterwards, "I took much to Shaw."
> We left St. Andrews about noon, and some miles from it observing at Leuchars a church with an old tower, we stopped to look at it. . . .

> We saw this day Dundee and Aberrothock, the last of which Dr. Johnson has celebrated in his *Journey*. (47, 48)

The second sentence shows that they are on the move. The first and third reveal a narrator able to use retrospection of a kind infeasible in a beginning. Both Boswell and his account have passed beyond beginning to the establishment, the realization of journeying.

By contrast, we can observe Bashō still in his beginning. As a seasoned traveler, he carried little. But he was seen off by friends (see fig. 5), who encumbered him with kindnesses:

> The pack of things on my bony, thin shoulders was giving me pain. Setting out with nothing but what I could bear myself, I carried a stout paper outer coat to keep out the chill at night, a cotton kimono, raingear, something in the way of ink and brush—and various things given me as farewell presents and therefore difficult to dispose of. It was the traveler's dilemma, knowing them a hindrance and unable to throw them away. (*Diaries*, 158–59; *Zenkō*, 96)

The mention of impedimenta is a common beginning, although awareness may be keener at later, trying moments. What is carried also tells something of the carrier, as Bashō's enumeration shows. Johnson carried a great stick, pistols, books, and other items testifying to his expectations of need. Boswell's gear included paper for his notes (not enough as it turned out), a Bible and, like us all, a luggage of ideas. Sora must have thought through what facts he was responsible for recording and the heavy duties he bore his poetic master and colleagues. Bashō's writing implements recorded prose notes or passages now lost, except what may survive unidentifiably in *The Narrow Road*. But they also enabled him to set down that which most fully defined him to himself and others, his poems.

The things that the travelers carried matter little to us, except when they enter into the narrative, as when Johnson presents someone with a book. But our own experience of travel shows that our impedimenta make a difference in comfort. Occasional details provide a glimpse of the human comedy. Boswell mentioned his carrying Ogden's sermons sufficiently often to be satirized for it.[1] (See figure 6 on their starting out

---

1. Samuel Ogden's *Sermons on the Efficacy of Prayer and Intercession* was published at Cambridge in 1770.

Fig. 5. Edo friends seeing off Bashō and Sora. (From Buson 1973.)

from Edinburgh.) Sora later displayed, almost as a relic, Bashō's soiled raincoat, given as a souvenir. His pride elicited some jeers and perhaps some envy. Those objects carried in 1689 or 1773 went over routes of considerable length, especially for the Japanese pair proceeding mostly on foot. (Johnson and Boswell traveled with far more luggage and more often with others as a party.) Our four travelers also bore what they assumed rather than noticed: their individual identities and their culture. We too assume them, or subsume them under their names. Without those names, it would be meaningless to speak of Bashō's *Narrow Road*, Sora's *Nikki*, Johnson's *Journey*, Boswell's *Tour*. The addition of those other proper names, or titles, brings the worlds of the writers into our ken.

We readers have taken likewise, with those travelers, our first step and committed ourselves thereby "to keep on going." We also carry our personal and cultural baggage, some of which has been the subject of matters discussed in the previous chapters. We are still fresh, fresh but

Fig. 6. Johnson and Boswell's departure from Edinburgh. In Rowlandson's caricature, Margaret Boswell waves, from right, to Joseph Ritter (Boswell's Bohemian servant), her husband, and Johnson. Boswell's frequent mention of Ogden's *Sermons* is gibed at here. (From Rowlandson 1786.)

accustomed to associating travel and names. Since travel is by definition a kind of movement through a spatial continuum, names of places
are as necessary as natural. Equally obviously, because spatial movement cannot be instantaneous, times must somehow be designated—at
least from time to time. The most important names of all, those of
people, appear equally naturally in diary literature. As our travelers
bear on, they meet a succession of people, some familiar and many
more new, as they recognize by accustomed or novel names: names that
acquire meaning for us as well as our four wayfarers. Anticipation or
recollection can summon, by thought of a name, an absent person to
present thought. But the typical crucial tension in diary literature is the
overwhelming presence of the almost completely unnamed diarist and
the often briefly known but necessarily designated persons newly met.
Downplay of the one normally emphasizes the other.

Travel literature has natural utility, then, for a study of the implications of literary and other naming. The utility is also one extending to
the very grounds of comparison itself, by being founded on the naturalness with which names of persons, places, and times become explicit in
travel literature. This explicitness in turn enables us to understand,
through adequately justifiable comparison, fundamental features of a
travel account. It is significant that the *Tosa Diary* (*Tosa Nikki,* ca. 935)
employs daily entries, whereas the raft journey down the Mississippi of
Huckleberry Finn seems almost to occur out of time, just as it is comparatively and intrinsically meaningful that Boswell's journal of a trip
in Scotland should employ daily entries and faithfully record places,
but always with an eye to named persons and that universally important unnamed person, oneself. The comparability is assisted by the high
degree of factuality of all four "records."[2]

Presuming that we can and do name according to cultural conventions and literary codes, it follows that we must be clear about what it is,
in the context of travel accounts, that we name. Although philosophers
feel greatest ease with singular proper names, philologically and philosophically speaking, names are not restricted to the singular or proper

---

2. Modern critics assign *The Narrow Road* to the class of *kikō bungaku,* recorded
travel literature, presumed to be factual in the absence of evidence to the contrary. Names
in fiction are often specially significant. In *Huckleberry Finn,* "Huckleberry" designates a
rude country boy, and "Finn" has an Irishness that makes the drunkenness of his father
appropriate—given the element of stereotype or prejudice. Twain's *Life on the Mississippi*
may be substituted for the novel, if a more factual account is desired.

for designating people and places, or for physical things and even subjective time. Since names are of somebody or something, the use of names of those three crucial categories—persons, places, and times—is reference to what the names are taken to designate. We are interested in names not only as three dimensions or coordinates of reality, but as deliberate means of indexing or conveying. In other words, the act of naming is intentional, whether involving humble immediate needs or deeply held cultural conceptions. For some reason, perhaps because of its subjectivity and its seeming elasticity (or compressibility), time has received most attention from literary critics.[3] In fact, since it can be shown to be the least important of these most important three, it may provide us with our visa.

An initial distinction must be drawn between the knowing process we use for the literary medium and the things we know by the process. As with music and dance, so with literature, the knowing process is radically temporal, as those for the other arts are not. Of course something conspicuous in a painting (in, say, a figure in a Dutch window scene or in a Japanese wood-block print) is likely to draw our attention first. It is customary to appreciate a cathedral's architecture by entering a set door and progressing through the nave toward the altar. But on entering further we are just as likely to look at the brass plate on, or the sign beside, the painting and to meander toward a side chapel or cloisters, away from those noisy tourists making routine progress through the church.

The literary medium is, on the other hand, a "spatial form" only metaphorically, as our memory, analysis, and anticipation combine. The literary object of such ill-termed "spatial" cognition may be thought of in terms of combinations, parallels, conclusions, and so forth that may be more or less taken out of the temporal medium for separate cognition. But the degree of possible extraction is limited and cannot be derived from a random scrambling of the words of a play, poem, or narrative. In other words, to make sense at all, poems, dances, and tunes must be known as not simply a continuum or as separated items, but as a continuous, established *sequence*. And the sequence must be of a

---

3. The Western locus classicus on time is Augustine, *Confessions*, 11 and 12, holding to a dominant present, as with the presence of the past and of the future. To Buddhists the three temporal "worlds" are mere terms of convenience, whereas time has no real existence. See Nakamura 1962, 207, s.v. "sanze." In practice, however, Japanese live by clock and calendar in as "realist" a fashion as do Westerners.

certain order, one steadily varying and yet continuously, intelligibly predicating. Dictionaries, gazetteers, and calendars all possess order, but not sufficient order to be literary or even full examples of language in use. For that a syntax and grammar are required. Calendars are the most completely ordered of the examples given, precisely because time is the simplest of the three radicals.

As with music and dance, the temporality of the literary medium derives of course from its nature as a continuing expression. The syntax and grammar that are metaphorical for them are literal for literature. In a sense, this is no more to say than that literature differs from music and dance (as well as the other arts) in being verbal. As with those other arts with temporally sustained media, however, literature is necessarily diachronic in expression: words all together would be noise and all apart silence. In some recent critical accounts, the linguistic nature of literature has been honored, like a royal baby, almost to suffocation. The other arts (and much else) show that thought need not be linguistic at all, and even for literature the linguistic dimension is but the verbal tip of the iceberg.

The least-examined condition for literature is that of something even more important than time: place. For if we can think without language, we obviously do not exist to think or do anything else if we are not somewhere—and a somewhere that is not simply a pin pricking a map or only a condition of being. The place is a matter of nurture (or culture) as well as nature. Time may be, as it were, interrupted, and we may speed or hasten performance, if only by the poet's craft and sullen art or by our most oracular ordinary experience, solitary reading— reading that if it is to be at all, must be somewhere. The specific some- wheres imply far more than the author's desk and the reader's arm- chair. They involve as well an interplay between the author's and reader's histories. The object of that interplay is what each understands in contemplating the given literary expression. We are given to charac- terizing that expression as factual or fictional, although the characteriz- ation refers only to what we think dominant in what is inevitably both a factual and fictional time-place-history encoded in the literary expression.

That multidimensional cultural history must be of something, something making more or less of place and of time, but necessarily even more of one or more persons. Aristotle famously or notoriously played down the poet's role in only one crucial respect, his preference for relation by characters (Plato's and his mimesis) over relation by a poet (Plato's diegesis). Because he held imitation by the characters preferable to imitation by the poet, he thought Homer the greatest epic writer in having his characters do so much imitation in what he regarded as a unique mixed style.[4] It is curious that even the most dramatic lyrics—those by a Donne or dramatic monologues by a Browning—commonly slight either time or place. And in those that slight both space and time, the speaking version of a person is all the more crucial. Moreover, although Paul de Man was too narrowly insistent on apostrophe as the radical of the lyric, his insight suggests the importance—often a shadowy presence—of the *other person* of lyric. Or to put matters differently, lyric offers a poetics of radical affective-expressive address that mimesis does not.[5]

These more or less empirical and certainly historical matters can be shown to demonstrate the logical priority of persons to space and time, and of space to time in literature. We may take as example narrative, because it is likely to share most with the other two: plot with drama, and unperformed relation with lyric.[6] Narrative can go for long stretches without dialogue, long stretches that sustain a continuum of sequence far beyond the shorter breaths of lyric. And for such reasons narrative normally develops multiple versions of specified persons, places, and times. A specified *person* is a character, and a specified (portion of) *space* is a place. We lack a common, natural term for literarily specified time, a fact that may itself hold some significance. *Specified times* will have to do. It is entirely just that the specification of time depends on use of names for some period (noon, Thursday, the Tang dynasty) or on temporal deictics (then, meanwhile, finally).

The argument as to the *descending* series of persons, places, and times is most simply presented in terms of plotted narrative, although it also holds for nonplotted writing in terms of characters, places, and

---

4. See Plato, *Republic*, 392d (Jowett 1892, 3, 77); and Aristotle 1947, *Poetics*, chaps. 23–24, 26 (pp. 657–61, 666–67).

5. For lyric apostrophe, see de Man 1985; and for affective-expressive poetics see Miner 1978–79. The really curious thing about Aristotle is his devotion to dramatic mimesis in a literary tradition of which Homeric narrative was and remained central. It is next odd that one could not infer from his *Poetics* the importance of the lyric odes in Greek tragedy.

6. The lack of a originating, systematic poetics based on narrative is discussed by Miner 1978–79 and 1991; the latter also discusses plotless narrative. Depending on the way plot is described (and very few critics have bothered to), all four of our accounts or only Sora's is plotless.

specified times in the given sequence, whether literary, historical, or otherwise. The telling fact is that time may be changed without change in place, in characters, or in plot line (sequence).[7] A narrative may simply have a gap signaled by something like, "Three weeks later" (name and deictic) or "On 28 July" (deictic and two names), when the last event dealt with was a birthday in April. Or steadily advancing time involves constant change as the plot process at its simplest: time simply passes, as we say, while the characters can remain themselves in the same place.

A change in place is more important, because it does entail a change in specified times or characters, or both. Characters cannot be in different places at the same time, although the same characters may be in the same or changed places at different times. Characters are the most important of all. An utter change of characters gives us a new story, lyric, or play; or it either introduces a subplot (subsequence) or reintroduces the main plot, depending on which had preceded. In plots of any length, there will inevitably be partial replacements of characters, some of whom may "depart" never to appear again (e.g., the Fool in *King Lear*), or others of whom leave the scene for return in yet more significant appearance (Achilles in the *Iliad*). These distinctions hold for unplotted lyrics as well. That is, in lyrics also there is an ascending order of importance from specified times to places to characters. It is one thing if Shakespeare thinks of his friend as a summer's day, or of summer having all too short a lease. It is another, more important thing for Donne to imagine "the round earth's imagin'd corners" or making "one little room an everywhere." Yet as we read the lyric ending of the greatest English narrative poem—

> Som natural tears they drop'd, but wip'd them soon;
> The World was all before them, where to choose
> Thir place of rest, and Providence thir guide:
> They hand in hand with wandring steps and slow,
> Through *Eden* took thir solitarie way—

the ascending importance from time to place to persons is indisputably clear.

---

7. Similarly, sequence is logically prior to plot. Plots not only can be but are told in an order different from their abstracted chronological sequence, and yet remain the same plots. But, ipso facto, any alteration of a sequence creates a new, different sequence. More simply still, all literary works have a sequence, but not all have a plot.

Since these are logical matters, they are true of any culture we can conceive of. But as the actual handling of our three entities differs to a lesser or greater degree from literary example to example and from age to age, so it may differ even more from culture to culture. This fact explains the desirability of comparative and, indeed, of intercultural evidence.

To facilitate discussion, persons, places, and specified times will be distinguished for convenience rather as grammarians distinguish nouns (although much more than convenience is involved). For example, there is common place, an unnamed, unidentified location. There is also proper place, that which is named and assumed to exist. There is also, frequently in literature, improper place—that which is taken not to exist, whether because it is fictional or because it has the problem of unreality possessed by Shakespeare's seacoast of Bohemia (*The Winter's Tale*, 3, 3, 1–2). The *relative* unimportance of time will be apparent in this giving "to airy nothing / A local habitation and a name": Shakespeare does not require Theseus even to mention *time*.

The logic of literary comparison requires further attending to. From Plato's *Cratylus* to Stoic allegorizing, to some recent theory, the derivation of words has often been given misleading significance. Such importance would not be assigned, however, if words, their derivations, their histories, and their associations lacked *interest*. So it may be fairly said that, although the fact has no probative value, it *is* a curiosity of coincidence that all four of our diaries of the road have a common derivation in their varying crucial terms. The "journey" of Johnson's title, the "journal" of Boswell's, and the "diary" used in English for Sora and for Bashō's "diaries of the road" as well all derive from the Latin *dies* or "day" (see also *diurnus* and *diurnum*). Although the Japanese *nikki*—as in Bashō's michi no nikki or "*diaries* of the road"—obviously does not come from *dies,* it does derive from a combination of *nichi* or "day" and *ki* or "record." His phrase can therefore be literalized beyond "diaries of the road" to "daily records of the road."[8]

Such coincidence aside, the logic of comparison here has another principal feature. By introducing naming to heighten sufficiency of likeness for justice of comparison, we also introduce another variable.

---

8. The phrase appears in his *Oi no Kobumi* (*Traveler's Book Satchel*), 1687; *Taisei*, 302. Although the plain sense of "nikki" is "daily records," most works in the rich Japanese tradition of diary literature, dating from about 935, do not feature daily entries, any more than do Bashō and Johnson, as distinguished from Sora and Boswell.

Names of people, and names adopted by writers (and other artists) in particular, have differing social as well as personal implications in Japan and (for example) England. For that matter, we shall be concerned in due course with differing properties distinguishing two of our four examples: the poetry so important to Bashō's account and an essay on Scottish and generalized human society inserted into Johnson's. Moreover, although names of persons and places are logically more important than denominations of temporalities, time may have recurrent prominence, or devotion to place may almost seem to exclude persons. It is always in season to remember that: literary comparison is pointless if it does not take into account literary evidence, actual literary creations. They alone provide meaningful grounds of comparison, providing of course there is sufficient likeness to make the comparison just and the differences illuminating.

Like most other comparative studies, this one has its historical and critical concerns along with the theoretical and comparative. To distinguish the four implies differentiation rather than opposition among these kinds of study. But to give some emphasis to the centrality of comparison and somewhat to downplay chronology, the rest of this second part leads—after some account of travel and travelers—into Johnson's and Boswell's eighteenth-century accounts before considering Bashō's and Sora's of a journey taken some eight decades earlier.

Hitting Stride

Travel is sufficiently central to human life for various features of wayfaring to be metaphorical for far more than moving from one place to another. *Odyssey* is a common as well as a proper noun. To the Roman Stoic, Epictetus, life was an inn on the way. The novel would be very different if its origins did not include travel literature and romances featuring travel. The Dao (Way) is a term or concept central to the major "ways" of Chinese thought. The three are of course the ways of Confucius, of the Buddhas and, most conspicuously, of the Daoist sages: our *Daoism* means "Way-ism." Of the Chinese triad, Japanese made most (and much more than the Chinese did) of the Way of the Buddhas, butsudō, but they never lost sight of Shintō, the way of their anciently worshiped divinities. Japanese "dō" (or, unvoiced, "tō") is obviously a Sinified word, adapting *Dao*.

In its native version, michi, the concept (and Chinese character) took on other meanings in addition to the Sinified. Reaching a climax in the twelfth and thirteenth centuries, these became rich, complex, and applicable to all as means of enlightenment (Konishi 1991, 139–65 or as in Miner 1985, 181–208). Travel (tabi) was a poetic topic or classification after the inspired codification of earlier thinking by the compilers of the first royal collection, the *Kokinshū* (ca. 910).

Certain features of these matters are quite striking. How readily we assume today that others in motion are tourists, whereas we ourselves are travelers. Our journeys may be nothing more than a weekly trip to customers in Sendai or in Nice. But it may be imaginary—space travel in a thick cartoon book (mangabon) read in an Osaka coffee shop or played with on a child's video game. Yet there remains a major difference between Japanese and Western ideas of travel. Japanese think of travel as ways to confirm what they know, what they assume to be important to their lives. Since their motive is far more such confirmation than the Western urge to discover the unknown, Japanese do not associate travelers with liars, as is proverbial in the West.

Of what, then, does travel consist? Of course the abstract answer holds it to be a congeries, within likeness, of different things, whether from person to person or from literature to literature. It is even possible to imagine travelers from other cultural areas visiting one's own, as with Montesquieu's Persian or Goldsmith's Chinese, each a "citizen of the world," to use Goldsmith's title. We may recall that Boswell, who was well acquainted with these writings, was not to be outdone: "I am, I flatter myself, completely a citizen of the world. In my travels through Holland, Germany, Switzerland, Italy, Corsica, France, I never felt myself from home" (*Tour*, 10).

One convenient way of distinguishing travel from other movement through space is by differentiating the ordinary from the special. To commute several hundreds of miles or kilometers a year from home to the office today is not travel in the sense meant here. But in the seventeenth or eighteenth century it was travel to leave home and go eighty miles by foot or horse to see a place known for its holiness or beauty. We are drivers or passengers in the one case. We become pilgrims or travelers in the other. The distinction is not at all a proper definition of travel, but a suggestion of general consensus. For anything exact dealing with centuries and cultures, more effort would be necessary than seems profitable. The empirical distinction suffices to explore differences. Travel was obviously more congenial to Boswell than to Johnson, who required at least a decade's urging to make a Scottish

journey (*Tour*, 3–6). (He did, however, long for more continental travel
than he had.) And, what is more to our point, although travel is still a
subject far from explaining all, it matters more in Japanese literature
than in any other of which I am aware. It has been well said of Bashō
that in view of such travel writings as *The Narrow Road* and his death in
Osaka on a journey to Kyushu, "we may form an image of him as a
person whose life was spent in journey after journey." That is all the
better said, because it is followed by the reminder that Bashō was not
exceptional in spending so much time on the road (Andō 1974, 53).

Earlier linked-poetry masters like Sōgi had spent much of their
lives in travel. His were times of grave social ruptures and incessant
war. Bashō lived in an age of very harshly imposed peace, and if he
wished, he could have easily settled down in Kyoto or Edo. As the
opening of *The Narrow Road* shows, the relation of travel to life required
him to take narrow or broader roads. That relation does not exhaust the
meaning of travel. In the first place, "relation" suggests metaphor, "the
journey of life." To Bashō, as to most Japanese poets before him, what
we consider the terms of metaphor (*a* signifies *b*) are matters of likeness
rather than of separateness. When Sei Shōnagon begins her *Pillow Book*
(*Makura no Sōshi*), "For spring, it is dawn," there is something stronger
than metaphor or preference, something sharing—if not quite
encompassing—identification.

That consideration leads to the second. We must add to Bashō's
semiassociation, semi-identification of travel and life, two further elements of equal matter: his art and death. In his *Sanzōshi*, Hattori Dohō
quotes a remark by Bashō that has come to seem more and more central
to understanding this complex individual (having requoted Boswell,
we may offer Bashō and the reader the same privilege):

> The Master said, "A kasen is to be thought of as thirty-six steps. In
> taking the first step, one has no thought of retracing a single
> footprint. The making new by devotion to travel derives solely
> from the desire to continue going." (*Taisei*, 628).[9]

---

9. See also Andō 1974, 71–72. The hokku is the first and most important stanza in a
haikai sequence and the grandparent, as it were, of haiku. A kasen is a thirty-six-stanza
haikai (sequence). The day will be welcome when discussions of Japanese literature need
not "name the parts" any more, or to repeat that Bashō's great pride lay in his orchestra-
tion as it were of sequences rather than composition of stanzas, or insist that he never
spoke of "haiku," because the word did not exist in his time.

As evidence, we can take a hokku Bashō wrote on the journey recorded in *A Traveler's Book Satchel*. It is the more interesting for including the second pace or step, another poet's second stanza of an unusual sequence. Unusual, that is, for Bashō's incorporating into his prose narration, not only a hokku (opening stanza), but also the waki or second stanza from a haikai sequence composed separately. This is so rare that we can only assume he does it because it clarifies, and extends, the meaning of his hokku in his prose narrative.

At the outset of the second month of winter, when all blue was covered in the sky, I felt myself a leaf in the wind, whirled to no set end.

> "O Traveler"
> they will call out as my name
> the first freezing drizzle

> winter camellias once again
> give color to house after house.

(*Taisei*, 302)

In effect, Bashō renames himself "Traveler" (tabibito), imagining others calling out to him by that address as he makes his way along the road, although those calling out that name know nothing further of him. He then adds the second stanza composed "by one called Chōtarō." With slight variation, that second stanza (waki) followed Bashō's hokku in a very rare example of a forty-four-stanza sequence (yoyoshi).[10] The added stanza connects by setting the scene for Mr. Traveler, a village where these wonderful winter blooms are bright with welcome, house after house, as if each plant calls out "Traveler!" to Bashō.

The example offers, in effect, two interpretations of Bashō's hokku. One is Bashō's own in the introductory prose, in which the unknown end, here of a leaf taken by the wind, is a figure for himself as traveler. In true haikai fashion, he combines an element of comedy (fūkyō) with

---

10. *Taisei*, 302 and 185–86, *Oi no Kobumi* and *Hatsushigure no Yoyoshi* respectively. The second stanza names the particular bushes imagined in bloom (sasanqua, autumn- to winter-blooming shrubs of the camellia species). The prose says its flowers are bright red. But the color may be paler, down to shades of pink and white, and the flowers vary in form from the single to multifoliate. (They are obviously one of my favorite plants.)

Buddhist evanescence, mujō, long since familiar in court poetry.[11] In contemplating Bashō's stanza, Chōtarō (proper haikai pen name Yūshi) saw something more. He understood that, in spite of Bashō's dismal scene and intimations of mortality, the itinerant haikai master gloried in the name of Traveler. His insight derived not merely from understanding of Bashō's highly complex personality. (We may discern beyond the near tearfulness of Bashō's prose and hokku there is a robust, ironic laughter that leads to yet further sorrow.) There was also the matter of the status of the stanza opening a sequence. "A hokku . . . has been held from times long past to be one elevated in its configuration"—so Bashō himself (*Taisei*, 628).

In a sense easily understood, travel—or the very name, Traveler— can be one of the major figures to represent human life, but only if it has multiple, complex, and even contradictory possibilities of meaning. Neither Japanese nor English literature has exclusive purchase on the multiplicities of meaningfulness expressible by travel and its namings. But it stands to reason that just as the configurings of meaning will vary from age to age, they will do so even more from one literature (and yet more from one culture) to another. Sorting out the constants from the differences is of course an essence of comparative study. Understanding so simple a fact, like travelers we are under way.

In fact, we discover that we have been considering no rigorous initial definition of travel, finding ourselves with Horace's poet among middle things. In the last chapter we observed our travelers' accounts of their setting forth. It remains for this chapter to consider something far more difficult to get at, whether in the art of writing or the art of reading about: the second stage.

This second phase (so far represented only by the quotations from Boswell opening this chapter) requires devising a method of continuing what has been begun. These second sections normally receive least attention and, in fact, are often of lesser impressiveness: it takes time to hit full stride in writing. So we may devote a few words to concede the claims of beginnings and endings before justifying attention to the crucial section when a travel writer finds the right way to describe the way. Long journeys are not sprints, and there is exertion, trial and error, to hitting stride.

---

11. See Ueda 1991, 166. He provides illuminating excerpts from comments on Bashō's hokku by critics ranging from Bashō's time to ours. Of the latter, Yamamoto Kenkichi is of special value to me. Ueda does not go into the waki added by "Chōtarō."

To end with, as it were, do we not presume that a great benefit of travel is reaching home, especially in safe and timely fashion? How good it is to be back! To know where things are kept, to eat familiar food, to see one's friends, even if they show too little interest in our experiences. Did not Odysseus use his many devices to get back to his own bed? There is also the special excitement in anticipating beginning, in planning travel to a new and distant (or otherwise *different*) place. Perhaps the people are as "new" or unfamiliar as the geography and weather. "The language problem, but you have to try" (William Empson). The curiosity of our friends heightens excitement. Emotion rises with thoughts of the unknown: *their* attitude toward us of different race or other appearance, *their* Immigration, *their* customs (as well as Customs), water, and police. Undeniably, our experience tells us that starting and finishing a journey are crucial.

To make an actual journey through space and time differs, however, from making a journey as an account. In writing about a lengthy journey, the writing of the beginning may be the most difficult act, as beginning almost always is in composition. But what follows the beginning is, in a closely related double sense, more telling. It is there that decisions must be made as to principles of order and presentation. The kind of thing deemed important, the voice of relation, the tone of telling, the attitude and atmosphere—all are founded in the decisions taken just after the beginning. *Getting under way* may lack appeal for the very natural reason that it deals with the stage of travel devoted to establishing the conventions for relating *this* journey to the exciting places and the remarkable people. But the very difficulty—which, to acknowledge fact, is often not wholly overcome—requires decisions about procedures that distinguish one travel account from another.

These difficulties may be brought more forcibly to us by considering the two who made the Highlands journey. Surely the baggage they carried as pocket gear and as culture more resembled that carried by us whose mother tongue is English than that borne by Bashō and Sora some eight decades before Boswell had, at last, the pleasure of welcoming—and showing off—Johnson in Edinburgh.

The complexities of hitting stride are shown by a major difference between Johnson and Boswell's accounts. Johnson omits any relation of those days in Edinburgh at the beginning and end of his Scottish visit that meant so much to Boswell. To Johnson, the periods in Edinburgh evidently did not constitute either the beginning or end of his journey.

The differences between the two friends meeting in Edinburgh is evident, as are the differences between them and us in our other places and times. If good fortune attends us, the demonstration, however implicitly, of those differences ought to serve two further ends. For one thing, it should remove any attribution of exoticism to Bashō's account. For another, that accommodation should lead not merely to the sense of the various ways of telling of travel but also to the realization that the variety speaks (with whatever strange accents at times) to genuine features of our own lives.

Johnson Placed

There were three basic methods available to our explorers of Scotland, ways remaining basic still. Although now as then susceptible to combination, they can be readily enough distinguished. We can readily think of examples in English classics prior to Johnson and Boswell. Pepys's diary obviously uses time as its principle. The imaginary journeys in Swift's *Gulliver's Travels* show how radically place matters— Lilliput, Brobdingnag, and the rest. Who reads of Gulliver's travels for their times? Who can fail to read them for its places—and characters? Defoe's novels show that a biography called a "life," or a "history" may be the principle. Any choice is one of emphasis, since an account wholly lacking *any* of the three—people, place, and time—is fundamentally infeasible and, if imaginable, almost inevitably of little credibility and therefore of interest.

Johnson and Boswell made different decisions. *A Journey to the Western Islands of Scotland,* Johnson's title, suggests what in fact is the case, that his account is an *itinerarium,* a succession of places. He is greatly interested in the people he meets, and days are distinguished from nights. But place is his principle, as the recollection of the beginnings of his first two paragraphs may suggest:

> I had desired to visit the *Hebrides,* or Western Islands of Scotland, so long. . . .
> On the eighteenth of August we left Edinburgh, a city too well known to admit description, and directed our course northward, along the eastern coast of Scotland. (*Journey,* 1)

By the end of the next page he has entered the first, St. Andrews, in the succession of place-names on which his brief chapters are founded. (See figs. 2 and 7, and app. 1.)

Johnson (and Boswell) felt obliged to relate their journey *to* the "Western Isles" as well as *among* them. For Johnson, that preamble, or preisles amble, established his method (places in succession) and identified matters of recurrent interest: historical legacies, poverty, emigration, government, education, and, in brief, the kinds of things that counted as civilization to him. That preamble accounts for almost a third (pp. 1–39) of the whole (137 pp.) and therefore must be taken seriously. Much in one lengthy later section, "Ostig in Sky" (pp. 63–99), reads so much as if written before setting foot in Scotland that it could be deducted from the whole. If so, the supposed preamble approaches half the length of the journey. We must revise our views: Johnson's overture is uncommonly brief, and almost before we realize it, we are in the second stage, getting under way. The more closely we attend to Johnson, the more art we uncover. It is difficult to avoid concluding, or rather starting, from the fact that the early stages engaged Johnson most. If his enthusiasm for his travels did not diminish in the Hebrides, his interest in *writing* about Scotland gradually did. He substitutes for stages of travel the relatively long essay in "Ostig on Sky."

Boswell's need for psychological aerobics results in a much slower process of working himself into form. But the very self-indulgence that he knows he requires without knowing why makes for absorbing reading. Of our two English accounts, my preference goes to Boswell's extraordinary ability, not simply to create the characters of others and himself, but to do so at once knowingly and unaware. There are those who prefer Johnson and who cannot abide Boswell, some who find it difficult to forgive Boswell for being so well liked by the great moralist and critic. It is not easy for any of us to hold a full and judicious view of these two remarkable men. The most successful attempt to do so is far from recent (Bronson 1944). My choice involves not the thoughts of angels but the experience of reading two versions of a Highlands journey. Those looking for authoritative reflections on eighteenth-century Scotland will do well to go to Johnson. The reason for going to the author of *Life of Samuel Johnson* is indeed for the life of Johnson—and of Boswell besides.

The preference certainly does not deny the merits of Johnson's writing. Close or repeated reading of it brings appreciation of two matters, his economy of means and his variations in style. On first or less than attentive reading, the economy may seem a weakness, and the style to be unvaried Johnsonese. But it is a kind of miracle that he covers so much so cogently. The labeled sections, or chapters on successive places, in the first forty-nine pages average only about three pages: there are fifteen named places as chapter titles (1–43) before reaching "The Highlands" (33–38) and "Glenelg" (38–39)—the point at which he nears his goal. After "Glenelg," he is located in "the Western Islands of Scotland," as his title puts it.

Johnson's problem is that he is in competition with Boswell over his own self-creation. Experienced readers of Johnson will observe his care with numerous tints and touches that fashion him into The Rambler. Yet if Johnson extracts and relates so compactly what he thought to be *importantly* true, Boswell seems to have exceeded mere fact—interpret that as we may. Johnson's formidable power of concentrated expression leads to a generality that verges on the symbolic, even in characterizing the lives of people quite unlike himself. Let us see how, at almost the beginning of his account, he can depict a befuddled old woman living among the ruins of ecclesiastical buildings in St. Andrews. (See fig. 9.)

> She thinks . . . she has a claim to something more than sufferance; for as her husband's name was Bruce, she is allied to royalty, and told Mr. Boswell that when there were persons of quality in the place, she was distinguished by some notice; that indeed she is now neglected, but she spins a thread, has the company of her cat, and is troublesome to nobody. (5)

There is subtlety not only in the light irony but also in the woman's anonymity beside two names that every reader recognizes. For all their homeliness, the images of the spinning and the cat approach poetry. The lyricism approaches the symbolic: here is much in little, a vignette that reveals Johnson's Scotland to us: romantic (in both the eighteenth and nineteenth-century senses) with the Bruce, the architectural ruins of a lost past glory, and our human condition as we spin on our dreams next to a quotidian cat.

A new paragraph is entered. With a shift and with austere economy of relation, Johnson declares that they had seen all of "this ancient city" and had been given pleasing "attention." We are told what we ought to have inferred. And we know that we are fully under way from the different register of what follows:

Fig. 7. The Tower and, *left,* the chapel of St. Salvator's College, University of St. Andrews (oldest in Britain after Oxford and Cambridge). Boswell (*Tour,* 43): "We looked at St. Salvator's College. . . . Dr. Johnson said it was the neatest place of worship he had seen."

But whoever surveys the world must see many things that give him pain. The kindness of the professors did not contribute to abate the uneasy remembrance of an university declining, a college alienated, and a church profaned and hastening to the ground. (5–6)

The closing series has the right mental rhythm, and I do not know how to improve upon the semichiasmus of those two verbs between those two nouns of the final clause. Nor do I see that, in the understanding of the world Johnson depicts, how we would benefit from learning what the professors taught. Likewise in the preceding quotation, hearing the old woman named, whether Mary or Moll, would do nothing but distract and therefore also subtract. Place comprehends people and time's ravages.

Johnson's range of means and ends can be exemplified by some of his own words. We can start from the zero degree: "We stopped a while at Dundee, where I remember nothing remarkable" (7). Many a traveler has had the experience but few the honesty to say so. Here is nearly the opposite:

To write of the cities of our own island with the solemnity of geographical description, as if we had been cast upon a newly discovered coast, has the appearance of very frivolous ostentation; yet as Scotland is little known to the greater part of those who may read these observations, it is not superfluous to relate, that under the name of Aberdeen are comprised two towns. (9–10)

The long opening clause (to the semicolon) puts us quite off balance, removing not only its own but the whole *Journey*'s reason for being— until we learn that what we had thought a single place is really two.

As they near the Highlands, they encounter less certain roads and harsher conditions. "Anoch" begins, "Early in the afternoon we came to Anoch, a village in *Glenmorrison* of three huts, one of which is distinguished by a chimney" (*Journey*, 27). From earlier places we remember that most Scottish "huts" (a designation Johnson uses consistently) have two openings: only an entrance and a hole for smoke in the thatched roofs. We experience yet again the realization that under the thatch are dark, dirty interiors. (See fig. 8.) Here the addition of names tells us that it is home to living creatures, but an "Anoch" might be in

Fig. 8. A poor weaver's cottage in Islay. Johnson called such meager dwellings huts. (From Pennant 1774.)

Palestine for all the name seems to say. In this all too in-the-way place on the journey, the travelers take their midday dinner, after which they are offered tea by the very pleasant and attractive daughter of their host.

We expect the easily stirred Boswell to be more sensitive to female presence than the great lexicographer. Yet it is Johnson who reports that he "presented her with a book, which I happened to have about me, and should not be pleased to think that she forgets me" (28). The unromantic book has been identified as Cocker's *Arithmetic*.[12] Johnson does not do what he could easily have done: give the book's title. It is only natural for us to presume that he omits it for the good reason that it would efface, as it were, the emotions he has inscribed between the lines. On reflection, we observe that he has also not named, as he might have done, the host (one Macqueen; 171) or his daughter. The blanks of namelessness creates a feeling that mingles romance with ghostliness. Rather as with the old woman and her cat, we are left decisively with a sense of human presence, with conviction of a world of things—then a cat, now a book. Time matters: Johnson wishes the young woman to remember him. It is certainly obvious that people exist. But the young woman is not dividually there: she is not named.

"Anoch" is in fact treated at length by Johnson's standards (27–32). "We" see this. "We" do that. "They" do what they do. And "I" did there what I did. But "Mr. Boswell . . . whose gaiety of conversation and civility of manners are sufficient to counteract the inconveniences of travel," as Johnson remarks at the outset of his account (1), is not quoted or described to be in what we suppose to be his usual liveliness.[13] In fact, he is not named in "Anoch." *Nobody is named.* The single proper name is that of the place.

Of course we owe to Boswell's ear and pen our sense of Johnson's speech. His accuracy was not faulted by their contemporaries, at least not as to that "æther" of Boswell's famous metaphor. Johnson's written styles are sometimes recognizably Boswellian Johnsonese, but there are also surprises—there is that supple variety of style that we have been

---

12. Fleeman relates information that Johnson had purchased the book at Inverness, and that Boswell learned later that the "pretty" daughter of the house married a watchmaker and died without children (*Journey*, 171). Lascelles 1971, 37 dates the book as published in 1678, then nearly a century old.

13. The importance of the description is apparent once we recall that there remained earlier, wider meanings to "conversation" (close human intercourse, including sexual) and "manners" (habitual, including moral, behavior).

observing. Although by no means predominant, his balanced, antitheti-
cal style does appear. It seems to be his vehicle of judgment, whether
satirical or moral. Here again is his orotund ridicule of those who might
wish to regard the Scots as noble savages: "Such is the effect of the late
regulations, that a longer journey than to the Highlands must be taken
by him whose curiosity pants for savage virtues and barbarous grandeur" (46). A more complex version of this theme appears early on,
between a condemnatory mention of the Scottish reformer, John Knox,
and a bare naming, "The city of St. Andrews" (3–4).

> The change of religion in Scotland, eager and vehement as it was,
> raised an epidemical enthusiasm, compounded of sullen scru-
> pulousness and warlike ferocity, which, in a people whom idleness
> resigned to their own thoughts, and who, conversing [having inti-
> mate contact] only with each other, suffered no dilution of their
> zeal from the gradual influx of new opinions, was long transmitted
> in its full strength from the old to the young, but by trade and
> intercourse with England, is now visibly abating, and giving way
> too fast to their laxity of practice and indifference of opinion, in
> which men, not sufficiently instructed to find the middle point, too
> easily shelter themselves from rigour and constraint.

That is a remarkable sentence-paragraph or, more accurately, rhetorical
period, in which the moral generalization on three centuries of history
is enacted by the very syntax.

The stylistic complexity testifies to the hard thought required, its
antithesis and balance to the judgment that must be exercised, and its
charged diction to the author's passion. The obvious stylistic discipline
offers a kind of exact moral pictography. One hue, one of the *colores
rhetoricae*, tinges the "merry" sarcastically ascribed to Knox's writing in
the sentence just before. And in the sentence just following, a bleaker
gray streaks the desolation of once "archepiscopal" St. Andrews: now
"the silence and solitude of active indigence and gloomy depopulation." "Knox" is a name for a cause, as "St. Andrews" is for an effect.
The namelessness in between is at once enacted with scholastic logic
and oratorical periodicity, as the namelessness of "Anoch" defines people, including Johnson, by place and what they do when placed. The
passage quoted could no doubt be reduced in other terms to the
prophet's grim comment that the fathers have eaten sour grapes, and

Fig. 9. The Ruins of St. Andrew's Cathedral. (From Grose 1797.)

the children's teeth are set on edge. But all about it is designedly more complex.

The fact that Johnson's places are all distinct suggests that his major stylistic principle is economy, even when he waxes eloquent or even when any moderately agreeable Scottish hospitality seems to him to require polite praise. If the characteristic economy of thought requires economy of words, his *Journey* does not lack for the crisply aphoristic.

They had the true military impatience of coin in their pockets. (28)

Such seems to be the disposition of man that whatever makes a distinction produces rivalry. (35)

Law is nothing without power. (36)

Countless other examples might be quoted, no doubt illustrative of Johnson's "grandeur of generality."[14] In these examples, the absence of names, whether of people or places or times, suggests a universal applicability that is one strain of the Johnsonian music.

It should not be thought, however, that Johnson fails to give his sense, and a strong one, of the experience of his *Journey*. To demonstrate what no attentive reader requires be proved, there are numerous arresting passages. Some of them gave pause to Boswell and his contemporaries long before seizing our attention. One was a condition of Scotland strikingly different from England. Johnson is under way from the decays of St. Andrews, bearing for "Aberbrothick" (that kind of name shows that Lemuel Gulliver lived in that century.) Here are three passages focused on that feature of Scotland which struck Johnson so forcibly.

As we knew sorrow and wishes to be vain, it was now our business to mind our way. The roads of Scotland afford little diversion to the traveller, who seldom sees himself either encountered or

14. The phrase is given in its full context by Hagstrum 1967, 86 as part of an acute analysis (83–89) of "Johnson's conception of literary pleasure" (83). Given the importance of Johnson's phrase, it is startling to find Boswell (*Tour*, 76) quoting—to explain a remark by Johnson—the tag, "Dolus latet in universalibus," loosely translatable for present purposes as "Generalizations make trouble." An aphorism that is itself a generalization!

overtaken, and who has nothing to contemplate but grounds that have no visible boundaries, or are separated by walls of loose stone. From the bank of the Tweed to St. Andrews I had never seen a single tree, which I did not believe to have grown up far within the present century. (6)

I had now travelled two hundred miles in Scotland and seen only one tree not younger than myself. (15)

The country [leading into the Highlands] is totally denuded of its wood, but the stumps both of oaks and firs, which are still found, shew that it has been once a forest of large timber. (26–27)

Johnson's expectations would seem prejudice to someone in an arid region of the earth. A Wisconsin boyhood leads me to share the prejudice, which has certainly affected my responses to Japan with its many ancient trees, to Korea thoroughly reforested after the devastations of war, and to China "totally denuded of its wood" (to exaggerate slightly and speak of places I saw) by urgent needs for fuel and even for food during Maoist extremities.

The three passages began, "As we knew sorrow and wishes to be vain," and ended with my head-nodding. As can well be imagined, Scottish sensitivities were pained, not because it is impossible to be good or wise without trees but because Johnson seemed to be suggesting that Scots inhabited an inferior place. As usual, Boswell is wordier on the matter.

We went and saw Colonel Nairne's garden and grotto. Here was a fine old plane-tree. Unluckily the Colonel said there was but this and another large tree in the county. This assertion was an excellent cue for Dr. Johnson, who laughed enormously, calling me to hear it. He expatiated to me on the nakedness of that part of Scotland which he had seen. His *Journey* has been violently abused for what he has said upon this subject. But let it be considered that when Dr. Johnson talks of trees, he means trees of good size, such as he was accustomed to see in England, and of these there are certainly very few upon the *eastern coast* of Scotland. (*Tour,* 46)

The Scots resemble other peoples in feeling irritated by foreign visitors who insinuate that some local difference is at best odd and more likely

Fig. 10. Slain's Castle. (From Cordimer 1788.)

the fault of the natives' way of life and thought. Whether we reside or whether we travel, we draw on our personal intellectual funds.[15] Whether visitor or host, we bear, even where it may not be needed, our sense of the human place. That sense is the stronger, certainly the more elusive, as a generalized set of assumptions, unnamed because presumed to be universal.

It would be cause for disbelief to argue that Johnson did not hold in himself great tensions, including not only pulls between the universal and the particular but also between the familiar and the novel.[16] In his entry for 26 August, Boswell says that Johnson "did not choose" to inspect a Scottish estate.

> He always said that he was not come to Scotland to see fine places, of which there were enough in England, but wild objects— mountains, waterfalls, peculiar manners: in short, *things which he had not seen before.* I have a notion that he at no time has had much taste for rural beauties. I have very little. (81; my emphasis)

In the competition between the picturesque, the beautiful, and the sublime, the sublime wins out, even if these two friends of Edmund Burke seemed to deprive his sublime of its full thrill of terror (Hagstrum 1967, 146, 151, 199 n. 21). The preference for the novel, distant, and unfamiliar is by no means Johnson's at all hours. The same Johnson who would have every man visit the Great Wall of China declared that to be tired of London was to be tired of life. In contrast to Japanese travelers (who seek to verify the known), Johnson seeks discovery, "things which he had not seen before."

A telling passage of another kind enables us to test the sentiments Boswell ascribes to Johnson and himself. As it happens, this most absorbing part of Johnson and Boswell's getting under way comes as its finale, provided in Johnson's version under the name of the place, "Glenelg." (Thereafter Johnson moves to the Hebrides and out of our immediate concern with getting under way.) Even a few excerpts show stylistically, cognitively, and emotionally (especially if we recall his great fear of death) how his seemingly generalized response ex-

---

15. There is the story of the Englishman's reaction to a Vermont mountainside brilliant with colored leaves: "Is there something the matter with them?" How one reacts to *that* is also telling.

16. Such tension is often a *discordia concors* that Johnson associated with one kind of wit (Hagstrum 1967, 155, 200).

Fig. 11. Buller of Buchan. This and figure 12 exemplify features of the sublime in the eighteenth century. (From Cordimer 1780.)

emplifies particulars coded by names of places and people and, remarkably, by their absence.

> We left *Auknascheals* and the *Macraes* in the afternoon, and in the evening came to *Ratiken*, a high hill on which a road is cut, but so steep and narrow, that it is very difficult. . . . Upon one of the precipices, my horse, weary with the steepness of the rise, staggered a little, and I called in haste to the Highlander [guide] to hold him. This was the only moment of my journey, in which I thought myself endangered. . . . At last we came to our inn [at Glenelg] weary and peavish, and began to inquire for meat and beds.
>
> Of the provisions the negative catalogue was very copious. . . .
>
> We were now to examine our lodging. Out of one of the beds, on which we were to repose, started up, at our entrance, a man black [i.e., dirty] as a Cyclops from the forge. Other circumstances of no elegant recital concurred to disgust us. We had been frighted by a lady [Boswell's wife] at Edinburgh, with discouraging representations of Highland lodgings. Sleep, however, was necessary. Our Highlanders had at last found some hay, with which the inn could not supply them. I directed them to bring a bundle into the room, and slept upon it in my riding coat. Mr. Boswell being more delicate, laid himself sheets with hay over and under him, and lay in linen like a gentleman. (*Journey*, 38–39)

Danger without hope and unrelieved filth are great deflaters of the sublime. Fortunately, Johnson found, in his guides and in himself the resources to cope. But the passage has more in common with the image of that self-imagined royal old woman with her spinning wheel and cat than it does with contemplations of Alpine grandeur. The resemblance holding importance is not that of squalor but of human nature as it is variously conceived and variously told.

For full appreciation of Johnson's experience, we must take into account a matter alluded to in passing, his fear of death. In fact his love of the bustle and society of London stemmed from a desire to put away moments of dark thought. As has been concisely said, "loneliness and idleness were both conditions that he deeply dreaded" (Quennell 1972, 67). In his *Life of Samuel Johnson*, Boswell writes about Johnson's dark thoughts with a special tone. He clearly expects confirmation from Johnson's other friends, and yet the impression made on him is so strong that he, in turn, cannot put the taboo subject from his mind. In a lengthy entry for 26 October 1769 (four years before their Scottish journey), Boswell has the ill judgment to persist in a line of questions and statements that clearly trouble Johnson.

> When we were alone, I introduced the subject of death, and endeavoured to maintain that the fear of it may be got over. I told him that David Hume said to me, he was no more uneasy to think he should *not be* after his life, than that he *had not been* before he began to exist.
>
> *Johnson:* "Sir, if he really thinks so, his perceptions are disturbed; he is mad; if he does not think so, he lies. . . ." *Boswell:* "But may we not fortify our minds for the approach of death?" Here I am sensible I was in the wrong, to bring before his view what he ever looked upon with horrour. . . .
>
> I attempted to continue the conversation. He was so provoked, that he said, "Give us no more of this"; and was thrown into such a state of agitation, that he expressed himself in a way that alarmed and distressed me; shewed an impatience that I should leave him, and when I was going away, called to me sternly, "Don't let us meet tomorrow."
>
> I went home exceedingly uneasy. All the harsh observations I had ever heard made upon his character crowded into my mind.[17]

Johnson's forgiving nature and Boswell's sociable address lead to an early reconciliation. But behind Johnson's account of that ride to Glenelg lies a combination of an exhausting day—a poor and corpulent horseman on an inadequate horse—and a feeling that he has been deserted just when there is a moment of danger. Two comparisons come irresistibly to mind. One is with Bashō, who half expects travel to lead to that bourne whence no traveler returns. Five years after his journey on the narrow road he did in fact take ill and die in Osaka on the longest trip he had planned: to the southern island of Kyushu. At some point in his final days, he composed a hokku that Johnson's agitation would not have allowed.

---

17. Boswell 1948, 1:404–405. Four years after their journey, in the entry for 16 December 1777, there is another incident that Boswell handles more delicately: "The horrour of death which I had always observed in Dr. Johnson, appeared strong to-night. . . . He said, "he never had a moment in which death was not terrible to him" (1948, 2:117).

> Stricken in travel
> and across wasted fields dreams
> chase about in vain whirl.

For the other comparison, we must turn to Boswell's version of that day's "journey."

What Boswell Heard on the Way

Boswell's *Tour* tells a different story. For one thing, his account is not of a place labeled "Glenelg" but of events dated 1–2 September 1773. For another—but for that other, only Boswell's words at length will serve:

> It grew dusky; and we had a very tedious ride for what was called five miles, but I am sure would measure ten. *We spoke none.* I was riding forward to the inn at Glenelg, that I might make some kind of preparation, or take some proper measures, before Mr. Johnson got up [closer], who was now advancing in silence, Hay [a guide] leading his horse. Mr. Johnson called me back with a tremendous shout, and was really in a passion with me for leaving him. I told him my intentions. But he was not satisfied, and said, "Do you know, I should as soon have thought of picking a pocket as doing so." "I'm diverted with you," said I. Said he, "I could never be diverted with incivility." . . . I justified myself but lamely to him. But my intentions were not improper. (*Tour*, 110; my emphasis)

It would be difficult to say what is more ominous in the Boswellian sphere, that lapse of conversation—"We spoke none"—or Johnson's "tremendous shout," no doubt a reverberating "Boswell!"[18]

In my opinion, the silence is the more threatening to Boswell, and the shout to Johnson. That emerges from what follows, where it is also made clear (as had Johnson's account of Glenelg, for that matter) that Boswell's apprehensions about their accommodations in Glenelg were all too well justified.

> A lass showed us upstairs into a room raw and dirty; bare walls, a variety of bad smells, a coarse black fir greasy table, [shelves] of the

---

18. This, with what follows, is one of the passages sanitized and debilitated in the printed version of Boswell's account.

same kind, and from a wretched bed started a fellow from his sleep like Edgar in *King Lear:* "Poor Tom's a-cold." . . . I was uneasy and almost fretful. Mr. Johnson was calm. I said he was so from vanity. "No," said he, " 'tis from philosophy." . . .

I resumed [the subject of] my riding forward, and wanted to defend it. Mr. Johnson was still violent upon that subject, and said, "Sir, had you gone on, I was thinking that I should have returned with you to Edinburgh, *and never spoke to you more.*"

I sent for fresh hay, with which we each made beds to ourselves . . . Mr. Johnson . . . lay down buttoned up in his greatcoat. I had my sheets spread on the hay [by Joseph Ritter, his Bohemian servant], and having stripped, I had my clothes and greatcoat and Joseph's greatcoat laid upon me, by way of blankets. . . .

I had slept ill. Mr. Johnson's anger had affected me much. I considered that, without any bad intention, I might suddenly forfeit his friendship. I was impatient to see him this morning. I told him how uneasy he made me by what he had said. He owed it was said in passion; that he would not have done it; that if he had done it, he would have been ten times worse than me . . . and said he, "Let's think no more on't." (*Tour,* 110–13)[19]

The central feature of this sustained episode common to both versions is the exhausting travel leading to a short temper and a night in filthy lodging: a named place at the close of their getting under way. They agree on the squalor of Glenelg. But Johnson does not see fit to include what makes Boswell's narration so much more memorable: speechlessness broken by a shout, what we may call after him the crisis of Johnson's "passion." To plumb the depths of the episode, we must consider, in Boswell's relation, his "points of attention."[20] Those are of course his of Johnson—and his of Johnson of himself. And we must enter what we know of both men from other sources than this remarkable passage alone.

A central if simple matter is this: Johnson's corpulence and physical awkwardness made him a very poor horseman. Boswell, who was so sensitive to almost everything about Johnson, somehow failed to

19. I have regretfully omitted much from these long passages, which are much the most revealing of this section. They also curiously occupy the same final position as in Bashō's counterpart of getting under way. (Emphasis mine.)

20. For "points of attention" as a concept complementary to "points of view," see Miner 1990, 182–212. Their importance here will be mentioned shortly.

observe on the narrow, uncertain road to Glenelg that Johnson felt "endangered." It was his great fear of death, and of Boswell's desertion of him in mortal danger, that led to his "tremendous shout." Johnson's philosophic calm begins to return once he is *indoors,* even in those wretched lodgings. By morning, he is fully restored, recomposed.

Poor Boswell is caught between conviction of his own good motives and admiration for Johnson. In an eerie fashion, however, his recording faculties never cease. In what other author could the most unexpected, the most threatening, and (to crown it all) the briefest sentence in the whole work be, "We spoke none"? The threat on his mind as he seeks sleep is that Johnson in fact may never *speak* to him again. If there be any doubt that talk, more than names, defined people in Boswell's onomasticon, one need only compare the two versions of the journey to Glenelg. Boswell's seems spoken even when nobody is quoted. Johnson's style is one of pure narrative, pure diegesis, to use Plato's fancy term, for even when he reports that people said something, in his account they speak none.

For Johnson the recorder of places under way, however, the issue raised by that shout is why he omits an incident so significant to Boswell and himself. Although negatives defy proof, it seems a mistake to think Johnson's motive was suppression of truth. It seems rather that he believed his subject to be Scotland rather than himself, at the same time thinking he should follow a certain decorum in reporting an English visitor's responses: the peculiarly personal was to be avoided. That is at least one likely inference from the first remarkable incident in Boswell's *Tour* (14 August), which begins with a triumphant and, for Boswell, unusually striking visual image.

> Mr. Johnson and I walked arm-in-arm up the High Street to my house in James's Court; it was a dusky night; I could not prevent his being assailed by the evening effluvia of Edinburgh. I heard a late baronet . . . observe that "walking the streets of Edinburgh at night was pretty perilous and a good deal odoriferous."

Officers tried "to enforce the city laws against throwing foul water from the windows." But many families were crowded in multistory buildings, "and there being no covered sewers, the odour still continues" (11). Even accustomed to filth we can barely imagine, our ancestors cannot have liked having a chamber pot emptied on them. Johnson's reaction?

As we marched slowly along, he grumbled in my ear, "I smell you
in the dark!" But he acknowledged that the breadth of the street
and the loftiness of the buildings on each side made a noble appearance. (12)

Johnson's remark implies that Boswell was yet more bespattered by the
"effluvia," and Boswell's addition that after their accident they moved
to the safer ground of the middle of the street. Since Johnson includes
no such incident in his whole *Journey* and omits his fearful, angry shout
on the way to Glenelg, the decorum seems clear. Boswell's response is
to take his friend's mild grumble as part of a remarkable occurrence
illustrative of Johnson's character.[21]

Johnson's account possesses remarkable composure. Boswell's is
far more given to nervous relation of actions, in what impresses us as
scenes that turn out on inspection to have very little of the visual about
them. It makes one wonder how Boswell could impart so strong a sense
of drama in his narrative. But whereas Johnson's *Journey* establishes a
world held firmly in place, Boswell's *Tour* swirls in a ceaseless agitation.
Some of Boswell's techniques by which he creates his effects are known
from the far closer study of them in his biography of Johnson. The most
obvious is the use he makes of dialogue, or at least of speech. That is
what makes so ominous the laconic "We spoke none." There is no need
for such a three-word sentence in Johnson's account, for in his version
all speak none: there is no dialogue or speech whatsoever. And where
there is not even the air or illusion of dialogue, any sense of drama can
only be mental, abstract. To Boswell, however, speech is so important
that he found ways of creating that air or illusion of dialogue even
where actual speech is not to be found. And on numerous occasions we
observe his foresight or Scottish thrift, saving up speech from occasions
of abundance for use at times of dearth.

Boswell also has a genius for creating scenes while yet keeping on
the move. Two relatively mechanical instances show the degree of planning or disposition usually artfully concealed. These are forecasts,
preparations:

The reason will appear when we come to the Isle of Skye. I shall
then insert my letter . . . ("Introduction," 6)

---

21. Since this passage was not excised by the more fastidious Edmond Malone for
the printed version, similar hazards would seem to have existed in London.

This imperfect sketch of . . . that Wonderful Man . . . will serve to introduce to the fancy [imagination] of my readers the capital object of the following Journal, in the course of which I trust they will attain to a considerable degree of acquaintance with him. (9)

To that "trust" or promise he ought to have added "and no little sense of myself."

The *Tour* is far longer and much more interesting than Johnson's version of the journey. Boswell's account begins (on 14 August 1773) four days before Johnson's, and at the outset of this chapter we saw that Boswell the narrator is under way by the twentieth. If that passage seems too quiet or restrained, there is no doubt that Boswell is in full stride on the twenty-sixth (p. 80 of the 403 in the edition used.) The Boswellian vitality emerges here with his sense of possible conflicts of personality. To be precise, it begins with a recollection of Lord Monboddo, to whose primitivism Johnson was utterly opposed, as Monboddo well knew. Yet Boswell had brought the two together on their best behavior (21 August, 53–58), and the recollection of that little triumph seems to energize his account.

What Boswell can achieve when in full stride can be illustrated by his account of one day, "SATURDAY 28 AUGUST." That day is recounted in fifteen paragraphs varying considerably in length, topic, and what is named. The most economical way of anatomizing Boswell's technique is by quotation from paragraph beginnings or endings, or both. Only his words can suggest what he considered worth presenting and his ways of doing so. (The ellipses will show whether an omission is of ensuing or preceding material.)

1. Mr. Johnson had brought a copy of Sallust with him in his pocket from Edinburgh. He gave it last night to Mr. Macaulay's son, a smart young lad about eleven. . . .
2. I should have mentioned that Mr. White, a Welshman who has been many years factor [agent, manager] on the estate of Cawdor, drank tea with us last night. . . .
3. After breakfast and a conversation about saying grace to breakfast as well as dinner and supper . . . we drove down to Fort George.
4. . . . This conversation passed after we had been some time together, But it comes in well here.

Fig. 12. The Fall of Fyers. A drought had reduced the sublimity of the sight for Johnson and Boswell. (From Cordimer 1788.)

5. Mr. Fern was a brisk civil man. . . .

6. . . . Mr. Johnson observed, "How seldom descriptions correspond with realities; and the reason is that people do not write them till some time after, and their imagination has added circumstances."

7. We talked of Sir Adolphus Oughton. . . .

8. I know not how the Major contrived to introduce the contest between [bishops] Warburton and Lowth. . . .

9. At three the drum beat for dinner. I could for a little fancy myself a military man, and it pleased me. . . . Lady Coote observed very well that we ought to know if there is not among the Arabs some punishment for not being faithful [to military duty]. . . .

10. We talked of the Stage [and players past and present].

11. Pennington said Garrick sometimes failed in emphasis. . . .

12. Sir Eyre had something between the Duke of Queensberry and my late worthy friend Captain Cunninghame in his manner. [Complete paragraph]

13. . . . I had a strong impression of the power and excellence of human art.

14. We left the fort between six and seven. . . .

15. Mr. Johnson wrote tonight both to Mrs. Thrale and Mrs. Williams [the blind woman he put up in his house], and I wrote to my wife. . . . The inn was dirty and ill furnished. The entertainment pretty good.

What, what, we may well ask, are the common elements holding such a seemingly random series together? One is the artfulness of the randomness itself, as for example the four paragraphs (9–12) on dinner. It is only natural that polite conversation should vary greatly to avoid tedium and to allow each person some chance to speak. Whether Boswell created the order of topics as well as reporting what was said cannot be known. But the result is felt.

Boswell's drama in those paragraphs involves named human actors speaking or spoken of. He does not exercise, as it were, equal civility as a narrator. He does not honor, among certain expectations of narrative, the names of time and place. There are indeed a few temporal markers (3, 9, 12, 15). Only the last ("tonight") serves as a genuinely named time, but we can add the subtler "I should have mentioned . . ."

(2), and could find some other traces in unquoted portions. For all that, and it is far from negligible, nobody would read this lengthy account for its temporalities, in spite of its being called a journal. Much less do we read Boswell for a consistent interest in place, which in fact requires for the day in question more effort than is repaid to get clear.

Problems are often clues, and so we may take that at first fully baffling sentence-paragraph (12), describing Sir Eyre (Coote, commanding officer of the regiment at Fort George) as "in his manner" something of a mean between "the Duke of Queensberry and my late worthy friend Captain Cunninghame." The assessment may be accurate. It may even show acute Boswellian insight. How can we judge? But it is certainly showing off, certainly Boswell dropping names. There are two essential reasons for him to drop names so trippingly. One is that people matter to him and his *Tour* incomparably more than do places or times. The other is that two of those people matter above all— Johnson most consistently and James Boswell even when he or we sometimes seem to forget it.

The shout Boswell heard reveals how presentation of Johnson also involves Boswell. Perhaps the most self-evident example occurs a bit beyond the day we are considering, a bit beyond the getting under way—although in fact it comes but two days later, 30 August. Two brief paragraphs—which may well be borne in mind when we turn to Bashō—record the progress of the two friends on horseback past perhaps the most popular place in the Highlands.

> It was a delightful day. Loch Ness, and the road upon the side of it, between birch trees, with the hills above, pleased us much. The scene was as remote and agreeably wild as could be desired. It was full [every bit] enough to occupy our minds for the time.
>
> To see Mr. Johnson in any new situation is an object of attention to me. As I saw him now for the first time ride along just like Lord Alemoor [unskillfully], I thought of *London, a Poem,* of *The Rambler,* of *The False Alarm;* and I cannot express the ideas which went across my imagination. (99)

The scene (with trees, we may be expected to note) suffices to fill the mind, but of course would not without Boswell's being there with Johnson. No visual perception of the loch is given, in any event. And it is evident that both travelers are necessary to the experience: the first

Fig. 13. Inverness in the distance from Fort George. The view suggests the Scottish bleakness of which Johnson complained.

sentence is ostensibly about Johnson but really more concerns Boswell, whereas the second more or less reverses the points of attention.

The final paragraph of the fifteen on 28 August is far more complex, more so than even Boswell imagined. Here it now is in full.

> Mr. Johnson wrote tonight both to Mrs. Thrale and Mrs. Williams, and I wrote to my wife. I value myself on having as constant a regard—nay, love—for her as any man ever had for a woman, and yet never troubling anybody else with it. I was somewhat uneasy that I found no letter here from her, though I could hardly expect it, as I had desired [asked] her to write to Skye. I could not help my mind from imaging it as dreary that I was to be yet for several weeks separated from her. Clouds passed over my imagination, and in these clouds I saw objects somewhat dismal. She might die or I might die; and I felt a momentary impatience to be home, but a sentence or two of the Rambler's conversation gave me firmness, and I saw that I was on an expedition which I had wished for for years, and the recollection of which would be a treasure to me for life. The inn was dirty and ill-furnished. The entertainment pretty good. (95)

The conclusion on the inn and their treatment is an inspired non sequitur, as if to say, "but no more now of that."

To Boswell and to us the crucial part of the paragraph is what follows the second sentence and precedes the comment on the inn. No special psychological training or suspicion of authors is necessary to understand that the crucial truth of Boswell's passage on his wife, Margaret, is that it *ought* to be true. I do believe that such ideas did come to his mind. I also believe that thought of his wife is not one of Boswell's obsessions on his journey. (There are not twenty passages on her in the 403 pages of the *Tour*). He sits down to write to his wife and imagine things about her, because if Johnson is writing even blind, difficult Mrs. Williams, he could hardly do less. Yet one of the conspicuous absences throughout his *Journal* is his wife's name, Margaret.

The ostensible point of *view* in the intermediate body of the paragraph is of course Boswell, as that of *attention* is his wife. The personal pronouns—which again contrast with Bashō's Japanese usage—tell, as one may say, a different story.[22] Boswell uses four third-person pronouns for his wife and fifteen first-person ones for himself. The real point of attention is James Boswell himself. The real point of view is shared by Boswell (of whose degree of self-understanding neither he nor we are certain), by the reader (who smiles with self-forgetful smugness at Boswell) and, as Boswell did know, God (who fortunately is as merciful as wise).

Perhaps the most fascinating element in this absorbing passage comes down to the unanswerable question of just how far, and in what ways, Boswell was self-aware. There is no need to dwell on Margaret Boswell's dislike of Johnson, which may have included some jealousy over the attention her husband paid the visitor.[23] It is just as well that Boswell was unaware of Johnson's troubled masochism in his relations with Hester Thrale. It is enough to attempt to follow Boswell's exploration of himself in his exploration of a world tacitly denominated, "I with him in Scotland."

The shout Boswell heard and the letter writing in that dirty inn are no less artistic than real, and in fact the powerful sense of real experience depends on the art of journal writing that Boswell had perfected. He names his successive dates and the places leading to the verge of the Highlands. But the flow of action makes the occurrences of days more chronometric than crucial. Places are far more important: Johnson would not have made that "tremendous shout" in London, and Boswell does not record writing his wife because of any local associations. Instead, as all readers who have as it were witnessed Boswell get under way toward the Highlands can testify, for him at least as much as Pope, "The proper study of mankind is man." He does present a *Journal*, and it does relate a *Tour to the Hebrides*. But the important thing about those days and places is the copresence: *with Samuel Johnson, LL.D.* Boswell gives us a much larger, rounder, fuller depiction than does Johnson himself of his learned and truly esteemed friend, that unerringly and multiply appropriately named Rambler of the passage just considered. By definition Johnson's copresence implies Boswell's presence.

---

22. Again there is a forecastable contrast with Bashō. He is even more subjective and self-aware than Boswell. But the personal nouns of Japanese that correspond to English pronouns in grammar are seldom employed in actual practice. Translation into English of course beclouds the difference.

23. Johnson alludes to Margaret Boswell's dislike of him in many of the letters Boswell prints in his *Life*. Something of a reconciliation seems to have occurred in later years.

Fig. 14. Fort Augustus. From here to Glenelg was the most trying portion of Johnson and Boswell's journey. (From Cordimer 1788.)

Some students of Johnson depreciate "Boswell's Johnson." Anyone sharing my skepticism about our powers to understand past or present can only concede that Boswell must have missed, colored, or distorted some things and have been mistaken about many others. Like the rest of us, Boswell may dally with false surmise, but unlike Homer, he does not nod. There were too many people one could know. Knowing required naming them, and naming required telling what was human and distinct by virtue of the name. No reader of Boswell is likely to overlook the presence of, or fail to speculate about, the meaning of Boswell's most often recurrent name, "I." No reader, certainly not this one, can vie in investing that brief name with the irresistible interest he did. Perhaps our highest tribute to his art of naming is our recognition, after all, of our lesser abilities (even with him as guide) to name and understand *ourselves.*

Bashō Enters the Narrow Road

It may be possible to find some good words for Sora later in this discussion. But after the interest we have discovered in the accounts by Johnson and Boswell it would tax ingenuity and coerce charity itself to claim his *Nikki* is literary. As we have seen in the quotation earlier of his disconnected observations at the beginning of his account, he faced none of the problems of the other three travelers in the difficult literary art of getting under way. What he had to offer, the Gradgrindian facts, were simple and classified at the outset, requiring only entry into his protocomputer. We observe the modesty of his claim, we see the modesty of his achievement, and we turn to the poet he accompanied: the self-styled Old Man (Okina).

Bashō spent perhaps a week in Sampū's cottage after he relinquished his Banana Plant Hermitage (Bashō An) to a family he knew, or perhaps imagined, to have one or more daughters. It was on III.27, as he left Senju with Sora that his journey truly began.[24] Four days later, the pair of travelers were in Nikkō, where the founder of the Edo military government (bakufu), Tokugawa Ieyasu (1542–1616) was enshrined. Another twenty days later, on IV.21, they arrived at last at one of the two places given special mention in the prose poem at the outset. This is the Shirakawa Barrier (Shirakawa no Seki), the point after which the narrow road was thought to begin.

---

24. We cannot be really confident of the exact dating of his moving from his small place to Sampū's and thence to Senju. See *Zenkō*, 102. See also figure 1 and appendix 1.

Bashō's complex personality and method allowed for some simplicities—and some things distinctly, deliberately odd. In his opening prose poem, he named but two of the places on the journey he envisioned—Shirakawa no Seki and Matsushima. We may take it therefore that the journey between those two points was crucial to him. Bearing these matters in mind, we need not dally over diligent Sora but seek to discover what Bashō made of the eighteen or so days (IV.21 to V.9) that he had led himself and his readers to consider would be so important.

The journey between Shirakawa Barrier and Matsushima posed literary problems—and possibilities—for him. The names of those two places were not simply localities but places poetically attested. In his art of linked poetry, and in the poetry of generations before him, they were storied for well-known features and associated with venerated poets of the past. They were more than mere places. They were poetic "places of name" (nadokoro; later Sinified to meisho), what it is no error to call doubly proper nouns or names, once grammatically and once again poetically. As such, they exerted claims on his literary powers unmatched by any place before or between.[25]

Our expectations for Bashō at Shirakawa Barrier have been aroused. Most details will be dealt with later in a consideration of stylistic riches. For present purposes, it is enough to say that the prose is given a poetic resonance, and the episode concludes with a hokku, just as we expect. That hokku is, however, a not particularly impressive one—and is by Sora. It seems incredible that the master poet of the age should pass this place of such fame without a poem. What he does is withhold his poem until the next episode, at Sukagawa, when he tells what the experience was like and gives us a decisive hokku. Such arousal and diversion of expectations is an astonishing example of haikai comedy at a place of poetic name. In retrospect, we shall see that it renders the stage of being under way as one of the strangest and most difficult passages in this complex work.[26]

---

25. It will not be amiss to stress again the special importance in Japanese literature of places of name. From their convenience to poets who never saw them but in the imagination, or used them as mere fillers, they were called poetic pillows (utamakura) or ornaments.

26. "Being under way" is meant to indicate that the getting under way had begun earlier; in fact haikai comedy first appears at Nikkō.

One measure of the difficulty is the bewildering fact that nobody claims this section of *The Narrow Road* as a favorite. The terminal places, those two places of high poetic name (nadokoro), have engendered great interest. No such claim can be made for what comes between. Critics do observe this or that felicity and do remark on the first allusions to the heroic, tragic, and highly romanticized figure of Yoshitsune.[27] Yet if the interval between Shirakawa no Seki and Matsushima does not arrest many readers—and seems in retrospect longer than it is—it is all the more important to interrogate for Bashō's purposes.

For one thing, time becomes unclear. Bashō uses few dates, and in fact the only means we have of ascertaining when he was in Shirakawa and when in Matsushima is to follow Sora's account. (Why do most Japanese editions not cite Sora's *Nikki* more thoroughly? See app. 1.) Bashō remarks on the summer rains (samidare) falling on the day they reach Iwanuma, and since summer begins with earlier poetic topics (dai; kigo) in the *fourth* month of the old calendar, a close reader realizes that dates are not fundamental to the prose of *Oku no Hosomichi*. (Past and present are other matters indeed.)

Bashō occasionally supplies a date: for example the passage devoted to relics of the family of Vice Governor Satō, so loyal in the doomed cause of Yoshitsune:

> we came at last to a hill called Maruyama, the site of the vice governor's palace. When people told us of the grand gate that had stood at the foot of the hill, the image of the past led me to tears. At an old temple nearby there remain the graves of the whole Satō household, and standing between those of the two brave young wives, I wiped my eyes. They may have been women, but they had left a name for bravery to the world. There is a famous Chinese monument that made all visitors weep, but we need not search so far for such a stone. Upon entering the temple to ask for tea, we were told that the sword of Yoshitsune and the pannier of [his loyal retainer] Benkei were kept there as treasures.

---

27. Minamoto Yoshitsune (1159–89) is almost impossible to recover as a historical person from the many stories and plays in which he is celebrated as a chivalric figure. He is so much the generic example of the doomed heroes Japanese have long favored that, from the title of hōgan he once held, the expression *hōgan biiki* (sympathy with the lieutenant) covers numerous others as well. He is the central figure of one of the peaks of *The Narrow Road*, the episode at Hiraizumi not long after Matsushima.

> Pannier and sword
> use them for the boys' festival
> along with carp streamers.

That happened on the first of the Fifth Month.[28]

But the date he gives is wrong. His "mistake" in saying V.1 for what is really V.2 is not gigantic. But it is almost certainly deliberate, since it goes with the statement that he and Sora entered a temple to see weaponry surviving from Yoshitsune and Benkei. Sora's diary states as matter of fact, which nobody disputes, the correct date and the fact that they did *not* enter the temple but heard of the weaponry (*Nikki*, 115).

We might hold that time becomes fictional—dream–like, unclear—as the romantic story of Yoshitsune unfolds. But it seems more accurate to say that, by the dominance of aestheticized place, poetic time refashions real time. One need only compare Sora's account to sense the difference.

If we are to have a hold on reality, such dreamlike aestheticizing of time must be compensated for by attention to persons and places. There are certainly names and other references to persons. Yet in this as well there is a curious detachment, a great distance of view that gives us little sense of people appearing here and now. After Shirakawa no Seki and before Matsushima, only three living people are even mentioned: Tōkyū, a holdover from the Shirakawa episode; Kyōhaku, an Edo haikai follower whose hokku on Takekuma Bashō recalls as a parting gift once he reaches that location; and the painter Kitano Kaemon from Sendai. Properly speaking, Kaemon alone counts as a name belonging to this interval. Otherwise, anonymous village children or fishers in boats may be mentioned. But we are not told how many there are, their sexes, or their ages. Moreover, on the stage of the journey from Edo to Shirakawa, Bashō had made much of Sora by name, often quoting his hokku. Neither happens between Shirakawa and Matsushima: Sora is not mentioned at all, and he is assigned no quoted verse.[29]

---

28. *Diaries*, 167; *Zenkō*, 205. A pannier is an archer's protective device. The Boys' Festival on V.5 is the counterpart of the girls' on III.3, which is referred to in Bashō's first hokku. The "double three" and the "double five" of these two festivals anticipate the "double seven" of the Tanabata celebration on VII.7, which Bashō mentions later in the Niigata area.

29. My translation in *Diaries*, 165–73 obscures the facts mentioned. It names Sora as composer of the third stanza because we have other knowledge that it was so.

Bashō also avoids use of his first-person noun, *yo*. (Translation into pronoun-ridden languages like English obscures this.) We know we are in Bashō's presence, because he speaks of his reactions from time to time. But we are hardly aware of Sora or any other living person actually present: only Kaemon is alive and there. Tōkyū and Kyōhaku must be recalled. Sora's *Nikki* is very different. As usual, he records the names of numerous people met.

Bashō's account of this stage of his journey empties the world of living, named, present people. It presents a world of successive place, or places, in a landscape with various features we dimly imagine—a landscape barely and anonymously inhabited. For readers wishing to visualize that ghostly landscape, the best examples are probably Bashō's own paintings of scenery for his *Kasshi Ginkō* (or *Nozarishi Kikō*, 1685).[30] Other than the poetic traveler, people, living people, are scarcely implied.

There is much more naming of, and allusions to, the people of the past, the "kojin" referred to in the passage opening *The Narrow Road*. To consider only the Yoshitsune story, there are: Yoshitsune and Benkei themselves; the Satō family—father, two sons, and wives—gallant and loyal to the death (near Maruyama); and the famously loyal Izumi Saburō (Fujiwara Tadahira), who will be mentioned again at Hiraizumi. The episode at Shiogama refers to blind reciters, reminding us of the "lute priests" (biwa hōshi) who recited famous episodes, including Yoshitsune's, in the Gempei wars of the second half of the twelfth century. There are also names of three people from the eighth century (Tsubo no Ishibumi episode) and otherwise a tenth-century figure, Fujiwara Sanekata. Sadness surrounds the story of each. The recent Date Masamune (1565–1636) is not named but identified as the lord of the area who had a shrine in Shiogama restored.

For poetic resonance, the Shiogama episode features an allusion to "Haku Rakuten's" *Chōgonka*. There is also an echo of an Azumauta in the *Kokinshū*.[31] These recollections are used to evoke feelings of the sufferings of human life no matter what the station, whether the emperor of China or Japanese fishers. In other words, from Shirakawa no

30. For samples of Bashō's paintings on that journey, see Miner and Odagairi 1985, figures 1 and 2. They will be found to convey visually much of the sense we gain from reading the section of *The Narrow Road* being discussed.

31. That is, Bo (or Bai) Juyi's *Changhenge* (*The Enduring Remorse*), the story of a Chinese monarch's ruinous fascination with a great beauty. Azumauta, "Eastern Poems," were from the Edo area, provincial in the view of those from the general Nara and Kyoto region, sites of successive courts.

Seki to Matsushima, Bashō reveals a marked inclination to flee the present, or rather to give meaning to it by peopling it with ideal but suffering people of the past. Whether human absence or human suffering, the depiction is part of the oblique political criticism of *Oku no Hosomichi*, which first appears in the Nikkō episode and will concern us in later pages.

Viewer and Viewed

Most of the natural scenery between Shirakawa and Matsushima is impossible to visualize from Bashō's account. With an exception we shall be considering shortly (Tsubo no Ishibumi), there is remarkably little sense of local presence. Time is largely indefinite. And, as we have seen, living people are absent to the point even of the poet's not mentioning his companion, Sora. It is instructive to compare this part of *Oku no Hosomichi* with Shiga Naoya's modern story, "At Kinosaki" ("Kinosaki nite"). In reading Shiga, we would have to lack visual imagination entirely not to feel we had seen and known the narrator's room, the stream, the rat, and the rest. By contrast, the liveliest imagination is unable to visualize most places, times, and people between Shirakawa and Matsushima. That absence characterizes this stage of Bashō's journey, and it deserves stress in order to emphasize what *is* experienced by Bashō and the careful reader. He hovers there. We feel very strongly the presence of the "Okina" (Old Man or Old Master) of Sora's *Nikki*. He is clearly present, envisioning former poets and responding—but how we have yet to determine—to the dimly described scenes.

Longing for the richer past and subjectively apprehending the world are hardly new in East Asian literature, or unknown in other literatures. Assessing the response is very difficult in this getting under way, and we shall have to dwell on some particularly Japanese details. Given the summer season and Bashō's mention of its monsoon rains, one may recall for example, a poem by Fujiwara Shunzei (1114–1204):

> Yearning for the past,
> Here at my grass thatched hermitage
> In the rain at night—
> Do not sing increase of my tears,
> Hototogisu from the hills.[32]

---

32. *Shinkokinshū*, 3:201. The hototogisu is the Asian gray-headed cuckoo, whose song, nesting habits, and associations differ radically from those of the Western cuckoo.

Shunzei was drawing on a venerable tradition, as in the very first part of the *Ise Monogatari,* which closes, "In bygone times, people exhibited this ready-witted elegance" (Watanabe 1976, 14). For his purposes, Bashō would have replaced that elegance (miyabi) with an art (fūryū) appropriate to his media of haikai and haibun.[33]

It seems clear that we must think, especially of this section of getting under way as a haikai version of another model. In naming, with their attributes, the succession of places visited, his account of travel, in his dream of figures from the past, Bashō presents a variation of the travel piece (michiyuki) familiar in nō.[34] The dream vision (mugen nō) variety is characterized by an absence of living people and present temporalities. (The absence is not complete, or we would find the account unintelligible.) The world of this stage of *Oku no Hosomichi* similarly seems at times to exist solely as named places narrated in succession by an unidentified voice. In itself, the analogy suggests high seriousness. But there is another feature of this strange account we are considering: who can recall more than one hokku from this segment of *The Narrow Road*? The absence, the blank is very strange.

What if, however, the blank is in our minds rather than Bashō's? If we see nothing of nature in a portion of this greatest prose creation by a poet of nature, is it not likely that we fail to see what Bashō saw there? As has been said, nature is always and everywhere taken to mean something crucial to the takers—something about ourselves. As centuries pass and from culture to culture, the conceptions differ, but as the early American Cotton Mather wrote, "Nature is the map and shadow [reflection] of the spiritual estate of the souls of men." And in every period of every culture there are favored ways of taking nature—our environmentalism is no more Bashō's concern than it is that of his English contemporaries, Milton and Dryden.

---

33. For simple clarity, we may distinguish three poetic eras in premodern Japan. The first, dominated by waka (lit., Japanese poetry), extended to the thirteenth century; the second, by renga, from the thirteenth through the sixteenth centuries; and the last, dominated by haikai, from the seventeenth through nineteenth centuries. Renga and haikai are linked-poetry forms. Renga shared with waka a high decorum of diction and conception. Haikai had a mixed or lower decorum; it originally signified the comic, a quality it never wholly lost. Haibun, the art of *The Narrow Road*, was a prose counterpart to haikai, but usually included poetry as well.

34. That drama features two chief characters. The secondary one, or waki, is commonly a priest who more or less begins by reciting a travel piece giving, with very brief descriptions, the names of places passed en route to the scene of the action.

As a haikai poet, Bashō was well aware of inheriting conceptions that go back through the high linked poetry (renga) of Sōgi and the court poetry (waka) of Saigyō. We have seen that he praises them for sharing a single true art. In renga—the earlier, more decorous linked poetry—critics classified four kinds of *place:* peaks (sanrui; hills or mountains, elevations), watersides (suihen), residences (kyosho), and places of poetic name or nadokoro (Konishi 1971, 87). In a prose sense any place-name must be a nadokoro. But that is not the poetic meaning in waka, renga, haikai, or *Oku no Hosomichi.*

The places of name in the three poetics of waka, renga, and haikai are well known to students of premodern Japanese literature, appearing in many a handbook and dictionary. Their number increases with time, even to the present day, and it is extremely difficult to specify the year status was accorded. Once the status was gained, Shinto animism infused a spirituality into the site. Even today talismans and charms are purchased in abundance from such localities. The association of temples with hills and shrines with groves is natural, given customs of location.

There is also the legacy of word magic inherited by Bashō. The realm of incantation, invocation, and spiritual efficacy of words is of an importance difficult to exaggerate and of a delicacy and even restriction difficult to get right. In a sense, what is involved are those just-mentioned temples on hills and shrines in sacred groves (cf. Latin *lucus*). The esoteric Buddhism (mikkyō) of the Shingon and Tendai sects could find or evoke spiritual magic in multiplicities—not in a single tree or hill or place, but a grouping that could be mentally or spiritually patterned. Yet farther back, and well beyond recoverable history, the animism of native Shinto provided an even more spiritualized view of language and place.

The spiritual and incantatory often were special speech-acts and were of course spoken, commonly in verse, in preliterate times, although written accounts of them have survived in considerable number. For our purposes, two of the most important manifestations of word magic were the spells or spell-songs (hoki, hokiuta) and the word spirit or kotodama that might be evoked by a special speech-act or kotoage. Shamanism was involved, and the effects might be malign as well as good. Given the highly permeable divide between human and divine, it is clear that word magic was thought to explain or even control powerful forces. Since such forces were present now, they must also have existed in the past, a presumption that led to the inclusion of incantations in recountings (narrative, ji) as well as in utterances (kotoba). Clearly, Japanese were receptive to the mandalas and mantras of esoteric Buddhism. (On these matters, see Konishi 1984, 94–110; and on esoteric Buddhism I rely on his correspondence.) No wonder the key concepts of Japanese poetics are kokoro, the human/divine heart or mind or spirit, and kotoba, words. No wonder Japanese literature is so highly aural and oral, even when literacy is widespread.

We can only assume a gradual diminution in the full belief in the spiritual strength and the efficacy of word-acts. But their connection to place names extended, with a degree of force difficult to ascertain, to Bashō's time. Appreciation of this depends on understanding of what came to be called pillow words (makurakotoba) and prefatory words (jokotoba). These celebratory enhancements might apply to things spiritual, human, and natural (although the three often defy distinguishing). Often they are so old that their meaning is presently obscure. Clearly, however, they were applied to places, although their force is difficult to translate if its existence cannot be assumed by a modern reader. Konishi gives as example a poem highly appreciated by Japanese (Konishi 1984, 208; translation revised). The pillow words are italicized (*Man'yōshū* 3:250).

Tamamo karu	We pass Minume
Minume o sugite	*Where they cut gem-like seaplants,*
Natsukusa no	And have now rowed near
Noshima ga saki ni	The Noshima promontory
Fune chikazukinu.	*Luxuriant with summer grasses.*

It may be difficult to describe any spiritual presence or even to say what the phrases mean. But take them away, and half the poem is gone. Take away the place-names, and nothing is left.

Bashō's narrative is not as formulaic as that poem from perhaps a millennium before him. But much the same temper can be found in a passage from the Shirakawa Barrier–to–Matsushima section that we are finding so difficult to understand.

> We inquired afterwards about the Tama River in Noda and the Stone of Oki. At the famous Sue no Matsuyama, a temple has been built with the same name rendered in Chinese fashion—

Matsushōzan. Graves dot the intervals between the pines of the grove. The most intimate promises of lovers, made never to change, have their outcomes in these graves, and the thought made time seem yet crueler, just as the vesper bell sounded from Shiogama Inlet. The sky, from which the summer rain had been falling, cleared somewhat, and in the faint glowing of the moon over the water in the early dark, the form of Magaki Isle seemed near at hand. (*Diaries*, 171–72; *Zenkō*, 246–47)

The Tama River at Noda was one of six famous Jewel Rivers (tamagawa). Shiogama Inlet is a place of poetic name (nadokoro, utamakura) famous—as the name suggests—for the making salt of sea brine there, and Magaki Isle is associated with it in poetry. Sue no Matsuyama is a famous place of poetic name. As Bashō suggests, lovers invoked it as a pledge to remain true (till the waves overspread its pines) and therefore also of gross infidelity: in *The Diary of Izumi Shikibu* there is a crisis when the heroine is accused by her princely lover of wanton unfaithfulness in a poem playing on the associations of Sue no Matsuyama (Miner 1969, 110). We should later recall that the poetic topic, love (koi), has made its first appearance here.

These considerations show that the blank is in our minds, not Bashō's. His naming of places evokes clusters of associations and is itself a meaningful act. In Western terms, it is less like a train announcement and more like a combination of names in a prayer. The associations of Shiogama ("brine kilns") with the miserable lives of salt makers and of Sue no Matsuyama with lovers are among the features giving a human dimension to what is observed. We see yet again the crucial importance of narrative points of attention (Miner 1990, 181–212).

In complementary fashion, once what is attended to is recognized (we may call it nature, place, a spiritual world), the attender and point of view gain significance. We should remember the name that was called out to him, "Traveler": *tabibito*, travel person. For, like the Man of the Past ("Mukashi otoko") early in *The Tales of Ise* (*Ise Monogatari*, dan 7–15), Bashō begins with a descent to the east (azuma kudari). This *is* travel, whereas, as the renga handbook *Ubuginu* puts it, even parting to visit a place of name in the vicinity of the capital is contrary to poetic travel (Yamada and Hoshika 1936, 208). This detail leads us to reflect on a significant absence: even when Bashō is miserable at Iizuka or later at

Shitomae no Seki, there is a total absence of nostalgia for Edo. That cannot be solely because Edo is the down east (azuma) from Kyoto.

Yet the aura of mystery remains. Is Bashō claiming that if he names a theretofore uncelebrated place it becomes a place of poetic name? The issue is further complicated by Bashō's making a point of introducing the names of places that he and Sora do *not* visit. Curiously enough, those comprise most of the best-established nadokoro between Shirakawa and Matsushima: Takakuma no Matsu, Natorigawa, Noda no Tamagawa, and Sue no Matsuyama. To a waka poet, to a renga poet, and to a haikai poet like Bashō, those are indisputably places of name. In an imaginary index they would appear under the head, "nadokoro, bypassed unseen." Such is the art of *The Narrow Road* that it is here, where the spiritual and high poetic associations are richest, that we catch first glimpse of that special thing, haikai comedy. That will concern us later.

Some places of name are visited. Abukumagawa is one well-established example. Yet all Bashō says—at the beginning of the Sukagawa episode—is "In such fashion we passed through, proceeding till we forded the Abukuma River" (*Diaries*, 165; *Zenkō*, 184). Why he says so little may be answered by *Ubuginu*: simply crossing a mountain or mountain peak (but not a hill) constitutes travel (Yamada and Hoshika 1936, 207). If that is the case, crossing a river like Abukumagawa, which is a nadokoro (and so close to Shirakawa no Seki), certainly constitutes travel, tabi.

The other place, Tsubo no Ishibumi, is both more complex and more revealing. It is particularly striking for being the one place between Shirakawa no Seki and Matsushima that is described in detail. And the very formality shows that Bashō took care to design his description to his purposes.

The Tsubo Stone Monument Is at Taga Castle in Ichikawa Village.

The monument is more than six feet high and just about three wide. Its surface is so covered by moss that one can only make out its inscription by the depressions. It tells of distances to the four corners of the country. There is also: "This castle was built in 724 by Lord Ōno Azumabito, provincial state secretary and military commander, and restored in 762 by Lord Emi Asakari, similarly a commander entrusted with pacifying the area, and also counselor and governor of the Eastern Provinces. The first day of the Twelfth Month." That would be in the reign of Shōmu [r. 724–49].

From long ago such monuments have been adornments of verse and the subject of numerous stories. Ours is a world in which in time even mountains crumble, rivers change their courses, and roads go in altered routes. Stones disappear beneath the surface of the earth, great trees wither away, and saplings take their place. There are seldom any certain vestiges of what has been. Yet in this place there are wholly trustworthy memorials of events a millennium ago and, as I stand here looking upon them with my own eyes, I have the feeling of actually seeing what motivated those of ancient times. Such an experience is a benefit of wayfaring, and rejoicing over the gift of life, I forgot the rigors of travel and was overcome even to tears. (*Diaries*, 171; *Zenkō*, 232–33)

The mathematical, prosaic description actually given of Tsubo no Ishibumi is evident. So also is the rise in tone when the style switches from what smacks of Chinese prose to Japanese fluency as Bashō mentions those "of ancient times" (mukashi; kojin). It is those of the past and suggested by the place that move him to tears.

What is not clear is what kind of *literary* claim Bashō is making. Superficially, quickly read, his words seem to say that Tsubo no Ishibumi is a poetic commonplace (utamakura) or, more precisely, a place of name, nadokoro. Closely read, the words say both less and more. Less, because he *compares* Tsubo no Ishibumi to other locations that, unlike it, are established places of name, nadokoro. More, because whereas many of them had actually disappeared, this place remains with the evidence of centuries. We cannot know which then-disappeared nadokoro Bashō had in mind, but a few examples may be given of poems celebrating famous places vanished in all but name as their poets wrote.

Fujiwara Shunzei. Senzaishū, *4:258. (Fushimi no Sato)*

As evening falls
From along the fields the autumn wind
    Pierces to the bone,
And the quails seem to cry in pain
In Fukakusa Village's deep grass.

(Allusion: see *Kokinshū*, 18:971–72; *Ise Monogatari*, dan 123)

Fujiwara Yoshitsune. Shinkokinshū, *17:1599. (Fuwa no Seki)*

Not a soul remains
At "everlasting" Fuwa Barrier
　Where the plank-roofed halls
Are devoid of all that was
Except for the autumn wind.[35]

Iio Sōgi. Sōgi Dokugin Nani Hito Hyakuin, *12–13. (Kiyomi)*

With utter clarity
and not a cloud to arrest the eye
　the moon shines on

and then the Kiyomi Barrier gate
opens as dawn moves on the waves

(Allusion: see *Shinkokinshū*, 3:259)

It is unlikely that these particular examples were on Bashō's mind, but they fit his category of places of name in a world in which "There are seldom any certain vestiges of what has been." By Shunzei's time, the location of Fukakusa was unclear. Yoshitsune plays on the literal meaning of Fuwa ("indestructible," "everlasting") and the fact of its obliteration. Sōgi's is the most brilliantly conceived. *Kiyomigata*, not Kiyomigaseki (gone after Heian times) was the nadokoro, for which the moon was the chief feature. Having written of the moon in stanza 12, Sōgi is free in 13 to innovate, playing on "sekido" (barrier gate) and "akeyuku" (dawn moves, or in Japanese night "opens" like the gate). In effect, he almost claims to be producing a new place of name. In the two waka, only the autumn wind remains, and in Sōgi's renga stanzas the waves are tinged by the first light of dawn and by lingering moonlight. At Tsubo no Ishibumi, Bashō reports actually seeing the stone memorial (ishibumi). To that extent, his Tsubo no Ishibumi gives (as it were) its own palpable evidence of being a poetic place: an utamakura, a nadokoro.

Without cognizance of these issues, much of importance would escape us. For example, we could not understand why Andō Tsuguo

---

35. The noble court poet Fujiwara Yoshitsune (1169–1206) should not be confused with the military hero, Minamoto Yoshitsune (1159–89).

uses "Utamakura" ("Places of Name") as the title for the chapter he devotes to the journey between Shirakawa no Seki and Matsushima (Andō 1974, 121–39). Precisely, and yet, just what is going on?

For one thing, we have here a striking example of that "haikai change" (haikaika) that is the basis of the comic in haikai, something we shall do well to bear in mind. Truly, dealing with Bashō raises difficult issues. He does not really say that Tsubo no Ishibumi is a place of poetic name. In fact, there were two places named Ishibumi (see *Kōjien*), which just does not do for a place of poetic name. On the other hand, Bashō clearly implies that in certain ways Tsubo no Ishibumi is superior to certain poetically established locations. That is not only because it is not lost, but because he has beheld with his own eyes (he says) what so deeply moved "kojin no kokoro" ("the hearts of those of old")—a phrase of very deep meaning for a Japanese poet and the premise of the existence of a nadokoro. Moreover, although the renga rule book, *Ubuginu,* says that Tsubo no Ishibumi is a mere place (tokoro) rather than a nadokoro, it goes on to associate it, "long ago," ("mukashi") with the important divinity Yamato Takeru no Mikoto and quotes a poem by Archbishop Jien (1155–1225), as if he had been reading Sōgi and as if it were a nadokoro (Yamada and Hoshika 1936, 218).

Bashō weeps because he is moved to find evidence of those of the past (kojin), of what once was (mukashi). In my opinion, he also weeps over his own life and ambitions. He wrote this account of his lengthy "descent" for himself, for members of his school, and for those who might think of him when he himself, the self-styled Old Man (Okina), joined the poetic past, when he became a kojin. In fact, that has pretty much been what has happened.

Perhaps we modern readers focus too much, however, on Okina and not enough on the place, Tsubo no Ishibumi. It is, after all, in the brief overture leading to *"The Tsubo Stone Monument"* that he uses his title phrase, "Oku no Hosomichi": "Following the route marked on the maps Kaemon had given us, we found along the narrow road to the remote provinces that the sedge of the ten-strand mat did exist. They say that even now the mats are presented to the lord of the Sendai fief."[36]

---

36. *Diaries,* 170–71. For military assistance in the struggles that led to the foundation of the Tokugawa Bakufu, Date Masamune (1567–1639) was granted the great Sendai fief. (A few sentences later, Bashō alludes to him again somewhat more explicitly.) The character for "oku" (as in *Oku no Hosomichi*) has specific associations with the large

Surely all readers observe the rise in tone in the course of the Tsubo no Ishibumi episode—it swells to bear us like a great wave to the ensuing episodes at those places of great poetic name, Sue no Matsuyama and at Matsushima. Of course, that is another way of saying that the episodes between Shirakawa no Seki and Tsubo no Ishibumi (and thence to Matsushima) are much less impressive. A modern reader may be tempted to conclude that those, so to speak, ordinary episodes are unimportant, better skipped in favor of the high points. To a reader schooled in renga or haikai, however, those "ordinary episodes" hold great aesthetic importance. It is they that give full value to the extraordinary episodes at Shirakawa before and at Tsubo no Ishibumi afterward. In renga terms, the ordinary episodes are the equivalent of ground (ji) and ground-design (jimon) stanzas, whereas the extraordinary episodes are the equivalents of the impressive design (mon) and design-ground (monji) stanzas of a linked-poetry sequence.[37]

Moreover, those ordinary episodes greatly assist our understanding of useful ways to read *Oku no Hosomichi*. No other section of the work shows as plainly as those "ordinary stanzas"—that is, episodes—how like a michiyuki (travel piece) this michi no nikki (diary of the road) is. Comparison with Sora's account is highly illuminating. It shows that Bashō usually omits what Sora writes down so unimaginatively: weather, times of the day, methods of travel, people met, gifts received, baths taken, and so on. In addition, between Shirakawa no Seki and Matsushima there is that omission of all but the rarest reference to people.

One of the very few things remaining in our memory is precisely what we recall about michiyuki: names of places with something about the associations the places arouse. To offer a simplification: it is as though Bashō is traveling alone along a route of named places and his narrow road draws a line across a map marked solely by place-names, as though only proper nouns are important and common nouns are disdained. Not only that. It is as though the only people who truly exist and are given names (proper nouns) are the dead, the "mukashi hito,"

---

province, Michinoku or Mutsu, in the extreme eastern and northern portion of the main island: a close counterpart of the Highlands and Hebrides visited in the next century by Johnson and Boswell.

37. For explanation of these terms, see Konishi 1986, 457–61 or, in English, Miner 1979a, 72–76.

the "kojin." As has been suggested, those emphases are shared with the travel pieces in nō.

Bashō did not invent the principles of places of poetic name and of travel pieces. Those are deep within the underground stream of Shinto as part of perennial Japanese belief, although it is not inaccurate to label them as features of the aesthetic of place-names (chimei bigaku) in Japanese literature. That aesthetic differs from the Western concepts in one direct and in one more contextual way. The direct reflects the existence of a Japanese aesthetic of poetic place-names in a sense and to a degree not true of most other cultures. Rome and Red Cliff mean much to Western or Chinese. But neither belongs to a systematic view of places as sacred to local divinities or to codification in literature over the centuries. Bashō is *required* somehow to recall the autumn wind at Shirakawa no Seki, although he has arrived in summer.

There is a similar problem triumphantly resolved in Sendai, which Bashō poses and partly resolves in two clauses: "Miyagi Moor was overgrown with bush clover and so gave rich promise of autumn scenery" (*Diaries*, 170; *Zenkō*, 226). Bush clover (hagi) is one of the seven autumn plants (aki no nanagusa). There was also a spring counterpart (haru no . . .). Of all Japan, Miyagi was known to poets as the best place to see bush clover in autumn bloom. One did not compose poems about peonies there or about bush clover along the Tatsuta River, which was aesthetically codified otherwise.

We have not yet seen the extent of Bashō's artistry. He also mentions another famous plant, Sendai bush clover (Sendai hagi) which must have bloomed two or three weeks before he and Sora arrived in Sendai. Poising summer's earlier Sendai bush clover with autumn's later Miyagi bush clover and his visit between, Bashō gives the feeling that, in his mind at least, both are in bloom. His contemporaries would have marveled at his poetic finesse, which implies total command of the aesthetic of place, of names—of place-names. His magic creates from a double absence a single presence.

This passage should give force to what has been said of the Japanese aesthetic of travel: its aim is more cognizance of the known rather than discovery of the unknown. Sora could not possibly have recorded of Bashō what Boswell said of Johnson, that he traveled with the aim of discovering "things which he had not seen before," any more than that "he at no time had much taste for rural beauties" (*Tour*, 81). Bashō most certainly sought out what were new and narrow roads, things he had not seen before. But it was not any surprise that was their attraction: it was rather proof of what he had learned to think poetically true and therefore empirically true when actually, personally beheld and proved.

The strong emphasis upon the qualities or features of place (with its times, flora, and fauna) is a related contextual matter, one so old that it cannot certainly be called the effect (or the cause) of the aesthetic coding. Both go back to prehistoric Shinto origins in concepts of sacral place and holiness in living things. These various factors combine with others to give rise to further aesthetic assumptions.

Of those others, none is more important for differentiating our two pairs of travelers than the relatively greater importance attributed by Japanese to aesthetic "points of attention" (Miner 1990, 181–212). The more familiar (and more Western in emphasis) reciprocal concept, narrative point of view, emphasizes the importance of the mind seeing or observing the world. That is distinctive of Western literature, mimesis, and "representation." Emphasis on literary points of attention lends greater importance to what is seen, experienced. The contrast may suggest a Japanese objectivity poised against Western subjectivity. But of course objectivity and subjectivity are interdependent, reciprocal. There are moments in the most subjective Western literature when we are concerned with the objective, when the very emphasis upon the seer leads the author and us readers to a heightened sense of what is seen. The counterpart is typical of Japanese literature. In his Japanese preface to the *Kokinshū*, Tsurayuki speaks of Japanese poetry in terms of the human affective faculty, the heart, spirit, or mind (kokoro) and of the human expressive resource, words, language, topics, and objects (kotoba). Unless it finds something in the world to move it, the heart will not be moved to expression in words.

This helps explain what is dreamlike after Shirakawa no Seki. In one sense, the account emphasizes Bashō's own subjective awareness of a factual succession of place-names. Clearly, we would have nothing about those places without him (or others like him). But equally clearly and yet more significantly, his record of that stage of the journey results in a dreamlike experience, because other persons and temporal markers have been minimized. The points of attention (places, many of which are places of name) seem almost to exclude point of view. We know, of course, that that is illogical, that what is seen can have importance solely because somebody sees it. But the relative stress upon points of attention over points of view is particularly Japanese. It sometimes

catches Western readers off balance and would certainly do so far more
if English translations could be written without adding all those pronouns so unnecessary in Japanese.

Another closely related contextual feature is the naturalness of
shifting points of attention. If places are what is valued, they can be
given in long succession, as in travel pieces (michiyuki) in drama or
narrative—or as in Bashō's account of the narrow road from Shirakawa
no Seki. A final feature is the naturalness of shifting, not only from one
point of attention to another, or even of one point of view to another, but
also from an emphasis upon point of attention to an emphasis on point
of view (or the reverse). Pronouns are not so necessary for this, and its
effect is therefore felt more by sensitized readers.[38]

The Tsubo no Ishibumi episode offers a striking example. The
monument and those of old have gripped us as a point of attention
more significant by far than point of view. At the close of the episode,
there is a defining moment like Boswell's "We spoke none." There
occurs a sudden sense of shift to the importance of point of view: Bashō
weeps. Point of attention still matters: his tears would not fall if the
point of attention, the stone monument, were a market or new castle.
But the emphasis has shifted as drastically as suddenly.

Bashō weeps over what he is led to feel by what he sees. Three
crucial clauses (Zenkō, 233) close the episode:

1. From long ago written about as an adornment of verse (Mukashi
   yori yomiokeru utamakura)
2. trustworthy memorials of events a millennium ago, and as I
   stand here looking upon them with my own eyes, I have the
   feeling of having seen what motivated those of ancient times
   (chitose no katami, ima me no mae ni kojin no kokoro)
3. I was overcome even to tears (namida mo otsuru bakari naru).

As Matsuo Yasuaki well observes, Bashō weeps at other times in *Oku no
Hosomichi*, both earlier at Sukagawa as also in thinking of the loyal Satō
household, and again later at Hiraizumi (Zenkō, 238).[39]

---

38. "Sensitized readers" is not meant condescendingly. Even people used to reading linked poetry in Japanese often have difficulty following extraordinary shifts of
points of view and attention.

39. More accurately, Bashō reports his weeping on those occasions. Does he report
weeping because he should have if he did not? Did he weep because it was the proper

In my view it is also worth observing how the Tsubo no Ishibumi passage, like the very beginning of *The Narrow Road,* moves from staccato drums of Chinese style to the flutelike flow of Japanese. Perhaps the parallel is a quiet reminder that Matsushima is mentioned at the beginning and that the travelers have drawn close to it. If Shirakawa no Seki marked the beginning of geography seen as art (fūryū), surely Matsushima will provide a climax.

The Meaning of Matsushima

After a briefly told account of one of the most famous of nadokoro, Sue no Matsuyama, Bashō and Sora arrived at last by boat at Matsushima (Ojima). According to Bashō, it was a journey of about five miles (2 ri bakari) to Ojima on the ninth of the Fifth Month, 1689. It was a summer's day in the old calendar, and Sora's entry begins, "Fine weather" (*Nikki,* 118). Conditions seem perfect for what he had envisioned before setting forth: "I could not put from my mind how lovely the moon must be at Matsushima" (*Diaries,* 157). Of course, in a sense it is the wrong season for a haikai poet, who would identify autumn as the natural poetic season to celebrate the moon. But, all in all, in following Bashō to arrival at beautiful Matsushima, we have two expectations: to fit the beauty of the place after those "ordinary stanzas" since Shirakawa or Tsubo no Ishibumi, Bashō's descriptive tone will be elevated; and he will write a hokku with its first or last line "the summer moon" ("natsu no tsuki").

Our expectations are altogether diverted. The description can be discussed in various ways that each of us would find to make sense: one could follow the temporal development, follow Bashō and Sora's path through the geography of the area, study Bashō's responses, and so on. All such discussions are important and no doubt necessary to full appreciation. The account here will proceed differently, emphasizing to begin with something so elementary that Japanese critics appear to have ignored it.

After an opening comparing Matsushima favorably with the finest Chinese beauty spots, Bashō turns to describing the innumerable is-

---

aesthetic response? Did he weep in a sudden rush of feeling? Should we think of Bashō the author as an entity closely related to? greatly at variance from? Bashō the stylized traveler (tabibito)? and linked-poetry master (haikaishi)? In lieu of answers, here is a note to this note: I have seen hard-bitten men weep copiously in the kabuki theater.

lands in the bay, and in the description we encounter the most sustained set of personifications of nature in all Bashō's writing, perhaps in Japanese. To consider but parts of it, we find:

> There are islands beyond counting, some tall ones pointing each its finger toward the heavens, and other low ones crawling on their bellies across the sea . . . some on the left stand aloof from each other, others join hands on the right. Some look as if they were children being carried on the back, yet others as if they were being hugged—in the manner in which parents or grandparents fondle their young ones. (*Diaries*, 173; *Zenkō*, 251)

The personification is striking for its "haikai change" (haikaika) of beautiful nature to familiar human relations and activities.[40] In Japanese aesthetics, that very sustaining of personification is comic in its excess and a potential comedy of deficiency in other matters. The waters are very deep at Matsushima.

It is striking that Bashō so celebrates the *human* qualities of the islands that their natural appearances seem lost. The comparison of Matsushima to a beautiful woman seems to emphasize the human over the place: it is more Chinese in its facial focus and its concept of beautifying the beautiful (yosohō). The Chinese personification of nature will be echoed when Kisagata, another lovely bay, will be compared with a woman's face—to the benefit of Matsushima.

The personification of islands gradually shifts to description of the pines on them. Then we suddenly note the narrative's crowding with ghostly figures: the dead monk Ungo, anonymous hermits, and, once in an inn for the night, recollection of friends left in Edo.

We must consider what Bashō does and does not include in the main part of his description of Matsushima. As lists of poetic places (nadokoro) show, Matsushima was an utamakura from poems like the first example in a royal collection, the *Goshūishū*, and it was a nadokoro

---

40. On the personification, the possible echo of Du Fu, and on the rhythmical prose rich in its art—in short, on the design along the lines of what was then termed a *fu* in Japanese usage, see the excellent commentary in *Zenkō*, 254–55. On haikai change in the precedent for this passage, the Shirakawa no Seki episode, see ibid., 182. In going on to trace elements of haikai comedy, I grapple with issues of tone that run throughout *The Narrow Road*. It will be clear that I am using this segment of Bashō's account to pose the most difficult questions. That is because they are most acute here, not because they exist nowhere else.

with several associations. Those were chiefly Ojima, fisherfolk (ama), and (in a familiar play on *matsu*) a lover's waiting in yearning (Katagiri 1983, 371–72). Other associations were plovers (chidori), the moon, and pines. Bashō has been anticipating the moon from the beginning, and in his description he deals with the famous pines. Why does he make so much of the many small (and by him unnamed) islands, never before a feature of Matsushima as a place of name?

One reason is that just as people say Osaka has 808 bridges, so the dictionaries say that Matsushima consists of "over 260 islands" (*Kōjien*, etc.). The islands really are there. But there is that other explanation so simple that critics have ignored it: the place-name *Matsushima* literally means "pines-islands." Bashō takes the literal meaning of the name to be fully descriptive. Or, to put it differently, the proper noun, the name, is an accurate designation of what its constituents mean as common nouns, which he writes at large and at length. This is extreme, whether as a Cratylus-like philosophical realism with names or unsettling haikai comedy.

The spirit of Cratylus achieves fullest realization in this description of Matsushima, but evidence of the same conception can be found from early to late in this work. For example, near the beginning there is Bashō's discussion of the Chinese characters changed from *Nikō* (futa-ara, double rough) to *Nikkō* (hi no hikari, sun's radiance). And the hokku at the very end plays on two meanings of the place-name Futami: both the place in the area he leaves for, Futami Bay, and the separation from friends, painful like tearing a clam's shell (futa) from its meat (mi).

Other examples abound. After Matsushima, they include (the list is not complete): Haguroyama, Komatsu, Nata, and Shirane. In these episodes, the significance of the name is explicitly referred to or accounted for (whether in prose, in verse, or in both) by the names' literal sense. This Cratylan philosophical realism in the treatment of places—and their names—implies that names mean just what they seem to say: Matsushima = matsu + shima (pines + islands); Shirane = shira + ne (white peak); and so forth. No other writer of travel known to me, Japanese or otherwise, does this so insistently. That it is deliberate is clear from the most extreme, astonishing example of all, the literalizing of the meaning—by prose description and by a hokku (which we shall see in the next chapter)—of the place-name Shitomae no Seki ("Before-Pissing Barrier").

Bashō's deliberate artistry can be also found in omissions and coinages. When he finds no use in names of two Chinese characters like *Matsushima*, he ignores the possibility (e.g., making nothing of *Kanazawa* as "Gold Marsh"). But with *Gassan*, he literalizes to the Japanese reading of the characters, producing "Tsuki no Yama" or "Mountain with Moonlight," so treating the image as a property that enables him to treat the place as a new one of poetic name. If literalizing a name adds nothing (e.g., Sado), Bashō requires other treatment to give the place a nadokoro-like importance. Matsushima is a very rare place: a nadokoro, a name literally meaningful, a place with both old and new properties of poetic name.

Once in their lodging at this most beautiful scene, Bashō and Sora understandably turn their thoughts to poetry. Bashō refers to Sodō's Chinese verses, Hara Anteki's waka, as also to Sampū and Dakushi's hokku on Matsushima. Bashō also includes a hokku by Sora. It is more significant for every reader that he emphasizes—with one of his rare uses of a first-person noun and a topic particle ("yo wa")—that *he* ("I myself") chose to make this no occasion for a hokku. Regarded as it is treated, without a hokku by the master poet of the age, Matsushima is certainly set apart. And this is all the stranger, especially after the sustained literalizing into islands and pines.

In my view, this odd matter actually completes the strange comedy begun at Shirakawa no Seki. It is not simply a matter of hokku. There, people were important—provided that they were of the past. As we have seen, in the journey from that beginning of poetic places (fūryū no hajime) to Matsushima, personal names—that is, designated people—grow increasingly rare, whether people of the valued past or the living present. By the eve of the travelers' arrival at Matsushima, the narrative of *Oku no Hosomichi* consists essentially of the voice or mind of an unself-designated narrator, whom we know to be Bashō, and otherwise of named places, some of which had long been nadokoro, with many others that had been uncelebrated in ambitious literature before.

Another elementary but to me crucial matter involves Bashō's reintroduction of the human element at Matsushima. We can recall that the first stage is personification of the islands as three generations of a family and of the whole of Matsushima as an unrivaled beauty whose loveliness has been increased by art. Next, Bashō introduces Monk Ungo (1582–1658), whose temple there was abandoned to ruin recently, along with certain present but unnamed religious hermits. The episode ends with a sudden naming of people: Sora reappears; poets in Edo are recalled by name; and Bashō identifies himself ("yo wa") as, of all things, a poetryless poet.

The surpassing beauty of Matsushima is stressed at great length in prose literalizing the place-name and going on and on with personified islands. But it is a mystery, a major crux of the account, that Bashō does not provide us with the hokku we expect on "the summer moon." The ensuing suite of answers is an interpretive drama in three acts. Its first is choral: what everybody seems to think. Its second shows the ideal hero most widely approved. The third seeks to reconcile tears with smiles.

Everybody seems to feel that Bashō of all people is extremely unlikely to have visited Matsushima without composing verse. He *must* have written one or more hokku there. After all, he records three at Obanazawa, three at Gassan, and five in the Kanazawa-Komatsu episode. Moreover, the one composed (after all) at Shirakawa no Seki led to a thirty-six-stanza haikai (kasen). It really is a puzzle: Sora's *Nikki* records no hokku by Bashō or himself. For all that, and remembering that this was Bashō's sole visit to the place, the fact is that other authentic sources do record hokku that he composed at Matsushima. (This is one of the ways in which understanding is assisted by the *Bashō Taisei.*) Attention to them may explain why Bashō might have composed them on his journey but excluded them from *The Narrow Road.*

The evidence is rather complicated, and it requires that we recall that *Oku no Hosomichi* was also not published in Bashō's lifetime. The range of alternatives being small but crucial, the various versions can be set forth in a column. No chronology is implied, whether of composition or publication.

1. A winter poem on Matsushima as a place of name (*Taisei*, 122); this has no connection with present concerns.
2. A prose account, "Matsushima no Fu" (*Taisei*, 349–50), nearly identical to *Oku no Hosomichi*; declaration that no poetry was composed.
3. Another, briefer prose account, "Matsushima no Ben" (*Taisei*, 350), with the same declaration.
4. Three almost identical hokku connected with the trip to Matsushima (*Taisei*, 53): "Islands upon islands! / Shattering into countless fragments / the summer sea."

5. Four hokku in three variant versions (*Taisei,* 121), beginning "Matsushima ya," relating either summer or clothes in the second line, and ending either "mizu to tsuki" ("water and the moon") or "natsu no tsuki" ("the summer moon").

Why should Bashō have written versions of two hokku (4 and 5) and then suppressed them from *The Narrow Road* with the fiction that he did not write any verse? Some answer is necessary, since it is perfectly clear that the "natsu no tsuki" version fulfills expectations aroused at the opening of this diary of the road. The other hokku ("Shimajima wa . . .") emphasizes the many islands the prose describes. Neither of them, nor both together—in whatever version—succeeds in combining the moon with the dominant images of the prose: islands and pines. That may explain why they were omitted. Or is the reason that the hokku are more optimistic (if they are) than the prose?

Or is not the answer, after all, simply their inadequacy? One need only compare the hokku written for Ryūshakuji or Hiraizumi with those we are considering. What verse he wrote at Matsushima simply does not fit, whether with this place of famous name or with the prose it accompanies.

There are other considerations. Among the most important is Bashō's naming of both kinds: giving a name and using a name already given. In this section of *The Narrow Road,* the most notable examples of Bashō's art are proper names, primarily of places (Matsushima). To be sure, there are a few proper names for time implied or used: for example, the Boy's Festival (Tango no Sechi). The matter of personal names requires special attention. We have seen how people seem to disappear from the narrative after Shirakawa no Seki and how Matsushima brings a final rush of names. In fact, the close of the Matsushima episode is unique (until the very end of the work) in *Oku no Hosomichi* in recalling by name more than one living person at a time in addition to Sora. Bashō did say, "Be careful about using the names of living people; there is no real problem about suitable use of the names of people of former times" (*Sanzōshi, Taisei,* 628). But that concerns canons for composing stanzas for the dignified front of the first sheet of a kasen or other major haikai form.

In other words, Bashō's omission of personal names and his stress on place-names, and further his sudden recollection at Matsushima of several Edo friends, are not decreed by rules but the result of his free

choice. The significant thing about all this is that the people named—
Sora, Sodō, Hara Anteki, Sampū, and Dakushi—are all introduced *as
poets*. He also is a poet, and a far greater one than those named. Paradox
that it is, and however filled his mind and however open his heart may
have been, at this crucial juncture Bashō found his poetic voice silenced.
    This is very strange.
    Naturally enough, Bashō's silence has been heard. Hattori Dohō
has an entry in his *Sanzōshi*: "The Master said he had no hokku at
Matsushima. This is an important matter" (*Taisei*, 655). He does not say
why. But with that omission there goes his rare introduction of names of
living persons.[41] Like the rare and striking stress on himself (yo wa),
this naming of others stresses all the more the poetic silence of the
greatest poet of the age. When Bashō really requires the resources of his
haikai art—at Matsushima—he seems to lose it. Has something gone
seriously wrong for Bashō at Matsushima?
    There seems to be a paradox, or perhaps rather something more
difficult, a dilemma. His prose is remarkable in what it does. His poetry
is remarkable in its absence from the episode. There may be a gloss in
one of his most famous comments: "Learn about what concerns pines
from pines; learn about what concerns bamboos from bamboos."[42] As a
gloss on the Matsushima episode, the passage suggests that, to some
degree or in some respect, Bashō the poet failed to learn from Matsushima what the prose writer learned from the pines and the "more
than 260" islands of Matsushima. The elaborately crafted prose reveals
that he had learned that the islands are almost human; the pines are
lovely and associated with religion; and the whole is like a lovely
woman made lovelier by her maid's and her jeweler's art. Where in the
rest of classical Japanese literature can we find a parallel for this unusual degree of personification of nature? And where else in Bashō do
we find, at the close of remarkably eloquent Japanese on nature, an
image so dominantly Chinese: that personification of natural loveliness
as a beautiful and beautified woman, "the loveliest face made lovelier"
by cosmetics and jewelry? (Two likely precedents in Chinese poetry are
given in *Zenkō*, 254.) To put it slightly differently, the personifications of

---

    41. Such a rush of names of living people is wholly appropriate in the third, final
part—the fast close or kyū—at the end of a linked-poetry sequence. See appendix 2.
    42. *Taisei*, 632. The aphorism only illustrates the problem. Its full application re-
quires attention to Bashō's metaphysics, which will be touched on later in this, and again
in the next, chapter.

individual islands are excessive, but the excess is Japanese. That Chinese, very much bedizened, lady, on the other hand seems neither very Japanese nor reassuring. Here is something different from what we see elsewhere in *The Narrow Road*. Has Bashō lost assurance and control? Or are we missing something?

We are now brought to the second and third acts of our drama. The second act shows the ideal poet at a moment of crisis. Its symptoms can be judged by comparison with the masterly handling of Shirakawa no Seki. Related to that, but so important as to deserve independent emphasis, is Bashō's loss of poetic voice. His failure to write a hokku for the episode as we have it is intensified with a sudden emphasis on poetry by others: Sodō and another four. Yet even that has its blank: the poems are mentioned, not quoted. Looking for other evidence of the strange or deficient, we observe that when (in his prose) he mentions the moon, he does not speak of the summer moon (natsu no tsuki) but simply the moon (tsuki). Plain *tsuki* poetically implies the *autumn* moon, as is traditional in waka about Matsushima. He is writing in summer, however. Perhaps that may be why he offers Sora's basically silly hokku: at least that hototogisu designates summer. To say the least, there is no real triumph there.

The irreducible fact is that if any place on Bashō and Sora's whole journey required a hokku, that was its most famous of places of name, Matsushima. The most steadfast, dedicated, responsible, and sensitive poet of the age is silent—or silenced, mute. In cases like this, Japanese commonly take recourse to factual or biographical circumstances. One possible biographical explanation for Bashō's poetic silence may be that he was disappointed by the totality of Matsushima (so have been many since) and found no way to put right what had gone wrong. On this view, it was not the beauty of Matsushima that kept him awake, but an unsettled sense of the difference between expectation and result, between his sense of what he ought to have discovered and felt and what he actually did. It may be an open question how far that disappointment was due to inadequacy in Matsushima and how far in himself. His uneasiness cannot have been assuaged by the unimpressive poems of his friends. That description seems to me to do justice both to the usual sense of Bashō and the unusual situation the ideal poet found himself in.

Our third and final act requires a radical concept of its hero founded on two reasonable assumptions. The first is that Bashō is more sophisticated than the ideal view allows for. The second is that he knew very well what he was doing. As has already been hinted in oversimple terms, the excessive artistry of the prose description—the extraordinarily extended initial personification of the islands and the bedizened Chinese beauty later—is part of a whole in which haikai change leads to a very special comedy. To explore this possibility, we must look back to the first episode in this section of *The Narrow Road*, Shirakawa no Seki.

Its opening differs in tone from what we have been seeing: "As the restless days of travel were piling up, we came at last to the Shirakawa Barrier, and my unsettled feelings gave way to calm" (*Diaries*, 164; *Zenkō*, 178). The reverse happens at Matsushima, even if the calm must endure another rather silly hokku by Sora. After that break for Sora, the prose and the travelers' motion pick up again:

> In such fashion we passed through [the site of Shirakawa Barrier], proceeding till we forded the Abukuma River. On the left Mount Aizu towered, and on the right lay the villages Iwaki, Sōma, and Miharu, which were divided by hills from Hitachi and Shimotsuke Provinces. We passed Kagenuma ["swamp of reflections"], but since the sky was clouded, we missed the chance to see the reflections in its waters. At the posting town of Sukagawa we visited Tōkyū, and we lingered on there for four or five days. (*Diaries*, 165; *Zenkō*, 184)

By the end of this passage, the travelers seem to be about a week out of the Shirakawa Barrier vicinity, and the sense of a considerable distance covered is conveyed by the names of a river and a mountain, of three villages and two provinces, of a legendary swamp, and at last of Sukagawa. The distance was in fact not great—some six ri, perhaps fourteen and a half miles. But the sense of distance is created: it is no accident that many editions (including *Zenkō*) treat this episode as one separate from Shirakawa no Seki.

Another way of putting the matter is to say that, although Bashō says nothing explicit, in contrast to his own declaration at Matsushima that he composed no poem, this narrative has taken us to, through, and well beyond Shirakawa no Seki without his offering a hokku—or, for that matter, his saying that he did or did not write verse. Thus far the episode (or episodes) seems almost an anticipation of his later poetic silence at Matsushima. It does seem that Bashō intends a connection between the opening and closing episodes of this stage of his journey.

It will be recalled that the comedy spoken of as a feature of the Shirakawa episode involved delaying introduction of the hokku. We must now recognize that the version of the comic in *The Narrow Road* is not farce but a high comedy consistent with, and an aid to, ultimate seriousness. This should be clear from the episode at Sukagawa following that at Shirakawa.

> At the posting town of Sukagawa we visited Tōkyū, and we lingered there for four or five days. When we met him, he asked, "How was it crossing the Shirakawa Barrier?"
>
> "The hardships of our long journey," I answered, "had left us exhausted and feeling oppressed. Added to that there was the almost overwhelming beauty of the area, the associations with those of former times, and what had been written about it long ago. There was so much to take in that I was able to write but little verse."
>
> > The places of high name
> > begin here—the way to far provinces
> > with a field-planting song.
>
> "I only wrote that, thinking that it would be a pity to cross the Shirakawa Barrier without writing something."
>
> Tōkyū responded by adding a second unit to my stanza, Sora the third. After a time we had written three sets of haikai. (*Diaries*, 165; *Zenkō*, 184)

So he had written a hokku, after all, and one justly famous (Miner 1992). It led to a burst of haikai composition (see fig. 18.) The parallel with Matsushima holds in a sense, but now the point is not likeness so much as contrast.

Considering this outcome, we may reasonably go back to the description of Shirakawa no Seki to discover what there is in lieu of the personifications at Matsushima. In fact, close examination reveals a remarkable description of that vanished barrier.

> As the restless days of travel were piling up, we came at last to the Shirakawa Barrier, and my unsettled feelings gave way to calm.

It surpasses what Taira Kanemori implied when he wrote from here, "If I could but convey / To those at home some hint of this." One of the three barriers in the northeastern provinces, Shirakawa has always had special appeal to poets and other writers. The richly leaved branches were the more precious because the autumn wind heard by Monk Nōin still lingers in the ears, and an image remains of its famous scarlet autumn leaves. The deutzia flowers are white as linen, and the wild roses vie for paleness, the whole giving the feeling of snow in its covering. Fujiwara Kiyosuke has set down how a man came to this barrier and tidied his headgear before he would cross it. (*Diaries*, 164–65; *Zenkō*, 178)

As the editors and commentators have shown, this passage is a dense, rich brocade of echo and allusion—all Japanese, unlike the cosmetically enhanced Chinese beauty of Matsushima. And Matsuo Yasuaki comments on the smooth rhythm of the prose as well as the haikai language.

It seems desirable to point out another remarkable feature that seems not to have been commented on and that my prose has certainly also failed to convey. That is, there is a quite special series of clauses beginning with the mention of the autumn wind. Its sound lingers in Bashō's mind (he says, ears) because of the poem by Nōin (*Goshūishū*, 9:518) that had begun to make the Shirakawa Barrier a place of name:

> From the capital
> I departed as companion
>   Of the haze of spring,
> And now the autumn wind blows here—
> The Barrier of Shirakawa.

Like Nōin, Bashō had started forth in the spring, but unlike Nōin, he has arrived in summer. That sad but beautiful sound of Nōin's autumn wind is what he hears poetically, even while seeing before him "the richly leaved branches" of trees in summer.

So far, all is standard use by Bashō of allusion to a valued past. But something much more remarkable also occurs. Mention of Nōin's autumn wind leads Bashō to clauses that are exceptional in *The Narrow Road* for being wholly of the pure Japanese of waka and renga. Not only that, Bashō manages to set them forth in units suggesting that the passage is some manner of poem, or perhaps one should say of prosodic prose: "Akikaze o / mimi ni nokoshi/ momiji o / omokage ni shite / aoba no sue / nao aware nari / u no hana no / shirotae ni / ibara no hana no / sakisoite / yuki ni mo koyuru / kokochi zo suru." This might be represented typographically in English as a version of a chōka.[43]

> with the autumn wind
> yet lingering in the ears,
> and the colored leaves
> yet a visionary image,
> the branches of green leaves
> bear a yet more poignant beauty;
> rich blooms of deutzia
> white as the purest linen
> are vied with for unblemished color
> by the wild rose blooms,
> and all conveys the feeling
> of color melting even as the snow.

Looking yet again at the plainer prose before and after this passage, one sees that although it is not prosodic, it is still remarkable for its purity of Japanese diction. (The one exception is "sankan no itsu ni shite fūsū no," or "one of three barriers and special in appeal.")

This takes our second explanation further and makes it contextually sounder. It posits that Bashō is very much in control throughout this section of his *Narrow Road*. Anyone can see that the joint Shirakawa-Sukagawa episode is as artful and mannered in its way as is the Matsushima episode.[44] The art and the manner differ radically, however. The earlier episode clarifies into the naturalness or purity of ages-old poetic language. The Matsushima episode is very differently marked:

---

43. Waka, the poetry of the court, has two main forms: chōka or longer poems, and tanka or shorter poems (in five lines). The prosody of both involves alternating five and seven lines, although in songs and dramatic passages the alternation is of sevens and fives. Bashō does not rigorously adhere to either of these rhythms, which explains the description, "prosodic prose." In that seemingly contradictory nature, the passage more closely resembles the Chinese version of *fu* or rhyme prose—although Bashō's diction is very pointedly un-Chinese.

44. Matsuo Yasuaki remarks on the haikai-like handling of language, the haikai change involved, and the emphasis upon the distinction drawn between waka and haikai assumptions (*Zenkō*, 182). Such alteration, such differentiation are means for the wit and high comedy that are being argued for here.

by the extraordinary distention of personification of the islands. By
received poetic standards, that sustained conceit is comic. As an example we may take one of the most powerful poems by Ono no Komachi
(fl. ca. 850).

> Unable to meet for love—
> No chance on a moonless night—
> I wake ablaze with passion,
> My breast consumed by racing fires,
> My heart reduced to glowing coals.

Komachi has drawn for her art on pivot words (kakekotoba) to make
words yield their metaphorical utmost. The result is that the sustaining
was viewed as excess and more or less comic: it is included among
poems labeled haikai.[45] In other words, a high comedy marks Bashō's
account of getting to Matsushima. Both the beginning with Shirakawa
no Seki and the ending with Matsushima are informed by a haikai wit
that turns a stretch of prose almost into verse here or turns islands and
the whole of Matsushima into personification.

To discover that does not explain all in the two episodes: the effects
of the manner and the wit seem very different. Where Matsushima
turns out to be anthropomorphized, to undergo what our rhetoricians
termed prosopopoeia, to be Sinified, to lack verse, and to deny assurance, Shirakawa no Seki had been translated into poetic allusiveness
and even, for some length, into Japanese poetic rhythms. It has verse
both in its prose and in the slyly delayed hokku. Verse and prose alike
affirm the beauty of an assured world.

What are the implications of so radical a reassessment? Perhaps
something can be learned from the other major episode of this series,
that at Tsubo no Ishibumi. There the movement is Bashō's usual one
and the reverse of that exemplified by the Matsushima episode. There
we find a beginning with an emphatic prosiness and Sinified language
and an ending with Japanese fluency.

The Tsubo no Ishibumi passage has another important feature. It
concerns *the past* as a powerful point of attention and ends with an
equally powerful point of view—with Bashō in tears. Shirakawa em-

---

45. The poem is *Kokinshū*, 19:1030 ("Hito ni awan / Tsuki no naki ni wa /
Omoiokite / Mune hashiribi ni / Kokoro yakeori"). Book 19 includes poems labeled
"haikai," with a character for "hai-" somewhat different from that for Bashō's. (See
Kuriyama 1963, 12–24.) But excess is a major source of the comic in Japanese.

bodies the past even more in some ways, but it is too wittily positive to allow for tears. Matsushima is, we now see, too much a present matter. The very tears at Tsubo no Ishibumi testify to the overwhelming value of the past. Haikai requires something of great value to alter into its lower sphere, somewhat as *Don Quijote* requires the romances and a putative Arab author for its comedy.

Such an interpretation of high comedy has a number of implications. Above all, it leads to conceiving a Bashō different from the sober, saintly figure who is most familiar and perhaps even precious to Japanese and other readers. The interpretation may lead some readers to posit as it were two Bashōs, one the author, Sora's Okina, and the other a character: Bashō as tabibito, traveler. Without deciding one way or another about that, one can surely assume that at some point the regression from fictional human agent to fictional human agent (or subjectivity) must cease and there be real human agency, an actual Bashō. Somebody must be, as it were, the Adam giving names.

Another nexus of matters involves haikai change. For that we can attend to the haikai poets themselves. In the words of Shikō (1665–1731), "haikai broadens art to that which is below the average, using a world lower in speech and conduct to guide the people of that lower road" (Kuriyama 1963, 163). And Bashō himself, after discussing the nature of three elements he identified in haikai—feeling, total effect, and language—concludes: "These three elements do not elevate a humble person to heights. They put an exalted person in a low place" (*Taisei,* 697; *Fūzoku Monzen*).

Bashō's three elements correspond to the three most important categories in Japanese poetic theory. For the traditional kokoro (heart, mind, spirit) he substitutes jō (i.e., nasake; feeling). His sugata (total effect) is an unchanged term. For kotoba (words, language, subjects) he substitutes gongo (language). And by far his most revealing remark in our present context is what he says of the last: "That language may be called aesthetic madness" (*Taisei,* 697). "Aesthetic madness" here renders "fūkyō." The first part, *fū,* recalls another compound, *fūryū,* which can be rendered most simply as "art" in Bashō's criticism. In this passage on the three elements of haikai, he says, "Its total effect may be termed aesthetic," that is, fūryū, the beauty or art of haikai. The second part of *fūkyō,* the *kyō,* is of crucial importance for consideration of Bashō's comedy. It basically means wildness or madness. In the compound kyōgen kigo, it was long familiar to Japanese from usage by Bo

Juyi, "wild words and fancy language" (Konishi 1991, 154), but of course that compound also designates the comic interludes of nō. "Aesthetic madness" is not the only possible rendering of "fūkyō," but it suggests both the deliberate art and the excess that the paradoxical term conveys.

Nakanishi Susumu, who has made the most thorough examination of the spirit of madness (kyō), concludes pointedly, "Truly Bashō was an aesthetically mad poet" (Nakanishi 1978, 167). He too treats "fūkyō" as an abbreviation of *fūryū no kyō*, what I have rendered "aesthetic madness." And he goes so far as to interpret Bashō to be suggesting, "I am a poet of mad stanzas" (159). A leading Bashō scholar, Ogata Tsutomu, has drawn similar conclusions. He remarks that these elements are not to be found in Sora's *Nikki,* and he posits an intimate relation between the poet's aesthetic madness and spiritual dedication to travel (dōnen).[46]

At Matsushima we discover the high comedy of aesthetic madness. It can be described in various terms, but here two versions will be offered, the first concerning its elements. Simply put, the bases of the comic are two contrary things. There is excess in description, and there is deficiency in poetic celebration. Excess and deficiency need not accompany each other, any more than the aesthetic and the mad. But these components resemble each other in that each presumes awareness of a standard by which both deviations are identifiable. We shall be seeing episodes farther on along the narrow road where one component is present without the other, as well as episodes in which the two again combine. And of course the proportions of the two components will vary, as they have varied during the stretch from Shirakawa-Sukagawa to Matsushima.

The comedy is, however, not merely one of elements but of human significance and artistic effect, features that may differ in principle but that for a careful artist like Bashō were united. At Matsushima the world, nature, exists in excess as a point of attention by the poet and reader alike. We do not need reminding that the point of attention

---

46. As recently as three years ago (See Miner, 1995, written in 1962), I could see no alternative to understanding the Matsushima episode as Bashō's expression of disappointment. But in the summer of 1994, in preparation for an October conference in Kyoto, I sent Konishi Jin'ichi an essay with the interpretation presented here, treating the episode as "high comedy" based on Bashō's concept of aesthetic madness, fūkyō. Professor Konishi arrived at the conference with a photocopy of Ogata 1994 (see pp. 174–78), showing that he had just come to a very like conclusion. Confirmation by Bashō scholars as eminent as Ogata and Konishi is very welcome.

which is the natural world is precisely that in the point of view of the poet and the reader. But if we did need reminding, the personification of the islands would jog us into understanding. In Bashō's account, nature is excessive to human view.

How can we know rightly the pines (matsu) and islands (shima) that constitute Matsushima? Bashō has an answer:

> Learn of the pine from the pine; learn of the bamboo from the bamboo . . . to learn is to enter into the thing, and the way to compose stanzas is through experiencing the fineness of its manifestations. For instance, even if you speak of the manifestations of something, if you do not derive its essential qualities from it naturally, it and yourself will be two separate things, and you will not attain the essential qualities. (*Taisei*, 632)

If we were to follow Bashō's advice and learn about the pines from the pines, and about the islands from those islands, our first lesson would be that pines are piney, islands insular, and human creatures human. The deficiency is human in lack of adequate poetic response to pines, islands, waves, and the summer moon in unity with them. The pines and islands as points of attention and the human response as point of view have become "two separate things." In the prose the separateness is marked by excess, and in the absence of poetry by deficiency.

The second lesson we learn from the pines and the rest is, then, that they are there and we are there, but in the separateness, their essential qualities have been lost. In itself, that situation is deplorable. But so carefully to devise that situation *and to make understanding of it the point* constitutes an aesthetic madness by which haikai change produces high comedy.

In short, Bashō understands perfectly well what he is doing.

To phrase things differently for the sake of clarity, we can and ought to begin with Bashō by understanding that his art is that of haikai. From the outset the haikai conception here involves an art by which the comic excess and the comic deficiency are apprehended in a tertium quid as aesthetic madness (fūkyō). Another way of putting the matter is to say that the Matsushima episode is after all a masterpiece of another kind, as it were. As nō has its kyōgen, so renga has its haikai renga version here. In standard renga composition (verse and prose), Bashō's Matsushima would be unceremoniously kicked out the back door. But this is haikai prose, a deliberate lowering. Let us recall Bashō on the three elements of haikai. Its feeling "plays with refined dishes but contents itself with humble fare." Its total effect is an elegance that "lives in figured silks and embroidered brocades but does not forget persons clad in woven straw." And more at length on the third, with a conclusion:

> Its language can be called aesthetic madness. Language resides in untruth and ought to comport with truth. It is difficult to reside in truth and sport with untruth. These three elements do not elevate a humble person to heights. They put an exalted person in a low place.

That seems almost to have been written for the Matsushima episode.

It has taken me a long time to get to the point, because in fact it has taken me years to get the point. The comedy of haikai change here is extremely complex. But it is comedy and indeed high comedy of a special haikai kind involving aesthetic madness, the high lowered, and much else in that vein showing—yes, showing what? Showing, then, that Bashō understood human excess and human deficiency, each of which might be imposed on the natural world by our too deliberate minds seeking to put it into solemn words. Bashō understood what it so complexly is to be human, and in other versions the comedy will be simpler. On occasion, it will disappear into the darkness of tragedy. For now, the difficulties he poses to our understanding yield finally to a deeper understanding than we thought or sought. Matsushima is after all the peak of the design "stanzas" among the episodes in *Oku no Hosomichi*.

Some eight decades or so before Boswell and Johnson faced their crisis on the road to Glenelg, Bashō discovered his difficulties in keeping under way. It is a problem that we readers share, and we participate in the high comedy of this stage of the *Narrow Road* only by recognizing the strange propriety of abundance of places of name with an absence of people and poetry. That yields the comedy of islands personified and the tears of a poet alone with people of the past. Once they fully understood how to convey the difficulties of getting under way, both pairs of travelers could glimpse at once the distance and the nature of their journeys' ends.

Chapter 4

The Journeys' Ends

[XI] 1st 2nd Arai 3rd Fukuroi 4th Fujieda 5th Nakatsu 6th Numazu 7th Odawara 8th Tozuka, arriving in Suzuki 4 P.M. Not one day of rain since Nagoya.

—Sora, traveling alone

The next morning we set out again on random travel over unknown roads.

—Bashō

I looked on this journey to the Hebrides as a co-partnery between Mr. Johnson and me.

—Boswell

All travel has its advantages. If the passenger visits better countries, he may learn to improve his own, and if fortune carries him to worse, he may learn to enjoy it.

—Johnson

Further Steps

As our pairs of travelers set out from Matsushima and from the region of Glenelg, they moved forward with very different motives. Sora's stenographic single-mindedness may have betokened a restricted imagination. But he had to set down for the rest of the Bashō school the facts of the journey. Others must have envied him for having been chosen Bashō's travel companion, and he had to justify being selected. Boswell's "co-partnery" with Johnson and his sense of the important, with his skill in conveying it, inhabit a realm above more people than Sora. But as the point of Sora's factual staccato and Boswell's stimulating of Johnson shows, these two were really less interested in where they went than in the fact that they went with Bashō (or Johnson).

Seeing Bashō up in the morning, moving with him during the day, and getting him to bed at night was Sora's duty and honor. Getting Johnson to play his roles as Johnson to entertain their hosts and to provide Boswell with glimpses of human possibility was Boswell's aim and pride. None of these things can be said without names.

We seldom think about names except when one eludes our recall. Yet names (onoma, nomina) may mean common as well as proper nouns. Even personal names come in numerous versions specific to a given person and culture. How many of us can name the parts of Africa—or Italy—these past three hundred years? Does anyone know all the appellations of "Matsuo Bashō"? Is it not winter in Sydney when it is summer in Sevastapol? What year is the present one by the Jewish or Japanese calendar? Does Constantinople exist? When is a nickname a real name? What differences exist between fictional and real names, between names in the news: of people and of corporations?

What does it mean that currency (and Christian sects) come in "denominations"? Or that a given unit of paper currency often depicts a figure with another name? (There are also Lutherans.) What, indeed, what *is* a name? The answers are various, complex, and by no means consistent. Some answers, the three in Plato's *Cratylus* for example, seem to assume that a name is any, or almost any, word. Some answers (Plato's own in that dialogue, for example) are so—so profound?—that it is sometimes difficult to agree with oneself as to what it all means.

When not baffled by nominal predicates, philosophers tend to accept them as names. By one of history's odd turns, English monarchs beginning with Henry VIII have been given the predicate, "Defender of the Faith," or "Defensor Fidei," or "DEF. FID." After pondering "Charlemagne" and "Karl der Grosse" (are they or are they not the same—and what do we mean by "the same"?), we return to the first English defender of the faith to ask whether "the Eighth" in "Henry VIII" is a predicate or part of a single nominal (and name). "The last of the Mohicans" is obviously a predicate, but if we agree that it designates somebody whose "baptismal" name we agree we cannot recall, is it then a name, or a pro-name, like a pronoun? How can there be (or how can there not be?) substantial differences merely by typographical conventions: *The Last of the Mohicans,* "The Last of the Mohicans," and the last of the Mohicans? What does it mean that the differences in those formulations cannot be shaped in Hebrew, Arabic, Chinese characters, Korean (hangul), or Japanese (katakana)?

Those English examples do not suggest a stark dualistic contrast between name and non-name but a sort of sliding nominal scale. They are only examples. But for logical reasons that independently govern the examples, many philosophers are led to decide that predicates are names without their nominal subject explicit. Once that (or the logic of the matter) is accepted and one goes on to issues like those posed by "le magne" and "der Grosse," a philosopher is heavily committed to consider all predicates, even those lacking their Charl/Karl, as names. That thinking leads some to accept as names all but "connectives" like prepositions, articles, and particles.

Why exclude even them? may be the question posed by the smiling libertine or the sarcastic linguistic puritan. Truly, does not another arguer for our verbal soul tell us that names and words cannot be coextensible terms, or we would not have two words (or is it terms?). After a certain amount of this, we may well be inclined to draw back from the giddy whirl, to give over questions, and to retreat to a firm, conservative proposition: nominal status is possessed solely by *singular proper nouns*. Or let us at least think of something else.

Lest after many a question die the thought, let us recall: our four travelers are now fully under way. Johnson and Boswell must have longed now and again for their own firesides; Sora must have looked forward to ending his responsibility for his Old Master and, if all went well, basking in the envy of those who had not walked the dusty or muddy leagues. Given to thinking and rethinking as he was, Bashō must have had assurance worth a smile at the thought of his disciples, who would welcome him to Ōgaki. He must have considered his travels thereafter to the Great Shrines of Ise, to his native province of Iga (now Mie Prefecture), and even beyond. As they thought from time to time of when their journeys would be done, they must also have asked themselves why they were traveling, what were their ends in strenuous motion. And they must have reflected at least as often on the gap in space and time between that *then* and *there* and their *now* and *here*.

After Glenelg, Johnson and Boswell readied their gear for boat travel from the west coast of Scotland to the isles of the Hebrides. Although this makes the compass directions or sequence strangely like those of Bashō and Sora eight decades earlier, to move any distance Johnson and Boswell had to turn to the uncertainties of navigation, often having to wait for better weather. On completing the Hebrides stage, the two friends would cross back to the main island and land travel, stopping off to see the Boswell family seat at Auchinleck, where Boswell's father, Alexander, was in residence. From there they continued back east, closing the circle of their travel at Edinburgh, where Johnson remained some days longer for Boswell to display proper attention to his friend as a token of gratitude to him—and as proof of his own importance.

Since the two stages were conceptions in the minds of the travelers, the reader of their accounts shares their distinctions. As we have seen in the preceding chapter, the first stages of travel draw us into sharing with the travelers their concern with the significance and the manner of telling of their journey as well as the details and sequence of it. With four such different tellers of the two journeys, we grow far more aware than we would in reading only one that the manner of telling is part of the significance of what is told: that the how is also part of the what and, as we shall be seeing, of the why.

It is difficult to give that how its proper name. One could borrow a term like *point of view* for a novel, perspective in painting, and the technical terms like *cuts* for film. For Bashō and Sora, the "what" of that "how" was the diary, or at any event, the nikki form.[1] Bashō's example with his diaries of the road (michi no nikki) reminds that what Japanese call diary literature (nikki bungaku) included poems from its first example, *The Tosa Diary* (ca. 935; Miner 1969, 20–30, 59–91). Bashō employs such a complex range of ways of presenting his account that, as we have found, we must read attentively to understand their usages. None of the others shared his problem, at least as intensely as he obviously conceived it, of entering into and becoming one with the pines and the islands, although he shared with them the problem of sustaining to journey's end the technique devised and the aims for which it was devised.

There were other complicating factors for him, not least Sora's departure after falling ill. (See fig. 15.) Bashō expresses no complaint; since he understands that loyal Sora had no choice, Bashō expresses only sympathy and regret. But if we can see the strangeness of the younger man falling out while the older—who associated travel with death among other things—is left to bear on his way, we may be sure

---

1. Some Western scholars argue that *diary* does not correspond sufficiently to *nikki* and have proposed *memoirs* and other terms as a substitute. *Diary* does not do *nikki* full justice, but the reverse is also true. Valor does not increase with exaggeration of difficulties: either one translates or one does not.

Fig. 15. Sora, fallen ill, taking leave of Bashō. (From Buson 1973.)

that Bashō did. And we can see that on his far more tiring journey, Bashō faced a physical trial that the cosseted and very much accompanied Johnson did not.[2]

Each Journey's Two Stages

When Bashō reached Matsushima after crossing Shirakawa Barrier, he had seen the two places that he specifies in his opening to be goals of his travel. That was the first sentence, the former main stage of his journey,

---

2. In *Oi no Kobumi*, Bashō had written of a strenuous day's journey on which "legs wholly weakened, body without strength . . . I was able to proceed no farther," adding a hokku: "Feeling exhausted / and at the time to rent lodging / wisteria in bloom" (*Taisei*, 303).

the getting fully under way as a traveler and as an artist of travel writing. A very long second stage follows. Similarly, Johnson and Boswell get under way in a first stage culminating in those dirty quarters in Glenelg. Thereafter, in their second stage, they are mostly in the Hebrides. By the time our four wayfarers had begun their second stage, each had developed the formal and other, more subtle, features of their travel accounts. Because maintaining an account may pall as day follows day, it would not be surprising if the second half treated the journey, on the whole, in less detail than the first. Let us see.

Sora's ease in plucking his single string was not shared by the others. If their ends as travelers were to see far places and to arrive safely at their destinations, their ends as writers lay in sustaining interest in what might easily turn into mere episodic repetition. These matters can be set forth in a simple set of terms that can lead to development and refinement in our understanding, as it did to begin with in the minds of those four developing their accounts.

The terms are simply those of the relative space devoted by each to the part of the journey past and the part that lay ahead. Art is not simply a matter of quantity, but there are things of import revealed by comparing the ratios of pages devoted to days before and after the dividing points, Matsushima and Glenelg. The order of inspection will be Sora, Boswell, Johnson, and Bashō.

Given his absence after falling ill, Sora's relative apportioning of pages to Matsushima and then beyond is not strictly comparable with Bashō's. As things stand, his proportion is about 40 percent from Edo to Matsushima (*Nikki*, 3–27) and the other 60 percent from Matsushima to Bashō's holding audience on IX.6 for the gathering of disciples in Ōgaki.[3]

Boswell's division is more certain: he devotes some 28 percent to the first part (to Glenelg) and 72 percent to what follows (*Tour*, 3–122 and 122–394). Johnson's proportions of the two legs were about one-quarter to three-quarters. That close resemblance to Boswell's supposes that we can include in Johnson's main narrative his lengthy essay on life in Scottish and other societies. The essay "Ostig in Sky" is by far the longest entry in Johnson's *Journey* (pp. 63–99 in the 137 of the whole).

---

3. The dates of Sora's illness and departure are not certain. As I read it, his *Nikki* first mentions illness on VIII.17, next on the twenty-second; when he does again the next day, he writes of return to Edo.

Bashō devotes only slightly more space to the second leg than to the first (seventeen columns vs. sixteen in the close print of *Taisei*, 307–18). That greatly emphasizes the first—and does not even take into account the far, far greater distance covered in the second. His Sakata episode provides a conspicuous example of the second part's disproportionately rapid coverage of *distance*, relative to words or pages. Bashō looks ahead somewhat wearily to the distance from Sakata to Kanazawa (where he will turn from west southwest to more directly south). It is, he says some 130 ri, or about 280 miles (ca. 450 km). Yet his account of that stretch of his narrow road requires less than two columns (*Taisei*, 316): it is only about a quarter longer than the Matsushima episode.

Geographical distances cannot found our comparisons, because they are not proportionate to the length or pace of narrative. We must consider, therefore, the proportions of days in travel with pages of the accounts. Omitting Sora, we arrive at the following proportions of *days* to *pages* in the remaining three narratives.

	Boswell	Johnson	Bashō
1st leg	18%	37%	48%
2nd leg	82%	63%	52%

Johnson and Bashō differ in proportions but are rather similar when Boswell's proportions are taken into account. Since Bashō's envisioned destinations, the Shirakawa Barrier and Matsushima, have been reached, it is not surprising that he should curtail the rest of his account. Boswell's is the distinctive narrative. It is clear that he warmed to his project, devoting (on the average) considerably more pages to a day in his second stage than in his first.

We must not lose sight of the fact that all four travelers kept on writing as they kept on going. In none do we feel that the narrative becomes perfunctory. One is struck by Sora's need for showing in a diary that a day had passed. It is not so much an art as a compulsion. We have evidence direct and indirect to show that when illness took him away from Bashō, he continued his diary and that when he rejoined Bashō, he rejoiced and kept record. Day, day, day and diary, diary, diary—he kept at it after leaving Bashō, recording place-names and only a bit more onto Nagoya and thence back to Edo, as the sample (*Nikki*, 71) chosen for an epigraph to this chapter shows.

Where poor Sora seems to have had an addiction, Boswell and Bashō had strong motives. For the son of Auchinleck, "Johnson in Scotland" was the best possible show for the peoples patronized by St. Andrew and St. George, provided that "Arranged by Mr. James Boswell" was wholly legible on the notices. In fact, one cannot but feel that had Johnson expressed an earnest desire to cross to Ireland, or Greenland, the impresario would have set to work at once to make necessary arrangements—for the English sage, for himself, and for his servant Joseph Ritter, who had done so well across Scotland. The exhibition of Johnson out of London was an experiment unlikely to be matched by any other diarist.

The foot-weary Bashō met a warm welcome in Ōgaki. Some rest would bring back restlessness, but the same reason that made it necessary to continue his "diary of the road" to its envisioned end in Ōgaki made it unnecessary to continue his account. The thirty-six-stanza (kasen) sequence begun with his first step out of Edo had its closing stanza (ageku) there in Mino province. Another poetically defined journey might be begun at any time. And in fact Bashō wrote more than one travel account before he returned to Edo to claim a house without dolls. But *the travel conceived as a haikai sequence of 1689* ended in Ōgaki.

The four markedly different accounts of the same or comparable sojourns testify to distinct personalities seeking differing ends. After considering their aesthetic purposes, we can attempt to deal with what will be termed ideology. Only with these further steps can we consider that we too have marked the ends of their journeys.

Four Arguments from Design

Let us begin with a design of our own: with Sora, who fashioned an account based on daily entries; then follow with Johnson, whose principle of titles for his brief chapters is place names; then Boswell, who transcended daily entries; and finally Bashō, who may literally and figuratively be said to have used a poetic conception and pattern. The chief comparative question, or category, in each case is the author's design: of self, of form, and of audience.

Some Good Words for Sora

We begin with that seemingly perpetual beginner, distance marker, and ender, Sora. And let me seek to be kinder and certainly more understanding than hitherto. Sora could not have known as he trudged on land or was steered by water with Bashō in Genroku 2 that about a century earlier Edmund Spenser had had one E. K. to comment on his *Shepheardes Calendar*, or that in somewhat over a century after him Goethe would have his Eckermann to preserve notable details about the Dichter, scientist, and public functionary of Weimar. We do know these things and knowing them, can assess the better Sora's conception of what his role was. The role is designated by the title of his diary: *Sora's Diary of Accompanying [Bashō] on [His Journey of] the Narrow Road through the Provinces (Sora Oku no Hosomichi Zuikō Nikki) (Nikki, 3–71)*.[4] In spite of the title, Sora does not close his diary as Bashō does on 1689.IX.6. His entry for the sixth shows that he also was on Bashō's boat as it went southwest along the coast and on to Ise. He records visiting the Great Shrines of Ise a week later. After further explorations, on X.6 he returned by boat to Nagashima near Ōgaki, where he had embarked with Bashō just a month earlier. The account closes with the entry for XI.13: "Returned to the Fukugawa hermitage" in Edo.

In continuing his diary for two months and a week after Bashō ends *The Narrow Road*, Sora makes a point we should hardly have taken otherwise. His *Diary of Accompanying* Bashō is indeed *his* diary, and all the names he gives are from his own experience. Bashō would visit here and there for another two years, and Sora would see him from time to time. Meanwhile, *his* journey of *The Narrow Road* would end with his completing a circle by returning to Edo. In that he resembles our travelers in Scotland rather than Bashō.

At some date, or dates, after 1689.XI.13, Sora sat down with his papers and fashioned a rich variety of other materials that considerably augment and illuminate features of what he records so telegraphically in his *Nikki*. Since a couple of these must be taken into account subsequently, the entire group of them (i.e., added to his diary) may be enumerated here with an initial brief characterization to assist recollection later in this chapter. (The ellipses in the translations of Sora's titles are of "*The Narrow Road through the Provinces*.")

1. Texts, specified by place and sometimes date of composition, of haikai composed on *The Narrow Road* journey, normally using as first stanza a hokku by Bashō quoted in his account, and some-

---

4. See figure 3 for the cover of Sora's diary, which includes the title just given.

times supplying information enabling dating of a given episode. *"Oku no Hosomichi* Haikai Kakitome" ("Haikai Register of . . .") (Sora 1943, 75–122)

2. Descriptions of various places of note—not necessarily of approved places of name (nadokoro) in the old senses of waka and renga poetry—often with details about routes of visit, what is to be found, and so forth. *"Oku no Hosomichi* Meishō Bibōroku" ("Reminder Notes of Famous Places in . . .") (Sora 1943, 125–44)

3. Compilation by shrines and their areas or locations of various divinities bearing relation to the journey. *"Engi Shiki* Jimmyō Chōshōroku" ("A Compilation of Names of Divinities According to the *Engi Shiki"*) (Sora 1943, 147–69)[5]

4. A diary running from III.4 to VIII.25 of accompanying Bashō in 1692 on another journey in the provinces thought central or near in relation to the old capital in Kyoto (cf. English "home counties") with many entries more detailed than those for *The Narrow Road*. "Sora Genroku Yonen Kinki Jun'yū Nikki" ("Sora's 1692 Diary of a Tour of Provinces in the Capital Area") (Sora 1943, 173–221)

5. A text of *The Narrow Road* that differs slightly from the received version. The major differences are given, in effect, as textual notes in *Zenkō*. *"Oku no Hosomichi* Zuikō Nikki Idō Hikakkō" ("The Companion's Variant Text of . . . Offered for Comparison") (Sora 1943, 225–63)

6. A compilation or index made by Sora from his original diary. ". . . Tenkō to Ryoshuku Ichiranhyō" ("A Simplified Chart of Weather and Lodging in . . ." (Sora 1943, 267–83)

These many supplements and redactions lead us to revise our sense of Sora's holding a passive, wholly unimaginative role. In a literal sense, he surely did plod, and one cannot entirely erase the figurative sense derived from acquaintance with the *Nikki* alone. The major

---

5. The *Engi Shiki* was ordered in 905 but not completed until 967. In fifty volumes, it fully reordered matters relating to the royal court. It was one of several major projects by Daigo (r. 897–930) to assert the authority of the throne. He was the last Japanese monarch truly to rule rather than mostly reign; for generations he was regarded as one of two or three men who best governed the nation. We shall see later the ideological importance to Bashō of such alternatives to the Edo military regime.

change in our conception and assessment will add no great spice of excitement to reading his *Nikki*. But I, at least, am affected in two ways. The first is gaining the sense that Sora knew what his purposes were. The supplementary titles just itemized show him making a claim to be an authority on Bashō's journey. His claim can be reduced to a fundamental axiom: *he knew the names.*

No small thing in itself, the claim displays a further end Sora held in view. That relates to his audience. It is not easy to conceive of candidates for that status other than those who wished to know everything possible about Bashō. In other words, Sora's audience, beyond Bashō and himself, was that of Bashō's followers, the members of his school. That is, he recorded all those things for those who sought to practice and be recognized as practitioners of the Bashō style—or the Shōfū "to give it proper name." It is difficult to imagine members of the rival Teimon or Danrin haikai schools finding any interest whatsoever in the results of Sora's diligence.

His own school is another matter. And given the Japanese tradition of arcanum represented by documents revealed to few and taught orally for a fee, Sora was essential to more important poets following Bashō as master. In what he sought, he was successful. And that was making certain that his privileged role in accompanying Bashō was incontestable by contemporaries and would be noted—as generations of Bashō's editors have testified (and as somebody I know is doing this very moment). Grant the element of vanity, of what a hostile observer might think puerility, in Sora's display of Bashō's soiled coat as a treasure for the ages. It was that kind of thing that made him something of a joke to the high-spirited Takarai Kikaku (1661–1707) and the witty Nozawa Bonchō (d. 1714).[6] Yes, a modest vanity, or vain modesty, must be granted. But I am also of the opinion that his sins are not the great offenders of humankind and even that some of us who accuse him of plodding might not outrun Achilles, either.

Johnson's Good Attentions

The mind of Samuel Johnson, LL.D. (as Boswell made sure it stood on his own title page) was certainly of another order. But what ends did he

---

6. They compiled and edited the most important collection of haikai of the Bashō school, *Sarumino Shū* (*The Monkey's Straw Raincoat Collection*), 1691, including hokku by Bashō and Sora from their journey. See n. 42.

have in view: why did he undergo the hardships of travel at an advanced age (he was born in 1709) for the eighteenth century, his midsixties? For all the exceptions he made—and we must always remember that he chose to "talk for victory" regardless of consistency—he was known to enjoy belittling Caledonia (he defined oats as fodder for horses in England, food for people in Scotland; he said that a Scot's best prospect was the road to England; etc.). Yet Boswell reports that Johnson told him a decade before their journey that he had been pleased by the copy of Martin Martin's book on Scotland (1703) that his father had given him while he was yet very young (*Tour*, 3). In his opening paragraph Johnson says that he had long wished to visit Scotland and was induced to make it by the prospect of traveling with one as lively as Boswell (ibid.). We may recall that he concludes his account with a survey including Scotland and himself.

> Such are the things which this journey has given me an opportunity of seeing, and such are the reflections which that sight has raised. Having passed my time almost wholly in cities, I may have been surprised by modes of life and appearances of nature that are familiar to men of wider survey and more varied conversation. (*Journey*, 137)

The generality of the opening and the humility topos of the close of this quotation do not convey, at least to me, either irrepressible or repressed feelings.

Perhaps one who has well studied him, his *Journey*, and his age can lend us assistance. The editor of the Oxford edition of Johnson's *Journey*, J. D. Fleeman, begins his account of Johnson's motivations with a comparison:

> Boswell's sense of the tour is chiefly theatrical: Johnson's is deeply personal. . . . Of course, he has a role in his own narrative as the philosophical observer of men and manners, and that role matches neatly with the writing of a formal travel book. Over a dozen years before he undertook his journey he had observed: "He that would travel for the entertainment of others, should remember that the great object of remark is human life." . . .

This submerged self-consciousness infuses the narrative with a strongly personal tone which is tinged with regret at the inevitable passing of an ancient and established system of life. (v)

And again: "Johnson's book is shot through with an undefined sense of the inevitable demise of the old Highland life" (xxxvii). Another authority, James Boswell, reports Johnson saying of his tour ten years later, "I got an acquisition of more ideas by it than by any thing that I remember" (Lascelles 1971, xvi). As usual, matters in our own lives draw many of the dimensions perceived in the lives of others.

It is widely agreed that Scottish emigration was one of Johnson's major concerns in assessing his experience. In a time of relatively easy travel like our own, we underestimate the distress caused by the thought of people taking the extreme measure of leaving their country and, more generally or theoretically, the gravity attributed to loss of population. Johnson's first charged remark on the topic appears to be made at Dunvegan. (For Dunvegan, see fig. 16.) In its harbor, "a ship lay waiting to dispeople *Sky*, by carrying the natives away to *America*" (54). "Lay waiting," "dispeople," "carrying . . . away," and no doubt "*America*" (a name opposed to "Sky") are freighted words. He earlier (51) and later (82) declares that some Scottish places, especially those governed in enlightened fashion, have suffered little loss. People in less well governed territories may either emigrate or undertake "a total secession" (82). That, and the larger passage (95–99) it concludes, are from Johnson's long essay inserted into "Ostig in Sky." Since Johnson's book of "Remarks" taken with him to Scotland has been lost, there can be no proof of my suspicion that the lengthy reflections offer a version of what he took with him. But it does seem to be true that emigration, whatever its evils, troubled him less than its causes: unjust, poor government and suffering from conditions political and economic. "Ill fares the land," as he and Goldsmith agreed in *The Deserted Village*, that suffers the misfortune of misgovernance (Miner 1959, 134–38). There lies Johnson's deepest concern.

The expression of that concern is, however, not connected with Ostig in "Ostig in Sky." Nor is it connected with Dunvegan on its first appearance in "Dunvegan" (54, quoted above). The abstracted nature of the problem may be a way of diverting Scottish anger. If so, Johnson had some success. But other, not necessarily conflicting explanations, may be equally possible.

Fig. 16. Dunvegan Castle on Skye. (From Grose 1797.)

Those can be approached by observing that the problems of (mis)governance, suffering, and depopulation are most strongly communicated by their temporality. That is, they are serious problems because they are present ones. They may have causes in the *past*, and they may lead to greater *future* difficulties. But their existence is *present*. The reason for emphasis is to observe that the single important existence of the problem is temporal. Of course it is in the nature of problems to trouble somebody presently. But elsewhere in Johnson's account it is rare that temporality matters.

Yet even here the places in Scotland matter more, and the people matter most—and not least, perhaps, because they can and often must be named. There are words for time and the times, too. Who does not know the Latin phrases, "Tempus fugit" and "Tempora mutantur"? But to say time flies is to personify for a greater effect. And the other phrase is but half the proverb: "Times change, *and we with them.*" In more than one sense, Johnson's sparing use of temporal names is understandable because he names each unit of his account with a place-name, and peoples his narrative with the names of people present and past.

That is the feature easy to describe. The causes of emigration and depopulation, like those effects themselves, produce the *present* dilemma of governance, a social crisis involving nobody named and occurring in no named place that is persistent in the narrative. None is named. Johnson saw a great deal of poverty. (His description of "huts" and the weaver's small cottage shown in fig. 8 are eloquent.) But the most fundamental, acute problem is curiously all but entirely abstracted from identifiable people in identified place. The abstraction implies generalized humanity in generalized Scotland now.

There is also a paradox about Johnson's dominant narrative. He presents a world not his. He is no Scot. The Scots themselves are absorbed into locations. Observation with extensive view surveys mankind in a succession of places from St. Andrews to last named Inch Kenneth (Iona). It is in place that the Scots are fixed and named. It is in successive places that Johnson comes upon them. It is in places named that Johnson subsumes his entire narrative, and one brief chapter–place name is the place where other places (and people) are included by being named. Is it not strange?

The decision that something is strange obviously assumes that something else, some alternative within the same kind, is normal. The search for the normal is complicated by the fact that what is strange

involves not only its identity in itself but in Johnson's manner of relation. Johnson and his contemporaries obviously assumed, as we assume, that he is describing Scotland. The obvious alternative to Scotland is England as Johnson understood it. What is obvious is, however,
not necessarily simple or consistent. In practice, his canons of judgment
vary somewhat with the locale and its inhabitants, and his application
of them is sometimes simpler at one time than another. These matters
can be shown by four passages typical of either the stage at which they
appear or even of what we discern of the whole.[7]

The first relates to the initial stage of travel north from Edinburgh.
They have just returned to their main road from the island of Inch Keith.

> When we landed, we found our chaise ready, and passed
> through *Kinghorn, Kirkaldy,* and *Cowpar,* places not unlike the small
> or straggling market-towns in those parts of England where com-
> merce and manufactures have not yet produced opulence. (2)

The double negative, "not unlike," confirms our assumption that
Johnson holds England as the norm, and that Scotland is judged inferior
by not meeting it. It is extremely difficult to judge for others how far that
comparison is assumed even when Johnson does not suggest it. It must
mean something that this explicit version (he names three towns) appears early and then fades out. It seems more important, however, that
subsequent passages suggest that some different calculus is involved.

The second example offers an alternative that appears frequently
in a variety of versions.

Ulinish

> Mr. *Macqueen* travelled with us, and directed our attention to all
> that was worthy of observation. With him we went to see an an-
> cient building, called a dun or borough. It was a circular inclosure,
> about forty-two feet in diameter, walled round with loose stones,
> perhaps to the height of nine feet. The walls are very thick.[8]

---

7. Since the text used for Johnson's *Journey* (Fleeman's excellent Oxford edition)
runs from pp. 1 to 137, citations here will suggest the relative location of a passage in
another edition.

8. *Journey,* 58. "Borough" is the English and "dun" the Gaelic for a fort, beacon,
watchtower or, perhaps, as Johnson thought, a refuge. The function is still debated
(*Journey,* 194).

By definition, there must also be some things, few or many, not "worthy of observation." And if this were not "ancient," it would hardly be worthy of traveling from afar to behold. Two other matters should not escape our "observation." One is crucial to Johnson's style, the subject of the controlling syntax, which here is "Mr. Macqueen." It is far less important that England exists at the moment than that a Scot of the area be the authority. The second matter is that of which Macqueen is the authority over: obviously "Ulinish," and first in order of the related sequence is this stony "ancient building." We shall badly deceive ourselves if we fail to understand Johnson's assumption about his subject: Scotland in all the reality of its presently adamantine existence. After all, the final decisive word of Johnson's title, the very end of his "Journey," is Scotland as knowable particularly from its "Western Islands." For "Islands" is here a place-name as well as word.

Visiting the castle area of Coll, Johnson offers a report giving us a third kind.

> The harvest in *Col*, and in *Lewis*, is ripe sooner than in *Sky*; and the winter in *Col* is never cold, but very tempestuous. I know not that I ever heard the wind so loud in any other place; and Mr. *Boswell* observed, that its noise was all its own, for there were no trees to increase it. (103)

From the first stages of his journey Johnson was struck by the deforested or, as he might have put it, nonarboreal Scottish landscape. Here it almost seems that Boswell is necessary for him to recall what he had made so much of in the first third or so of the *Journey*.

The distinctive feature in the paragraph is something else, however. Johnson has encountered something utterly quotidian, the common wind, yet in a version quite out of his previous experience.[9] Moreover, this extraordinary event is presented in the context of a comparison wholly Scottish, and in fact more closely limited to the Hebridean: the climate of the island of Coll (and of Lewis) in relation to that of the largest island, Skye. Johnson (and therefore we) have actually reached the point of no longer comparing Scotland with England

---

9. Had he wished, Johnson could have developed the importance of the temporal from thoughts of earliness of harvest. But he did not wish, and place is so much more important a basis of reality that the temporal is merely one of the attributes, one even less striking than the wind: perhaps because it has no name?

but one remote Scottish island with two other remote Scottish islands. Johnson and we with him have come a long way when not only is "here" Scotland but so also is "there."

Our fourth example comes from the travelers' return to Mull, the second largest of the three main Hebridean islands and the last visited. (Here we take up in their due contexts two passages considered earlier in shorter versions.) Johnson finds he must understand something special about local naming customs. On the evening of arrival, he and his party "were entertained for the night by Mr. *Maclean*, a Minister." On the following day, they "dined with Dr. *Maclean* . . . and then travelled on to the house of a very powerful laird, *Maclean* of *Lochbuy*, for in this country every man's name is *Maclean*."[10] Two arresting paragraphs follow.

> Where races are thus numerous, and thus combined, none but the chief of a clan is addressed by his name. The Laird of *Dunvegan* is called *Macleod*, but other gentlemen of the same family are denominated by the places where they reside, as *Raasay*, or *Talisker*. The distinction of the meaner people is made by their Christian names. . . .
>
> Our afternoon journey was through a country of such gloomy desolation, that Mr. *Boswell* thought no [other] part of the Highlands equally terrifick [terrifying], yet we came without any difficulty, at evening, to *Lochbuy*, where we found a true Highland Laird, rough and haughty, and tenacious of his dignity; who, hearing my name, inquired whether I was of the *Johnstons* of *Glencoe*, or of *Ardnamurchan*. (127–28)

Here, too, Johnson gives an overpowering sense of Scottish atmosphere in the places where he finds himself.[11] This passage also shares with the others an unstressed but nonetheless dominant present, issues of "is"

---

10. Boswell wrote Johnson, Lascelles notes (1971, 153), to point out that the first person mentioned, the minister, was Neil Macleod. Johnson is not the first, or last, traveler to be so struck by something unusual as to exaggerate its extent carelessly. Or, as it has been said by somebody recognizable by his style, "To this dilatory notation must be imputed the false relations of travellers, where there is no imaginable motive to deceive" (*Journey*, 122).

11. Sometimes reading Boswell's and Johnson's versions of the same event gives a special pleasure beyond even the considerable powers of each singly. This episode provides one example: cf. Boswell on 21 October (*Tour*, 342–44). A return from that passage to the one just quoted will also heighten one's appreciation of Johnson's comedy.

and "are." What is this place? What are the people? It is as if Johnson is all attention to that existing, named reality which is Scotland. Scots could only have been flattered by this accurate attention—or would have been, that is, if England were not so strongly if implicitly the norm and Scotland the variation, somehow inadequate because not England. This is surely the reason why Johnson's account aroused a storm of Scottish criticism.[12]

The last example proves particularly telling: *the Scots name themselves differently,* and by implication abnormally. There is even that comic moment when the crusty laird, "tenacious of his dignity," asks the English visitor which of two local Scottish families he belongs to.[13] Or, more precisely, Johnson writes of "a true Highland Laird . . . who, hearing my name, inquired whether I was of the *Johnstons* of *Glencoe,* or of *Ardnamurchan.*" This is as close as Johnson gets to allowing those present people he names in the places he names the gift of human speech. It is impossible to identify Johnson's motives. Yet it is easy enough to understand why Scottish sensibilities should be wounded. Johnson "speaks" throughout of Scots who clearly exist in places that clearly exist. But as Boswell might have put it, in Johnson's *Journey,* the Scots speak none. For that matter, nobody does, except the author of the narration. Johnson's attentiveness and his exertion of the power of naming allow him to speak decisively. How can those who object to being depicted as inferior to the English find a means of rebuttal when their names are the sole words they are allowed? It helps but little to protest with Boswell that there are some fine old trees in some parts of Scotland. And it is not easy to dismiss the whole account of the greatest authority on the language. Two centuries and an ocean apart, it is still easier (although not very easy) to describe Johnson's account than to find words for a people denied them but identified by them in terms of names of people and places.

Boswell himself must have been disappointed that Johnson did not choose to give any extended treatment, as a major point of attention, to

---

12. As Fleeman discreetly puts it, "Not all Scottish opinion was adverse" (*Journey,* xxxi).

13. The comedy is heightened in *Boswell's* next paragraph. In what turns out to be a description of Lochbuie's legal dodge to back out of a lease, Boswell begins with the wonderfully droll clause, "Lochbuie tried not long ago to prove himself a fool." His failure with this device in Scottish law is altogether successful in Boswell's court (*Tour,* 343). His legal training had such unexpected benefits.

Edinburgh. They certainly were great days for him to show off his famous friend from London. Johnson chose instead to attend to "the western islands," to what he mentions in his final paragraph as unfamiliar "modes of life and appearances of nature." But in the opening of the final clause of his *Journey* he stresses that it is *his* art of attending that matters: "I," he says, "cannot but be conscious that my thoughts on national manners . . ." (137). That end of the design begins with the same agent that had begun the design, and with the same particular object of his attention. I am not suggesting anything unnatural but rather something we should not miss. The same word begins the last clause as had begun the first paragraph of his *Journey:* "I," he says again, "had desired to visit the *Hebrides,* or Western Islands of Scotland, so long . . ." (1; emphasis added) Read aright, in that beginning Johnson simply and clearly designs his end.

Boswell's Designs

Johnson's self-construction in his *Journey* is consistent with the personality and the understanding expressed in his most famous couplet: "Let Observation, with extensive view / Survey mankind from China to Peru." *Pace* Wordsworth, there is ample point. He observes the distant. He contemplates that which does not really impinge on him. That is at least the impression he gives to any but the closest inspection. One telling point of the "Observation" by that observer is that the entry of Boswell as narrator creates a different Johnson. In Coll on 11 October, Boswell discovers a thin skin. Talk of "one of the hardest-favoured women that I ever saw, swarthy and marked with the smallpox, and of very ungainly manners" leads to the consideration of her never having been "upon the mainland" and to Johnson's unkind suggestion that she should visit lowly Glenelg. Boswell tells of his response.

> "Why," said I, "you have never seen, till now, anything but your native island." [We are meant to recall Boswell's extensive travels on the continent.] "But," said he, "by seeing London I have seen as much of life as the world can show." "You have not seen Pekin," said I. "Sir," said he in a sort of anger, "what is Pekin?" (*Tour,* 291)

Here names decline to pronouns, with the exception of two places not in Scotland. In this we observe the fact and spirit of human speech. When people so seriously cross words, the security of the extensive view vanishes.

There is no need to suggest any falsehood in Johnson or Boswell, but it is evident that their senses of human design serve differing ends. So much should be clear from the contexts of the last quotations from Johnson (the opening and close of his *Journey*) and of this from Boswell. Nor is there a need to be solemn or ignore the humblest human needs. Boswell's recounting continues with talk of the importance of providing toilets in houses: Johnson says that that is where one thinks, Boswell that there one is always happy, which Johnson doubts—and so on in one of the many passages omitted from the published version.

Three days later, in Erray, the two friends again talk of their Hebridean travel. Johnson observes, with a certain satisfaction, "sir, we have seen enough to give us a pretty good notion of the system of insular life." "And so," as Samuel Pepys had so often said, "to bed." Boswell is shocked by the filthy sheets. He throws off (his expression) his boots, uses his "greatcoat as a night-gown" and lies down, only to discover that "The mixture of brandy punch at the inn and rum punch here, joined with the comfortless bed, made me rest very poorly." When his servant, Joseph Ritter, wakes him up, he discovers "I was not well at all." Like Bashō, Boswell depicts himself wilting under poor reception. Unlike Bashō, he has a remedy to hand: "but I got up, sat down to my Journal, and soon was better."

A heavy rain keeps them with the Macleans. Johnson improves his spirits by writing "to the mainland," no doubt to Mrs. Thrale. Boswell shifts attention back to himself and thence to others: "I wrote to my dear wife. . . . I also wrote to my father" (14 October, *Tour*, 303). Those were in fact his two most troubled relationships, as his ensuing reflections show. By contrast, there is a definite sense of self-mastery and ease two paragraphs later: "I wrote journal a good part of the forenoon" (*Tour*, 304).

Boswell revives his spirits by writing journal, as he puts it. It seems that he recovers yet more by writing about writing his journal. He takes obvious delight in being able to state, in his 19 September Dunvegan entry, that after himself Johnson was his first reader.

> He came to my room this morning before breakfast to read my Journal, which he has done all along. He often before said, "I take great delight in reading it." Today he said, "You improve. It grows

better and better." I said there was a danger of my getting a habit of writing in a slovenly manner. "Sir," said he, "it is not written in a slovenly manner. It might be printed, were the subject fit for printing." (188)[14]

The travelers understand each other. At least Boswell clearly understands that Johnson, who concedes without saying so that he is the point of attention—the end—of so much of the diary, cannot politely urge the printing of what is, on balance, so flattering a portrait of himself. The subjunctives of the final sentence amount to a humility topos.[15]

These several quotations are hardly highlights of Boswell's account, and yet it is in their very plainness that they are revealing, particularly of Boswell's purposes, of his methods, and (if we can work them out) of his ends. One by no means trivial significance of these plain episodes can be understood by a glance back at their quotation marks. In the last, Boswell skillfully uses direct quotation for Johnson and indirect for himself. And at this juncture it is no mere repetition to insist on a point made before. Surely there is not one reader of Boswell's *Tour* who could be expected to guess that, in the whole of his *Journey* Johnson, who was also very much there, uses not one word of dialogue.

Boswell certainly has unusual gifts for conveying the air of talk, even of the sounds of different voices. So one feels, but on revisiting a passage it is often very difficult to tell what it is in the reported talk that has given one the impression or conviction of actual conversation. It usually turns out that Johnson dominates a group by his talk, and that Boswell is the stimulant. It will appear shortly that Boswell thought so himself, or says so in passages having to do with his method.

He and Sora follow the pattern of the diary as diurnal. Sora does so because no alternative entered his mind. Boswell does so in order best to meet his personal needs. To him, the daily-entry device provides the ability to re-create the steady flow of time by marking intervals in it, rather than the reverse. Otherwise, a given series of incidents continues as if the entry for a new day were merely the reminder of what's o'clock

---

14. "It grows better and better." As observed earlier in this chapter, only Boswell's account swells in this long second part. Length and quality correspond with Boswell, a far from universal talent.

15. I take that to be one of the implications of the note Boswell added to this passage when his *Journal of a Tour* was printed: "As I have faithfully recorded so many minute particulars, I hope I shall be pardoned for inserting so flattering an encomium on what is now offered to the public" (*Tour*, 188).

on a day or that it is late summer: germane but not crucial. As with Johnson, place seems more important, and yet that is not crucial either, although it is more than germane in being necessary. In the end, there is no escaping the fact that Boswell could flourish in a world without days, and even in a world of either monotonous or bizarre places. What he cannot do without is people, and two of those in particular, Johnson and the other great name, "I."

Boswell's awareness of this emerges from his remarks on his method. A few of them can be offered with minimal initial comment. For the date 9 September at Raasay he writes:

> When we returned [from visiting an island], Mr. Johnson came out with us to see the old chapel. But before quitting the island in my Journal (as I am now far behind with it, for I am writing on the 15 September), I shall put down all my observations upon it at once. Mr. Johnson was in fine spirits. He said, "This is truly the patriarchal [as in Genesis] life. This is what we came to find." (*Tour*, 135)

For the same place the next day, he exhorts, or apostrophizes:

> Let me gather here some gold dust, some gleanings of Mr. Johnson's conversation without regard to order of time. (140)

Still at Raasay, he writes of 11 September about Dr. Johnson's admiration of the debt-inheriting Norman MacLeod of Raasay, who works so hard to free his estate. We pick up with Johnson's final remark on the laird:

> "I've seen nobody that I wish more to do a kindness to than MacLeod." I do not observe exact chronology in Mr. Johnson's sayings. There is no occasion. (151)

Two days later, now at Greshornish, Boswell tells that he "took the liberty to observe to Mr. Johnson" that he ate his fish with his fingers.

> "Yes," said he, "but it is because I am short-sighted, and afraid of bones, for which reason I'm not fond of eating many kinds of fish, because I must take [?it with] my fingers." Perhaps I put down too many things in this Journal. I have no fanners in my head, at least

no good ones, to separate wheat from chaff. Yet for what I put
down, what is written falls greatly short of the quantity of thought.
A page of my Journal is like a cake of portable soup. A little may be
diffused into a considerable portion. (165)

From the first example we observe that to be putting his journal
into what may be termed a readable draft, Boswell felt six days to be
"far behind," as if things important might escape him or qualitative
features be lost. From the second and third, moreover, we infer that
Boswell either had a surplus of materials that he would set aside or
perhaps a category of "Johnson's sayings." These might be drawn on as
needed from those supplies of gold dust or from the gleanings once the
harvest had gone in with the main business of the entries. He makes no
complaint of lack of materials. Rather there are "too many things"
insufficiently sorted, as he says, "in my head."

Of course we cannot winnow the minds of other people less mercurial than Boswell. But the passages just quoted amount to something
like a discourse on method, and other evidence is not lacking. The
editors of Boswell's *Tour,* Frederick A. Pottle and Charles H. Bennett,
have established that Boswell set down what we have in four sets of
physically separate papers. Boswell went on the journey with two note-
books, borrowed a third from Johnson, and bought loose sheets when
the earlier bound ones were filled. He also carried a packet of letters.[16]
Not only from these remarks but from the entire journal, I believe we
can reconstruct Boswell's usual if not invariable method. The early
version, or *Tour,* that resulted from his perfected method of setting
down events and conversation seemingly as they occurred is the version that is for most of us the most vigorous, open, and revealing. There
are conversational moments improved on in the version prepared for
publication after Johnson's death by him and, increasingly as revision
went on, by Edmond Malone. That later version suited a politer taste,
and perhaps was based on necessary refinements for the public. But, as
will be apparent, I believe that Boswell's ends, and our own, are better

---

16. For details, see, in the introduction the section labeled "Documentation": *Tour,*
xii–xxvii, especially xii–xiii. And although the journals discussed in Pottle 1966 predate
that of the Scottish journey, pp. 86–94 offer a most helpful account by one who knows
Boswell's methods thoroughly: "The distinguishing structural features of Boswell's journal can be summed up in the one word *dramatic*" (90); and his characterizing of "the
highest mode" of Boswell's art as that "in which the conversation of two or more speakers
is cast and given stage-directions" (91).

met by a method culminating in the *Tour* version than the later-revised, tamed version published in 1785.

Each of the four passages quoted before my excursus on Boswell's method is embedded. That is, none is an independent unit, a separate paragraph. They are *part of a continuum*. More precisely, each of them is part of an episode, a larger context, featuring Johnson, who may appear before, after, or in the middle again. The return to what had preceded the digression on method reaches an extraordinary point in the fourth passage, which had begun (before the quotation) with Johnson's querying Scots "about the use of the dirk." No, it was not to eat with, since the Highlanders had cutlery—although some did eat with their fingers. That leads Boswell to his question about Johnson's eating habits, to his comment on his journal, and then with a far-fetched metaphor ("my journal is like a cake of portable soup") back to food.

The passages also share something that seems to me yet more important. It is not enough to say that they are concerned with readers. Each is essentially an address to readers. Boswell on method—Boswell (we might almost say) on himself—is not something furtive. It is not even enough to say that he wishes to gain his reader's consent. Not even enough to say that he needs it. The desire and the need are features of an incident in which Johnson is central—central as a fountain is central—and in which Boswell is the mechanism to start and sustain the flow. (In fact he claims as much in the passage from which his epigraph to this chapter was taken.)

As quotation will suggest, the entire larger passage would provide another Auerbach with a chapter for another *Mimesis*. On 2 October at Armadale, in a rather close and frantic air, Boswell spends the morning writing letters. "It was a very bad day, and at night there was a great deal of lightning." That is the outside. The inside story requires a good deal of the first person.

> I was fatigued with violent dancing. I do not like dancing. But I force myself to it, when it promotes social happiness, as in the country . . . so I danced a reel tonight . . . I thought it was better that I should engage the people of Skye by taking a cheerful glass with them and dancing with them rather than play the abstract scholar. I looked on this tour to the Hebrides as a co-partnery between Mr. Johnson and me. Each was to do all he could to promote its success; and I am certain that my gayer exertions were of

much service to us. Mr. Johnson's immense fund of knowledge and
wit was a wonderful source of admiration and delight to them. But
they had it only at times; and they required to have interstices
agreeably filled up, and even little elucidations of his grand text.
Besides, they observed that it was I who always "set him a-going."
The fountain was locked up till I interfered. (243–44)

Many things may be said of this and similar passages. One is that it, like
the others we have just seen, are addresses: Mr. James (and at times
plain Jemmy) Boswell speaks to the reader. In certain passages like this,
however, where Johnson is not the central figure, readers (certainly one
of them) may feel a certain vertigo. Boswell, I feel, is speaking words
that are true all right in their way. But there are other, unmentioned
ways that seem at least as important.

A reader dizzied by Boswell can sort out the reasons only by attentive reading. Not that anybody sets out to be inattentive. Of course we
cannot pretend to take ourselves seriously, much less expect that consideration of others, if we do not invest in them from our stocks of
solipsism. Whether we are aware of it or not, others can tell that our
interpretations, even our willingness to interpret others, reflect ourselves. By the same token, we can find Boswell himself in his interpretations of others, particularly of Johnson. To paraphrase Quintilian, there
are those who prefer Johnson, and there are even those who cannot
abide our protean Scot. They, too, are interpreting themselves. Fortunately, interpretations are like those reprint rights termed nonexclu-
sive: they do not preclude others, and they provide a new context.

So let us seek to locate, to identify some features of what that name
Boswell conveys to us, and as a first step do so by attention to his
depiction of Johnson. In a sense that requires the whole of his *Tour* and
his life of Johnson besides. But if our attention is directed, as it presently
is, to Boswell, then it may be possible to pick especially revelatory
passages. Those that follow begin with a characterization of Johnson by
someone other than Boswell; from there we move to occasions when
Johnson affected Boswell in very different ways. And, to project to the
end of this Boswellian design, there will be a few other unforgettable
passages.

Johnson was so extraordinary in his individual features as well as
their combinations that Boswell was far from the only person of the
time who sought to capture the titan in words. Yet our first passage

shows why it is proper to speak of the Boswellian "aether." The scene is an inn at Inverness on 29 August.

> I am, as Mr. Johnson observed, one who has all the old principles, good and bad. That of attention to relations in the remotest degree, or to worthy people in every state whom I have once known, I inherit from my father. It gave me greater satisfaction to hear everybody here speak of him with uncommon regard. Mr. Keith and Mr. Grant supped with us at the inn. We had roasted kid. (98)

Boswell is probably unaware of his introducing the two great authority figures of his life in order to delineate his charitable virtues. In fact, his father and Johnson seem useful even more for framing, arresting, making a tableau vivant that holds his personality from slipping away. His last four words provide him with a certification of the genuineness of that time and place, of those people present and his father absent. They provide a stamp of reassurance that this is kosher Boswell.

Boswell's editors supply a note to this passage. Robert Carruthers, a very able editor of the printed version of Boswell's account, relates from some source an account of Johnson told by one of Boswell and Johnson's fellow diners, the Rev. Alexander Grant.

> Mr. Grant used to relate that on this occasion [of dinner at the inn] Johnson was in high spirits. In the course of conversation, he mentioned that Mr. Banks (afterwards Sir Joseph) had, in his travels in New South Wales, discovered an extraordinary animal called the kangaroo. The appearance, conformation, and habits of this quadruped were of a most singular kind; and, in order to render his description more vivid and graphic, Johnson rose from his chair and volunteered an imitation of the animal. The company stared; and Mr. Grant said nothing could be more ludicrous than the appearance of a tall, heavy, grave-looking man, like Dr. Johnson, standing up to mimic the shape and motions of a kangaroo. He stood erect, put out his hands like feelers, and, gathering up the tails of his huge brown coat so as to resemble the pouch of the animal, made two or three vigorous bounds across the room. (98 n. 6)

It is impossible to prove that this did not happen, that it is all fabrication. But our point is that here is not the Johnson that Boswell saw and shows us. Boswell's Johnson is not in pantomime but dialogue. He is ungainly, awkward, even downright crude at times, but he is not ridiculous. And his presence is guaranteed by, as it also guarantees, Boswell's presence. What we have from Grant is a story, no doubt embellished in retelling, told from an uninvolved distance. There is nothing like, "*We* had roasted kid" (with or without my emphasis).

Boswell has a much later passage dated 28 October at Cameron that seems more significant to me than it seems to be to others.

> We were shown a Latin inscription for this monument [to the novelist Smollett]. Dr. Johnson sat down with an ardent and liberal earnest to revise it, and greatly improved it by several additions and variations. I unfortunately did not take a copy of it as it originally stood, but I have happily preserved every fragment of what Dr. Johnson wrote.
>
> We had this morning a singular proof of Dr. Johnson's quick and retentive memory. Hay's translation of Martial was lying in a window. I said I thought it was pretty well done, and showed him a particular epigram, I think of ten, but am certain of eight, lines. He read it, and tossed away the book, saying, "No, it is *not* pretty well done." As I persisted in my opinion, he said, "Why, sir, the original is thus" (and he repeated it); "and this man's translation is thus" and he repeated that also, exactly, though he had never seen it before, and read it over only once, without any intention of getting it by heart.[17]

Boswell certainly succeeds in his aim of convincing this reader of Johnson's "quick and retentive memory."

The whole passage is very revealing, of Boswell as well as of Johnson. Boswell wishes to illustrate every remarkable trait his friend possessed, and that memory is certainly not a negligible one. Although I doubt that he adds certain touches in any calculated way, he provides a copybook example of what the rhetoricians called ethical proof. His personal testimony to Johnson's memory carries complete conviction, because he includes examples of his own less perfect memory: he cannot remember even which epigram it was, how long it was, or what Hay's version was. With no preparation and simply out of a desire to

---

17. *Tour,* 363. Boswell's editors note that in the ms. Boswell gave the "fragments" of Johnson's revisions of the epitaph to Smollett along with the whole text.

convince Boswell of what the truth of the matter is, Johnson calls on that truly extraordinary memory. Boswell also intensely and convincingly shows his memory of an incident demonstrating Johnson's superior powers to retain and recall. Yes. But we should not fail to observe as well the connections between those two paragraphs. As the incident of the epigram shows, Johnson has by innate gifts the power, not possessed by Boswell, to summon the necessary facts. The preceding paragraph subtly makes two points related to that. One is that Boswell must use a cultivated method to preserve, as he puts it, what Johnson can summon at will. The implied praise of Johnson is obvious. What is not apparent is Boswell's self-praise, or perhaps it is better to say self-confidence. Indolent as he knew he was, Johnson usually does not put his extraordinary talent to profitable use. Boswell's method triumphantly demonstrates itself by its altogether evident success in the process of use.

None of us will forget, any more than Boswell, Johnson's shout on the uncertain road to Glenelg. And we recall Boswell's hurt, chagrin, and anxiety when Johnson impugns his behavior. There is another incident, which has caught more attention, that shows us Johnson's ability to wound without a shout. At Dunvegan on 16 September, cold, windy rain continues. After supper at the Macleods, the company retires to the drawing room, which has the house's only fireplace that does not smoke. Boswell and some others savor their port. Johnson does not drink. Then, "After the ladies were gone," the conversation, in which Johnson so memorably participates, turns on various textiles.

> And then he came out with this saying: "I have often thought that if I kept a seraglio, the ladies should all wear linen gowns or cotton; I mean stuffs made out of vegetables. I would have no silk; you cannot tell when it is clean. It will be very nasty before it is perceived to be so. Linen detects its own dirtiness."
>
> To hear Mr. Johnson, while sitting solemn in an arm-chair, talk of keeping a seraglio, and saying too, "I have *often* thought," was truly curious. Mr. Macqueen asked him if he would admit me. "Yes," said he, "if he were properly prepared; and he'd make a very good eunuch. He'd be a fine gay animal. He'd do his part well." "I take it," said I, "better than you would do your part." Though he treats his friends with uncommon freedom, he does not like a return. He seemed to me to be a little angry. He got off from

my joke by saying, "I have not yet told you what was to be my part"—and then at once he returned to my office as eunuch and expatiated on it with such fluency that it really hurt me. He made me quite contemptible for the moment. Luckily the company did not take it so clearly as I did. Perhaps, too, I imagined him to be more serious in this extraordinary raillery than he was. But I am of a firmer metal than Langton and can stand a rub better.

This morning he described Langton's house. He said the old house of the family was burnt. A temporary building was erected; and to this they have been always adding as the family increased. It was like a shirt made for a man when he was a child, and enlarged always as he grew older.[18]

There is a prodigious skill in moving from Johnson's lengthy remark on textiles (only the close is given here) to the clothing of those ladies in Johnson's oft imagined seraglio, and on to Langton with the closing shirt simile.

Obviously something serious is going on. It is curiously out of Boswell's usual practice that he uses Johnson's name but once in this lengthy passage. Boswell's feelings are understandably hurt, and it truly is unjust that Johnson should feel free to use his sharp wit on Boswell and yet resent any return in kind. But the heart of the passage is Boswell's uncertainty about Johnson's motives, and I believe that is the reason why he relies on pronouns rather than on Mr. Johnsons. He cannot decide a crucial issue. Others did not take Johnson's gibe "so *clearly* as I did." But maybe Boswell thought Johnson "more serious" than he was. Johnson cannot have known Boswell's sexual behavior in great detail, but he must have had some idea. Boswell clearly fears that Johnson is accusing him of sexual profligacy. And castration, the measure proposed for admission to the seraglio, is a veiled threat to Boswell, who greatly prized, and slightly feared, his virility along with its appeal to women. Who can pretend to outguess Boswell in this extraordinary scene?

Those are memorable passages, but there are three others that remain freshest, most vivacious in my memory of Boswell's *Tour.* They vary from brief to lengthy. The first has a lengthy preamble, but in itself

---

18. *Tour,* 176–77. The editors observe that, of the second paragraph, all after the first sentence was heavily inked out by Boswell in a style different from his usual manner of deletion. They speculate that it was preparation for lending the ms. to Mrs. Thrale.

possesses a magic or supererogation of a kind I do not discover in the other three "diaries of the road."

Johnson and Boswell first set foot on a Hebridean isle on 2 September 1773. It is a Thursday. The place is Armadale, on Skye, the largest island of the group. Boswell is gravely disappointed, and nothing promises to brighten the experience.

[Thursday, 2 Sept.] We had an ill-dressed dinner. . . . I observed that when Captain Macdonald and Mr. Macqueen came in after we were sat down to dinner, [their host] Sir Alexander [Macdonald] let them stand round the room and stuck his fork into a liver pudding, instead of getting room made for them. I took care to act as he ought to have done. . . .

I was quite hurt with the meanness and unsuitable appearance of everything. . . .

[Friday, 3 September] The day was very wet. . . . It was really melancholy to see the manly, gallant, and generous attachment of clanship going to ruin. . . . After dinner the Knight [Sir Alexander] and I met in Mr. Johnson's room . . . I fell upon him with perhaps too great violence upon his behaviour to his people; on the meanness of his appearance here. . . . In short, I gave him a volley. He was thrown into a violent passion. . . . Had he been a man of more mind, he and I must have had a quarrel for life. . . .

Mr. Johnson was vexed that he could get no distinct information about anything from any of the people here. . . .

[Saturday, 3 September] I set Mr. Johnson upon [Macdonald] this morning. . . . It was in vain to try to inspirit him. Mr. Johnson said [to me], "Sir we shall make nothing of him. . . . All is wrong. He has nothing to say to the people when they come about him." My beauty of a cousin, too, did not escape. Indeed, I was quite disgusted with her nothingness and insipidity. Mr. Johnson said, "This woman would sink a ninety-gun ship. She is so dull—so heavy." . . . The evening was heavy enough. (114–18)

Unhappy enough on his own account, Boswell is clearly deeply depressed that Johnson's first impression of the islands he had come so far to see should be this dismal. Johnson could not have been pleased. But the account he published (*Journey*, 49–52) is handsomely restrained. Without Boswell's angry remarks, one could not guess Johnson's exasperation behind "Many of my subsequent inquiries upon more interesting topicks ended in the like uncertainty" (51). And he handsomely translates Macdonald's irresponsible mismanagement of his lands and tenants into humane concern: "This is not the description of a cruel climate, yet the dark months are here a time of great distress; because the summer can do little more than feed itself, and winter comes with its cold and its scarcity upon families very slenderly provided" (52). Both comments are wholly credible and altogether humane.

The end comes two days later. On Sunday, 5 September, Boswell ends his diurnal with a report of drinking too much "by way of keeping off a *taedium vitae*" and of Sir Alexander "again in a passion" (*Tour*, 119). From all that damp and mud, and although quite consonant with them in its negation, there is nonetheless that one beautiful, long-waited-for and much-needed contrasting lyric sentence illuminating all that was Skye: "There are no church-bells in the island" (118). There is more than a touch here of the conclusion to George Herbert's "Prayer": "Church bells beyond the stars heard . . . Something understood."

Lyric moments are so very rare in the two accounts of the Scottish journey that we need to inquire elsewhere in the literary emporium for Boswell's characteristic finest work. It will not be found in descriptions such as Austen's heroines admired in a Cowper. It might have been, since it is just at this stage of eighteenth-century England that the earlier nature as divine order yields to nature localized into Austen's hedges, hills, and the "English verdure" Emma observes at Mr. Knightley's sun-filled strawberry picnic. It is therefore the more remarkable that Boswell should provide such a passage, although we can well understand that after the heaviness of Armadale the brightness of Raasay should call on his descriptive talents and therefore give us a second passage to discourage any easy cynicism toward Boswell.

> It was a most pleasing approach to Raasay. We saw before us a beautiful bay, well defended with a rocky coast; a good gentleman's house, a fine verdure about it, a considerable number of trees, and beyond it hills and mountains in gradation of wildness. Our boatmen sung with great spirit. Mr. Johnson observed that naval music was very ancient. As we came to shore, the music of rowers was succeeded by that of reapers, who were busy at work, and who seemed to shout as much as to sing, while they worked with a bounding vigour. Just as we landed, I observed a cross, or

rather the ruins of one, upon a rock, which had to me a pleasing vestige of religion. (132–33)

This is a miscellany, but ordered in its ascending description from a rocky coast to the human and, finally, a "vestige" of the divine. There is another progression, as the lyric stress on the immediate presence of beauty leads, as lyric description so easily does, to narration, Boswell's indisputably greatest talent, a medium transcending Johnson's emphasis on place and his own apparent dependence on dates.

With this gradation, in two examples, from lyric to narrative we are ready to consider what I think the high moment in Boswell's *Tour.* His editors call it "the most amusing, and at the same time the most touching passage" in the *Tour.* I do not really agree, unless "amusing" be taken in its older sense (i.e., to reflect). Whether others consent with the editors or me, everyone must regret that the published version reduces the remarkable narration and a moment of prayer to a mere "devout meditation" (*Tour,* 336 n. 8). The "passage" consists of but one paragraph from the account of a visit to that ancient site of Christianity, Iona (Icolmkill), on 20 October.

> I then went into the cathedral, which is really grand enough when one thinks of its antiquity and of the remoteness of the place; and at the end, I offered up my adorations to God. I again addressed a few words to St. Columbus; and I warmed my soul with religious resolutions. I felt a kind of exultation in thinking that the solemn scenes of piety ever remain the same, though the cares and follies of life may prevent us from visiting them, or may even make us fancy that their effects were only "as yesterday when it is past," and never again to be perceived. I hoped that ever after having been in this holy place, I should maintain an exemplary conduct. One has a strange propensity to fix upon some point from whence a better course of life may be said to begin. I read with an audible voice the fifth chapter of St. James, and Dr. Ogden's tenth sermon. I suppose there has not been a sermon preached in this Church since the Reformation. I had a serious joy in hearing my voice, while it was filled with Ogden's admirable eloquence, resounding in the ancient cathedral of Icolmkill. (336)[19]

---

19. For a picture of the ancient site, see figure 17.

Fig. 17. Iona (in Icolmkill, also called Inch Colm, Inch Kenneth). The ruins of the ancient Christian settlement were termed monastery, abbey, cathedral, etc. (From Grose 1797.)

Many besides Boswell's editors will find the tone of this passage mixed. Indeed, it is not easily described.

Two of the brightly colored threads in this texture are the biblical passage and the sermon. Since Boswell's editors do not supply either one, we ought at least to consider a part. Here, then, are the first seven verses of James 4:

> From whence come wars and fightings among you? come they not hence, even of your lusts that war in your members? Ye lust, and have not; ye kill, and desire to have, and cannot obtain; ye fight and war, yet ye have not, because ye ask not. Ye ask, and receive not, because ye ask amiss, that ye may consume it upon your lusts. Ye adulterers and adulteresses, know ye not that the friendship of the world is enmity with God? whosoever therefore will be a friend of the world is the enemy of God. Do ye think that the scripture saith in vain, The spirit that dwelleth in us lusteth to envy? but he giveth more grace. Wherefore he saith, God resisteth the proud, but giveth grace unto the humble. Submit yourselves therefore to God. Resist the Devil, and he will flee from you.

There must have seemed to Boswell all too clear an application of these verses to his "amorous propensities"—to use a phrase that Johnson had applied to himself for far less recurrent inclinations. To say so implies that Boswell knew so, and there is no sin in a fresh resolve as part of repentance. Both his resolve and his far from painful self-dramatizing make him, in his wayfaring, a Christian of the Boswellian-Ionian chapel of ease.

Those who know Boswell will think that he had good reason to dedicate himself to his far from beaten path of "exemplary conduct." Those who know themselves as well as Boswell may wish to breathe a fellow sigh. But it is the climactic ending that interests Boswell most and ought to interest us most, for in it we discover the end of his visit to Iona. In fact the whole passage is an effort to redesign his life to a worthy Christian end, and although that cannot be said accurately to be true of his *Tour*, it is true that being with Johnson repeatedly heated him with an holy flame. As the passage rises toward its *O altitudo!* we imagine Boswell reading that chapter first in a soft voice and listening to hear whether others are about. Finding they are not, he reads more loudly. Opening Ogden's tenth sermon, he reads it with full voice and all the eloquence he can imagine Garrick summoning, more and more loudly until his voice is "resounding in the ancient cathedral."

There are two essential features of this remarkable scene. The first is by no means abstruse but apt to be overlooked, in spite of its importance. Boswell does have remarkable ability to distinguish Johnson from himself by quoted or imputed speech—and to create the accent of Johnson in particular. But that ability is all too likely to make us slight those remarkable gifts for narrative. The scene presently before us shows as much. The intensity of emotion does not simply come at a call. It is built up detail by detail, clause by clause and stage by stage, sentence by sentence in masterful fashion. Not only that. The narrative is enlarged by a dramatic element as well. It really makes one wonder whether the novelist's art is not easier than Boswell's literary capacity with factuality. Unusual, strange, and finally embarrassing as the scene is, it is a masterly achievement that confirms our conviction of Boswell's abilities throughout the *Tour*.

The second essential feature of this scene of performance among the ruins at Iona is, if not obvious, simple enough. *Boswell is alone*. He writes from time to time that Johnson reads his *Journal* and likes it. I do not think Johnson read this, and perhaps Boswell hid it from Malone as well. In any event, ours is a strange world in which Boswell's pious elevations should seem stranger than his sexual ones in his *London Journal*. But it is also Boswell's world—at least on the terms presented here—and we can only ask what response he expected from any reader. His reason for fearing knowledge by others is that he knows even better than we that he is motivated by pious guile, although we no more than he can measure the parts of piety and of guile. And any person with his insight into others should know that others would also detect the tampering with piety. He should have known. But did he? What is his understanding of others and himself here?

Surely he knew, and that an attentive reader would know, that there was a gap between Boswell in ordinary and Boswell in robes, between Boswell the fallible and Boswell the preacher of sermons, the font of eloquence, and the reviver of piety in Iona. The question is why, knowing those things, he delivers this vision of himself. None of us really knows the answers, but two possibilities come to mind. One is only this: Boswell is experimenting with a role that befits a Scot at the time and place and beyond that really cannot explain himself any better than we can. He knows the design he wishes to create and the end he wishes to realize by completing the design. He can convince neither himself nor us that he has done or can do so completely. But of course he wants the conviction he knows he cannot reach—by whatever extraordinary effort he shows himself capable of performing. The aim misses, the design is incomplete, the end is unobtained.

Because Boswell is alone.

Sora was almost a mute to begin with. Johnson's far-reaching intelligence is sullied by no dialogue, and it works on condition of separateness. Boswell requires others to confirm precisely what he seeks to confirm in this passage and fails to do, his real existent self. That is a quicksilver thing, to be sure, but it is present magnificently and subtly in most of the *Tour*. To alter Bacon's phrasing, Boswell fears being alone as men fear to go into death. His darkness falls in the absence of others. He loses himself in the absence of other persons necessary to his person as a means to generate the light, the understanding, and the conviction he mistakenly seeks to create, alone, in Iona.

Anyone accepting this reasoning will find that Boswell recovers his existence and usual narrative power in what immediately follows his account of reading among the ruins:

> I had promised to write to my worthy old friend [the Edinburgh attorney, Boswell's close friend John Johnston of] Grange from Icolmkill. While I was writing it, Mr. Johnson entered, that he might attentively view and even measure the ruins. I left him there, as I was to take a ride to the shore where [St.] Columbus landed, as it is said, and where the green pebbles called Icolmkill stones are found. I eat some eggs for breakfast, while Sir Allan sat by me. (337)

Although this might deserve a stage direction such as *[Enter Johnson]*, its straightforward narrative no longer requires buskins. Also, although this is a descent from dizzying heights to stones on a far shore, it bears the conviction that—no longer alone—the gifted author is once more sure he is there, carrying our conviction of his return, and carrying his own conviction as well.

Bashō's Poetics of Travel

The great popularity of Horace's *Ars Poetica* in eighteenth-century England led to numerous translations, imitations, and would-be witty

Fig. 18. Composing haikai at the residence of Nagayama Shigeyuki. It is
not known whether Buson's informal scene was typical of Bashō's time.
(From Buson 1973.)

variations such as *The Art of Cookery*. In our age of solemn theory, it has
been desirable to have a poetics of any activity requiring advertising. It
will not be amiss to begin this discussion of Bashō's design of *The
Narrow Road through the Provinces* with an insistence that the design
entails a genuine poetics of travel. Of course, other descriptions are
possible. *The Narrow Road* is also, in Bashō's phrase, a diary of the road,
which is to say an example of the peculiarly Japanese kind, a literary
diary and, more particularly of a haikai poetic diary (kunikki). Or again,
as its famous opening shows, travel constitutes not merely movement
but an art of life and death.

Within his literary heritage, Bashō may be original, but in sanc-
tioned ways. About seven and a half centuries before him, the first royal
poetic collection, the *Kokinshū* (ca. 910), had established travel (tabi) as a
poetic topic, devoting one of its twenty scrolls to the subject. The

Kokinshū itself gave formal recognition to what had had lengthy prior existence, and as time went on, Chinese lore was incorporated. Some male poets took orders as monks in order to move among all conditions of people. Only by such a change in life could Monks Nōin and Saigyō now enter the royal presence and then travel freely to outlying country.[20] As we have seen in the Shirakawa episode, those two figures served as models for Bashō, who was well aware also of precedents among the renga linked-poetry masters, with Iio Sōgi (1421–1502) being his ideal example.

The principle of a poetics of travel is, then, by no means new in *The Narrow Road* or in Bashō's other writings. The novelty, the changes, are to be found instead in the metamorphoses brought about by his insistence on three things: literal, actual travel; the aesthetic codes of travel; and the equivalence of a stanza of his linked poetry to a stage of a journey. Each of the three is interchangeable. Recollection of two examples encountered earlier will take us by easy steps to Bashō's profoundest innovation.

To begin with, as Bashō begins, it will be recalled that the opening words of *The Narrow Road* may be rendered, "The months and days are the wayfarers of the centuries, and as yet another year comes around it, too, turns traveler." Travel has become so important a constituent and condition—almost indeed a definition—of life that instead of its being something for which time is a dimension, we discover that the units of time themselves travel. Secondly, as discussed at length in the preceding chapter in terms of "Bashō's poetic places," at the stage of the journey culminating in Matsushima, Bashō insists so strongly on the aesthetics of place that strange things happen. Places can literally be said to displace the usual priority of people in travel accounts and to render time a consideration almost solely of the seasonal topics of hokku primarily about places. Not only that. As the climax, the famous poetic place, Matsushima, is depicted at great length and in great detail to be significant precisely as *Matsushima*, that is, as its name means, pines (matsu) and islands (shima). We shall be seeing more of these

---

20. Women also found taking orders gave them freedom of movement. Ukō (lay name Tome; d. ca. 1716–35), the wife of one of the principal poets in Bashō's school, Nozawa Bonchō, used illness as an excuse to take orders, enabling her to move among men and exercise her talent as a hokku poet. Recent study has revealed that, in spite of the rigid antifemale policy of the Edo regime, many women became respected writers. In time we shall have a fuller literary history.

matters shortly, but at present they lead us to consider a reversal like
time taken to be traveler. Although introduced before, Bashō's principal
example of a radical poetics of inversion now requires close attention.

It will be recalled that he said of his haikai art, "A kasen is to be
thought of as thirty-six steps. In taking the first, there is no thought of
return" (*Taisei*, 628). A first stanza written during travel becomes the
first stage of travel.[21] That shift is accompanied by a larger logical
consequence: his *poetic art* of linked poetry is defined as a *journey* with
each of the thirty-six stanzas being taken as a stride or stage of the
travel.[22] So intently does he take the poetic conception of travel that his
poetry becomes a journey. Although this is similar to the inversion or
metamorphosis of the opening words of *The Narrow Road*, it leads to a
further transformation, a further metamorphosis in the application of
travel as poetry. And it is that which sets Bashō wholly apart from our
other three travelers.

In recent decades, Japanese scholars have come to interpret *The
Narrow Road through the Provinces* as no less than a version of a linked-
poetry (haikai) sequence. Just what that means has been a matter of
gradual definition and of change from a rather generalized conception
of *The Narrow Road* as an analogue to a haikai sequence to a bolder and
detailed working out of formal resemblance.[23]

Understanding of what is entailed requires technical details, but it
is well worth the effort. (For the matter summarized here, see appendixes 1 and 2.) For the earlier, renga, version of linked poetry, the
standard sequence is the hyakuin or one-hundred-stanza length—a
century of stanzas was set down on the fronts and backs of four folded
sheets of paper. The hundred-stanza unit was also commonly used in
haikai, but Bashō's favorite and habitual length was that of thirty-six
stanzas (kasen), written on the fronts and backs of two sheets. Six

---

21. As "stanza" is the Italian word for "room," Bashō posits what has been termed
"stanza" here—"ku"—as a step or stage of a journey. It is a pity English does not stretch
that far.

22. Bashō's lexicon had a second term lacking in English: "ginkō." The word means
taking a journey with the purpose of composing renga or haikai: the "gin" means "to
compose linked poetry," and the "kō" means "to go (in travel)."

23. Compare Andō's detailed analysis of 1974, which is set out below, with Sugiura
Shōichirō's rather more hesitant version fifteen years earlier: *The Narrow Road* was "well
fashioned into the method of haikai sequences; even if it was not the author's conscious
aim to use the kasen form, the abounding of sequential fluctuations and the intermixture
of fact and fiction gave form to a haikai whole [sekai]" (Bashō 1959, 22). And see appendix
2 for details.

stanzas were written on the front of the first sheet and the back of the second; twelve stanzas were written on the other two sides, so yielding the thirty-six.

In this allocation of stanzas, there are three large divisions marking a rhythm of three movements. The musical analogy is just, since the rhythm was adapted from court music by the renga poets, who bequeathed it to nō and haikai. The Japanese name for this three-stage rhythm, jo-ha-kyū, requires translation and explanation. The jo may be termed an introduction, and it is the stateliest or most continuously elevated part of the three. The ha constitutes what is commonly translated "development." The Japanese for this longest of the three movements means something rather more like "breakage": it is the most agitated. The kyū is a kind of presto or fast close. Of course the speed is metaphorical and may be conveyed in various ways: by frequent or "quick" change of subjects, by shifting to a more prosaic or didactic tone, by using names of places at great distances from each other, and so forth. A simple diagram for a thirty-six-stanza sequence will assist perception of these matters:

Stanzas 1–6	Introduction (jo)	Elevated tone
Stanzas 7–29	Development (ha)	Agitation
Stanzas 30–36	Fast close (kyū)	"Speed"

In the opening of *The Narrow Road* Bashō says he left a first side of eight stanzas (omote hakku) on the pillar of his grass-thatched hermitage when leaving it for his journey on the narrow road. That is more or less to say that he had composed that part or the whole of a solo hundred-stanza sequence, since it is for a sequence of that length that eight stanzas constitute an introduction. That might be taken as a hint that we should read *The Narrow Road* as a hundred-stanza sequence, something that an influential critic of Bashō, Andō Tsuguo, has done for us.

His proposal can be found in more than one place in his books but nowhere more specifically than in his chapter "Moon and Flowers" (Andō 1974, 179–88). That discussion has been well prepared for in his earlier chapters, and details of his proposal to read *The Narrow Road* on the model of a hundred-stanza sequence are given in appendix 2.

His striking proposal is, unfortunately, impossible to understand without considering some of the conventions or rules of linked poetry,

Fig. 19. With their guide, the young prostitutes at Ichiburi. (From Buson 1973.)

and for fullest sense, both appendixes must be consulted. Some of the linked-poetry canons must be identified here, however, if what he and others have proposed is to make sense. We must recur, then, to the point that linked poems were considered to have an organization based on sheets and their sides.

Each *side*, except the last, was to have a moon stanza; each *sheet* was to have a flower stanza. That was the minimum. Moreover, there was an appointed place for each moon and flower, although in haikai practice of a kasen only the second flower uniformly appears in its appointed place, the thirty-fifth or penultimate stanza. Andō strikingly adds that, given the parallel, we discover "no great departure" from the expected pattern of moon and flower stanzas. It is a strong proposal.

The great art of linked poetry involves creation of a constantly varying but nonetheless integral sequence. Since variation without art or integrity was altogether too likely when the usual three or four poets composed their stanzas in alterations of only a few minutes, it was necessary to introduce an elaborate code for discipline. The code extended to many features of stanzas. Three conceptions of stanzas mattered most. One was the closeness or the distance (the heaviness or lightness) of a stanza's relation to its predecessor. Variation was crucial to avoid monotony. A second conception was that of the impressiveness of an individual stanza, and again variety was sought. Such is the Japanese appreciation of asymmetry in art that a sequence artfully mixing plain or middling among impressive stanzas was favored over another uniform in brilliance (or, of course, in plainness). The third conception was of topics, possible subtopics, and motifs.[24] Each stanza had as a topic a season or was "miscellaneous" in topic. For our purposes, the best example of a subtopic is travel (tabi) and of a motif, places of poetic name (nadokoro). Spring and autumn topics were to be sustained for at least three stanzas, and seasonal topics predominate in the introduction. A rise in the number of miscellaneous stanzas helps create the agitation of the development section.

Andō's chapter "Moon and Flowers" concerns Bashō and Sora's meeting the two penitent young prostitutes. At Ichiburi Barrier Bashō reports that he and Sora are approached in the morning by the two women with whom they had shared an inn the previous night. Readers have long found that an arresting incident. When Sora's lost *Nikki* was recovered and then published, in 1943, no other passage aroused as much comment as this one. In that episode what seemed explosive was the following, in which Bashō replies to the prostitutes' polite request to follow, on their pilgrimage to the Great Shrines of Ise, the two monklike men.

> "I regret it very much," I told them, "but we are not so much traveling somewhere as stopping here and there for periods of time. It would really be better for you if you accompanied ordinary travelers. The favor of the gods should enable you to get to Ise without trouble." With that we set out on our way, but the great pity of their situation troubled me for some time.
>
> Under a single roof

---

24. Some disagreement exists among Japanese about a number of matters, particularly as to topics. I follow the canons given by Konishi Jin'ichi, the last living person to be taught renga composition. See Konishi 1971.

> the prostitutes and I for one night:
> bush clover and the moon.

I spoke out the verses to Sora, who copied them down.[25]

There was shock when it was realized that the stanza was not to be found in Sora's registry of the stanzas and sequences composed on the trip, or in his diary. Clearly, the whole episode was made up.

The expectation of literary factuality (of course in the absence of countervailing evidence of fiction) is that strong in Japan: even witty Buson clearly believed the event occurred. The presumption of sober, solemn Bashō had grown to a commonplace still widely held. (His aesthetic madness and high comedy are clearly not the first things his name betokens.) In the revision required by the recovery of Sora's diary, however, two reinforcing conclusions were reached. One was that this passage—like some others less striking as well—was fictional. The other, which is particularly important to Andō's thesis, was that the episode occurs at a stage in a sequence where stanzas on love could be expected. (As also in connection with Sue no Matsuyama, where love is first touched on: see p. 127.) This is admittedly an odd love episode, but that is not strange in haikai, and especially in Bashō's carefully pre-pared context, as Andō shows.

Of course nobody argues that *The Narrow Road through the Provinces* is an actual haikai sequence. But the chief reason, prosody apart, why that is so depends on the criteria of linked poetry itself. In the nature of the continuance of his diary, Bashō violates a central rule of linked poetry, renga and haikai alike: that no stanza is related semantically to any but its predecessor (and hence its successor). That is the reason for the metaphor of links in a chain. Western readers find it impossible to read linked poetry at first without presuming recollections, parallels, repetitions, and other connections (as in two separated stanzas dealing with soft spring rains or betrayal in love). *The Narrow Road* differs in this respect. Bashō's repeated evocation of the doomed heroic figure, Minamoto Yoshitsune, and his explicit comparison of Kisa Bay to Mat-sushima show that his diary of the road is not fully a linked-poetry sequence. On the other hand, his haikai gaps or leaps show that a simple, tidy plot was far from preoccupying him.

---

25. *Diaries*, 187–88. The force of this episode is testified to by Buson's selecting it as a major scene in his text and illustrations of *The Narrow Road*, as is evident from figure 19.

With so much preamble, we may now follow the spirit, rather than the letter, of Andō's thesis. As explained in appendix 2, I believe that the model of the thirty-six-stanza kasen sequence preserves Andō's insight without being subject to some of its problems, particularly in accounting for the jo-ha-kyū rhythm. All that we have seen still holds, as for example that difficult section from the Shirakawa Barrier to Matsushima or, again, the great rise in the Hiraizumi passage and the great fall to Shitomae Barrier. These units and sequential surprises fit in with the kasen design, and they perfectly accommodate Bashō's poetics of place from Edo to Ōgaki.

The haikai design of *The Narrow Road* develops beyond the poetics of place, although never omitting it. But specified places, named places introduce other important features of *The Narrow Road*, features we do not expect to see combined in Western literature, including the travel accounts by Johnson and Boswell. First, *The Narrow Road* is basically factual. (Although it is but one of many fictional passages in the account, that on the prostitutes is by far the lengthiest and most narrative.) We can verify Bashō's detail from Sora's *Diary* or personal experience: many of us have followed Bashō along some portions of his travel. The second feature is yet more important: as Andō recognized, the design on the basis of a haikai sequence enables Bashō to aestheticize fact and fiction alike.

Bashō is not unique in this. His contemporary Ihara Saikaku (1642–93), a Danrin school haikai poet before he became a writer of "books of worldly life" (ukiyozōshi), also sometimes used the haikai design. The conspicuous example is that of *One Man Who Devoted His Life to Love*, which falls into two halves, each modeled on a haikai one-hundred-stanza sequence. In the first, the amorous hero, Yonosuke, begins a triumphant (and highly precocious) series of sexual adventures constituting the jo or introduction. The development section, the ha, features some ups and a definite penultimate down, until in the triumphant fast close or kyū Yonosuke is summoned home to wealth on his father's death. The second half has greater bravura in some ways but also a highly ironic affirmation in its fast close.[26] The differing aims of

---

26. I share the view that the haikai design can also be discerned, less comprehensively, in Saikaku's *Five Women Who Devoted Their Lives to Love*. I do not see the design elsewhere in his work. For the haikai equivalent of these examples, see Nishiyama Sōin's *Hana de Soro no Maki* (*I Am Called Blossom*) labeled a "koi haikai"—that is, a hundred-stanza sequence every stanza of which has love as a subtopic.

the two writers in their haikai aestheticizing of prose narrative can be variously characterized. One way is to say that Bashō's journey was, on balance, as factual as Saikaku's was fictional.[27]

That is not understood by all readers. For example, there is the not greatly conspicuous episode after Bashō and Sora leave beautiful Matsushima for a visit to Temple Suiganji. Bashō dates the event V.11 and their next setting out for Hiraizumi as an event of the twelfth. As we know from Sora's *Diary*, those steps really were taken two days earlier, V.9 and 10. Heads have been scratched over the discrepancy. No answer in the usual sense of that word is possible, but explanation is readily feasible.

There is no expectation that a Japanese literary, poetic diary will utilize daily entries. That is true both of the court diaries (utanikki) and of Bashō's "diaries of the road" (or kunikki).[28] Dating is not a matter of oath. But Bashō is so highly venerated that each declaration is taken as literally true. Actually, we often do not know what he has in mind. The matter at hand is an instance: there is no apparent reason. His dating throughout *The Narrow Road* is peculiar—or indifferent. He provides dates for but seventeen events or occasions, and of that number only eight can be verified. Five are wrong, and four are simply unclear. After the stricken Sora had to go on ahead, there is really no way of verifying or falsifying the few dates Bashō gives. There are other ways of honoring time, and he uses them. But we see here the extent to which people, places, and seasons mattered so much more to him than did exact dating.

Another haikai feature must be recognized. Bashō's ignoring of exact dates gives an unusual artistic significance to haikai gaps or intervals (haikai no ma). The usual sense of the term is repeatedly emphasized in *The Narrow Road*—and becomes inescapable as we near the end—by transitionless leaps in space and therefore time.

---

27. Because all the stanzas after the first (hokku) in a linked poetry sequence were expected to be fictional, Saikaku's made-up adventures of an amorous man are, in that respect at least, closer to haikai than is Bashō's dominantly factual account.

28. There is one exception. Bashō's account of a period after that of *The Narrow Road* spent traveling from a base at the Rakushisha hermitage of his loyal follower Mukai Kyorai is called *The Saga Diary* and utilizes daily entries. But Bashō could not treat that as "a diary of the road" like the others. By aesthetic definition, moving from point to point in the area of the capital, Kyoto, was not travel. Travel (tabi) required that the motion be from the capital or between other points. One *returned* to the capital.

There is another, double haikai gap or omission that involves two *unmentioned* anniversaries. Bashō's respect for Monk Saigyō did not require that poet's preceding him on this journey for Bashō to allude to "the waka of Saigyō" (*Taisei*, 301, *Oi no Kobumi*). But Saigyō's dates, 1118–90, made Bashō's journey in 1689 an event of the five hundredth anniversary of Saigyō's death (by Japanese count of years included). It was also the five hundredth anniversary (plus one year in Japanese account) of another death on Bashō's mind. As he went on to Hiraizumi, he knew that the legendary Minamoto Yoshitsune (b. 1159) had tragically died there a victim of the ill intent of his brother, Yoritomo, in 1189. Since no other historical figures are at all as important to *The Narrow Road* as these two, they obviously matter, Saigyō for poetic and Yoshitsune for political reasons.

The most profoundly important matter in this for Bashō's ends is that the poetry of Saigyō and the political struggle of Yoshitsune are at once discrete and relatable, and that both (like factuality and fictionality) are unified by the ground of his haikai art. As we shall now see, the haikai gaps and the downward transformation of haikai change (haikaika) sometimes lead to extreme fluctuation of tone. Although in a general sense that varying gives evidence of Bashō's genius and practice as a haikai writer, the marked shifts attest in particular (as Andō and others have recognized) to this portion of *The Narrow Road* as the counterpart to the lengthy ha or development section of a linked-poetry sequence.

We can now understand better the richness of the magnificent Hiraizumi episode (*Diaries*, 175–77; *Zenkō*, 278–79). We begin by situating Bashō. He lived (1644–94) during the early and most repressive stage of what Japanese term the Edo Bakufu or military government ruling in the name of by now marginalized monarchs. That government followed other bakufu.

1. Kamakura Bakufu. 1185–1333. Founded by Minamoto Yoritomo (1147–99) after the Minamoto (or Genji) victory over the Taira (or Heike) in the Gempei Wars. This is the setting for Yoshitsune, as has been mentioned.
2. Muromachi or Ashikaga Bakufu, 1358–ca. 1573. Civil war, chaos, and (surely it is a paradox) an outburst of artistic splendors continuing into the next.

3. Azuchi-Momoyama era. 1573–1600. More splendor, more chaos.
4. Edo Bakufu. 1603–1867. Founded by Tokugawa Ieyasu (1542–1616), military victor, dictator, restorer of peace and order after the chaos (punctuated by temporary centralizings of power) from the twelfth century.

In the Asian fashion, it was possible for Bashō to write adversely (or positively if he had chosen) about the Edo Bakufu by discussing details, drawing parallels, or writing allegorically about an earlier bakufu. By writing sympathetically of those who opposed—or those like Yoshitsune who were victimized by—Yoritomo, the founder of the Kamakura Bakufu, he criticizes the repressive Tokugawa or Edo regime of his day.

The passage on Hiraizumi is preceded by three and followed by two others that relate to the Kamakura Bakufu and to Yoshitsune. In the earlier Kurobane episode (*Diaries*, 162; *Zenkō*, 152), Bashō refers to an episode in the largely naval battle of Yashima, at which the Minamoto won a crucial victory over the Taira. This passage reads like praise of the Minamoto and, by implication, of the Edo regime under which Bashō lived.[29] Any such implication is dispelled by the second passage involved, that praising the loyalty to Yoshitsune, even to death, of Vice Governor Satō, his sons, and their intrepid wives (in 1189, the year of Yoshitsune's death; *Diaries*, 162; *Zenkō*, 205). The last of the three pre-Hiraizumi episodes is that at Shiogama (*Diaries*, 173; *Zenkō*, 246–47), which praises the famous loyalty of Izumi Saburō to Yoshitsune.

From that exemplar of loyalty we can look beyond the Hiraizumi episode to two further references to the Yoshitsune story. Bashō later glances at the Pavilion of the Immortals (Sennindō), where Yoshitsune hid for a time in refuge (*Diaries*, 180; *Zenkō*, 326–28). Near the end of *The Narrow Road*, in the account of Komatsu, Bashō refers to two further figures in the Yoshitsune story, both of whom supported Yoritomo until his behavior forfeited their allegiance. These are Saitō Sanemori (1111–83) who was said to have dyed his white hair so as to participate in the battle of Shinohara, where he was killed; and the impetuous Minamoto

---

29. At Nikkō, the praise of the Edo Bakufu for "peaceable and prosperous" influence throughout the country is a pro forma or ironic gesture, a cover for the criticism actually conveyed.

(better known as Kiso) Yoshinaka (1154–84), killed by Yoritomo's order (*Diaries*, 189–90; *Zenkō*, 406).[30]

These five passages are foothills to the tragic grandeur of Hiraizumi, the account of which requires some last information. Hiraizumi was the site of a splendid rebel fortress or court founded by Fujiwara Kiyohira (d. 1126) in 1094. He was followed by his son, Motohira (d. 1157) and grandson, Hidehira (d. 1187). Hidehira swore his three sons in loyalty to the cause of Yoshitsune, who had taken refuge in Hiraizumi. His son Tadahira or Izumi Saburō held to his pledge, but the eldest son, Yasuhira, did not, betraying the Yoshitsune cause. The betrayal did not arouse the calculating Yoritomo's trust, admiration, or gratitude: he had the betrayer of Yoshitsune destroyed with Hiraizumi in 1189.

These historical details are foothills of another kind to the great rise in tragic beauty effected by the Hiraizumi episode. After describing an exhausting journey from Matsushima, Bashō reports arriving at Hiraizumi. Sora dated the occasion V.13 (29 June in modern reckoning).

The splendors of the three generations of Hiraizumi now constitute the briefest of dreams, and of the grand facade there are only faint remains stretching out for two and a half miles. Hidehira's castle is now levelled to overgrown fields, and of all the splendors of the past, only Mount Kinkei retains its form. Climbing up to the high ramparts of what had been Yoshitsune's stronghold, one can see below the Kitakami River flowing in a wide stream from the south. The Koromo River pours past the site of loyal Izumi Saburō's castle, then beneath these ramparts, and at last into the Kitakami. The old relics of others like Yasuhira are to be found separated to the west at Koromo Barrier, which controlled the approach from the north and probably was meant to protect the area against incursions by the northern tribesmen. Yoshitsune and his brave adherents took refuge in this citadel. But the most famous

---

30. During the two years remaining of his travels after the six or seven months recorded in *The Narrow Road*, Bashō spent a large portion of his time in the general Kyoto area. His frequent visits to the Temple Gichūji (also pronounced Yoshinakadera) in nearby Ōtsu made that temple famous. His favor of Yoshinaka was understood as an anti-bakufu gesture.

names claim the world only a little while, and now the level grasses cover their traces. Du Fu's words came to mind—

> The country crumbles, but mountains and rivers endure;
> A late spring visits the castle, replacing it with
> > green grasses—

and sitting down on my pilgrim's hat, I wept over the ruins of time.

> Summer grasses rampant
> the common soldiers' aftermath
> in traces of dreams . . .

I saw at last with astonishment the wonders of the temple Chūsonji, of which I had heard before. . . . the seven treasures had been scattered, the jeweled door was broken by the wind, and the gilt pillars were moldered by frost and snow. Yet a place that ought long since to have been utterly reduced and left level under the turf has been enclosed not long ago, and with the roof retiled it withstands the wind and the rain. It is preserved for a time as a remembrance of the past:

> Have ages of summer rain
> left undimmed this radiance
> the Temple of Light.

More than any other passage in *The Narrow Road*, this on Hiraizumi (*Diaries*, 176–77; *Zenkō*, 278–79, 288–89) combines mastery of prose and verse with immediacy of appeal and great depth. Its force derives from Bashō's convictions about the harsh government of his time. He had visited Suma the year before, deeply aware of its associations with real and fictional exile.[31] From it he wrote to his fellow townsman and poetic disciple Ensui (1640–1704), referring to Atsumori as he does to Yoshitsune later: "The loss on that day and the pain of this—I shall never forget you among thoughts of life and death, the subservience of the

---

31. Among the exiles are: Ariwara Yukihira (?818–?93); Hikaru Genji, hero of *The Tale of Genji*, and Taira Atsumori (1169–84). Yukihira's and Atsumori's sufferings (observe Atsumori's youth at death) were often treated in narrative and drama and alluded to by poets. Even today, at the Shingon Temple Sumadera in Suma, relics purported to be Atsumori's (including his famous flute) are on display.

weak to the powerful, mutability, and swift time" (Miner 1979a, 115). That moving attention to "the subservience of the weak to the powerful" speaks of the basis of injustice in every society that ever was, although sometimes in crueler versions.

There is a related matter, Bashō's hokku on the summer grasses at Hiraizumi: "Natsugusa ya / tsuwamonodomo ga / yume no ato." Interpretations vary. (See Ueda 1991, 242–43.) Most readers take the mention of dreams as an echo of the opening of the passage and the references to grasses as a connection with Du Fu's couplet. That seems incontestable. But it does not follow that in his hokku Bashō is still writing about Yoshitsune and the other romantic figures. *Tsuwamono* are common soldiers, men who have had to take up arms for battle, not named heroes. This implication is powerfully enforced by the termination, -domo, a suffix that conveys possible plurality and definite depreciation. The axis is Du Fu's couplet. One of the hallmarks of Du's greatness is his vision of the nation and people at large, not just the great heroes like Yoshitsune. Bashō brilliantly uses the couplet to switch from the few great to the countless anonymous men pressed into war and slain, their bodies left to rot under the coarse summer grasses stirring so thickly before him. Many a mute inglorious Yoshitsune left behind bones to mingle with the earth, all too well illustrating "the subservience of the weak to the powerful." The bakufu of ruthless Yoritomo is a stand-in for the bakufu of Bashō's own time, and he mourns for a whole nation. Only religion avails, leaving us with the undimmed hope of Hikaridō, the Temple of Light.

Tragedy and moral judgment may accompany romance. Bashō's haikai gap and move to his next step or stanza is remarkable, one of the most extraordinary descents imaginable (*Diaries*, 177–78; *Zenkō*, 294). Bashō says that he and Sora made their way

> past Narugo Hot Springs to the Barrier of Shitomae, then crossing the mountains to Dewa Province. Because there are so few travelers on this route, the barrier guards treated us with great suspicion, and we were let through only after much delay. We struggled up a steep mountain trail and, finding that the day had grown dark, stumbled into the house of a provincial border guard and asked to be given lodging for the night. A fierce rainstorm howled for three days, keeping us in those worthless lodgings in the mountains.

Fleas and lice
with the sound of horses pissing
right by my pillow.

Bashō often reveals a grumpy or displeased reaction to ill treatment. But
the evidence available shows that things were by no means so bad. (See
fig. 20.) What is he up to?

Three matters are involved. One is that haikai requires a shift in
tone from the grandeur of Hiraizumi and the Temple of Light. In haikai
terms, Hiraizumi is a splendid design-stanza, and the Shitomae Barrier
episode that follows an extreme ground-stanza. Variety is crucial. There
is a second matter. Bashō exploits one of the several place-names he
mentions. But it is extraordinary that from the many barrier points
established around the country, he should select Shitomae no Seki and
emphasize that it means "before-pissing barrier," all in a manner as
literal as with Matsushima and several other locations. Hiraizumi
names great names. It names a temple whose literal meaning Bashō
seizes on. But why name and poetically literalize Shitomae no Seki?
Why does he not choose Hiraizumi ("broad spring head") to literalize
instead? The answer has been given in principle: haikai change. Here its
effects include an unusually low example of haikai comedy. Another,
milder way of putting it is that the sudden descent from Hiraizumi
underscores the importance to haikai of the principle of fluctuating
impressiveness. Yet another consideration shows the true greatness of
Bashō: his real and imagined misery in filth is the counterpart of the
unburied corpses of common soldiers at Hiraizumi. One need not share
Bashō's Buddhist outlook to appreciate the close relation of greatness
and degradation in the human estate.

The example of the Hiraizumi–Shitomae no Seki sequence also
inescapably shows that Bashō was working with a poetics of place-
names. Of course Western place-names may be evocative. Goethe's love
of Italy is well known. It is richly implied in the familiar query from the
song, "Kennst du das Land wo die Citronen blüh'n?" and famously
expressed by his remark, that spelled backward, Rome becomes love
(Roma, amor). Yet there is a difference.

Bashō wrote in a tradition sometimes holding that less means
more, a tradition requiring "Neither those bright blooms nor colored
leaves"—not the best the world offers. Or, to take that line in its context:

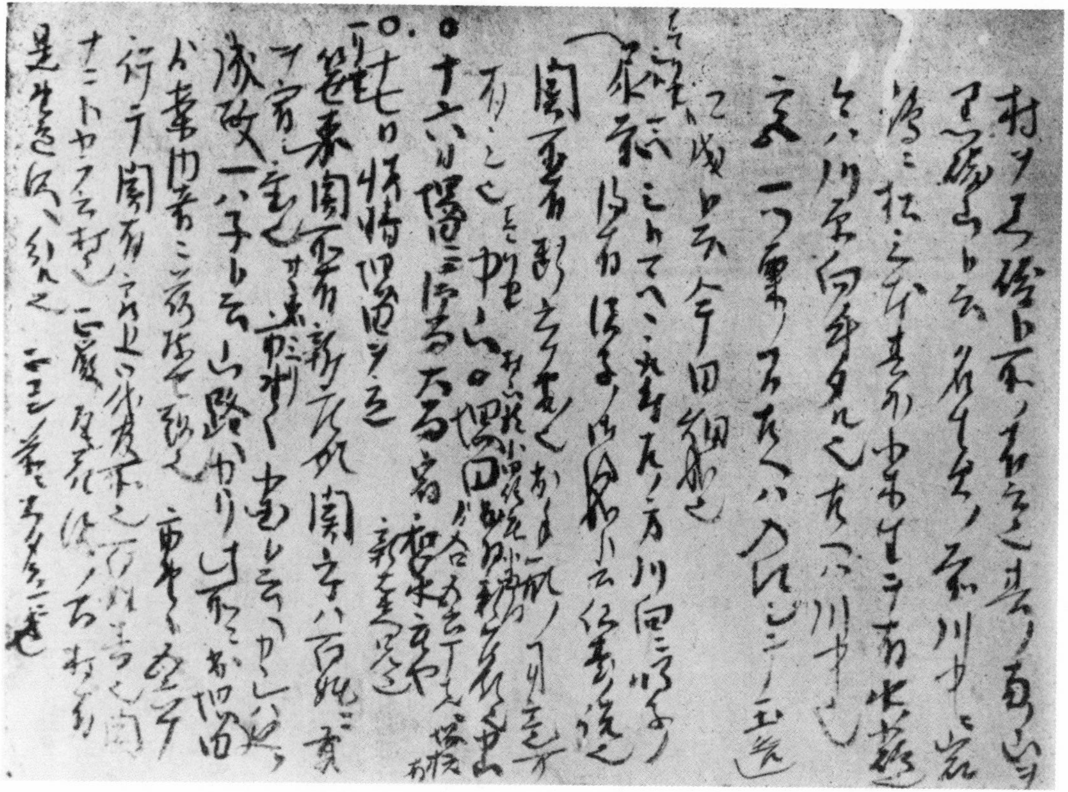

Fig. 20. Sora's diary, Month V, 15–17. His account of Shitomae no Seki tells of much less squalor than Bashō describes.

Gazing wide and far
Neither those bright blooms nor colored leaves
   Are seen or needed.
Upon the inlet's rush-thatched huts
Closes the dark of autumn dusk.[32]

As we have observed before, however, Monk Saigyō was Bashō's favorite waka poet, and indeed he has poems like this winter one (*Shinkokinshū*, 6:625) that more closely resembles Bashō's poetry in use of place-names.

In Tsu Province,
Naniwa with all its springtime
   Is now no more than dream!
The reeds' frost-withered leaves
Show how the winds have blown their course.

Bashō may well have thought, with some modern critics, that Saigyō had history in mind: the vanished grandeur of a former capital. We ought to recall, as a last precedent, stanzas 69–70 from Bashō's favorite renga poet, Sōgi:

I long to see you
oh moon do not delay your rising
   bright upon the waves

after only the long autumn night
dawn breaks on the Akashi shore[33]

These examples and the Hiraizumi passage show clearly that there need be no disjunction in Japanese poetry between deprivation or suffering and beauty. Bashō's account of the faint remains of Hiraizumi, of its summer grasses, and of its nearby Temple of Light is (in the original

---

32. Fujiwara Teika (1162–1241), *Shinkokinshū*, 4:363.

33. Stanzas 69 and 70 of *A Hundred Stanzas Related to "Person" by Sōgi Alone*. Sōgi deliberately leaves unclear why the speaker fails to see the moon: e.g., whether it had already set, whether the sky was overcast, or whatever. But evening was considered the most meaningful time for autumn; dawn (suggested to many an earlier poet as well by the sound of "Akashi") the most meaningful for spring. (See chap. 1 n. 31.) The meaning of time must yield here to the meaning of place.

at least) one of the high points in Japanese literature. If he had been a waka or renga poet, the passage would have added Hiraizumi to the list of places of name (nadokoro, meisho). Because he was a haikai poet, his achievement was simply ignored by the arbiters of taste in his time, a judgment that now makes no sense. The passage on Shitomae Barrier—a most remarkable "ground stanza" after the preceding "design stanza"—conveys an insight into human history that all can understand. Yet it is effected by means available only from haikai.

In fact, the more one thinks of it, the more natural that shocking Shitomae episode seems. It conforms to the rule that the meaning of a place can be derived by literalizing its name, just as with Matsushima and other places. We are returned yet again at the crucial juncture to the importance of naming. (*Naming properties* is the title of this study.) If it is not too emphatic to phrase it so, the aesthetic place of names becomes inescapable when we attend to the Japanese aesthetic of poetic place-names.

As Andō recognized, fluctuations like that between Hiraizumi and Shitomae no Seki are appropriate to the long development or breakage section, the ha, of a linked-poetry sequence. Those fluctuations will not continue in the same vein. That would contradict the very principle of variety on which they are founded.

Let us move on as the travelers themselves cross westward to the Sea of Japan side. They see beautifully described places like the temple Ryūshakuji; they go by boat down the Mogami River and visit temples in the area of Mounts Haguro and Yudono and Gassan ("moon mountain"); and back on the Mogami again, go to Sakata on the far coast. As with the journey earlier from Shirakawa no Seki to Matsushima, there is an emphasis on place and travel; the difference now lies in the importance of temples to this later stage.

We are ready for the rise in tone that comes with the description of Kisa Bay, which required a trip up the coast from Sakata (*Diaries*, 184– 85; *Zenkō*, 354–80):

> we could see a wide panorama lying before us. To the south—islands, the sea, and Mount Chōkai looming up to support the heavens and reflected below in the waters of Kisa Bay. . . . it reminds me of Matsushima, but with this difference: Matsushima carried an air of people smiling. Kisa Bay suggests rather the gloom of a frown. It is not just that it is melancholy—more than that, there

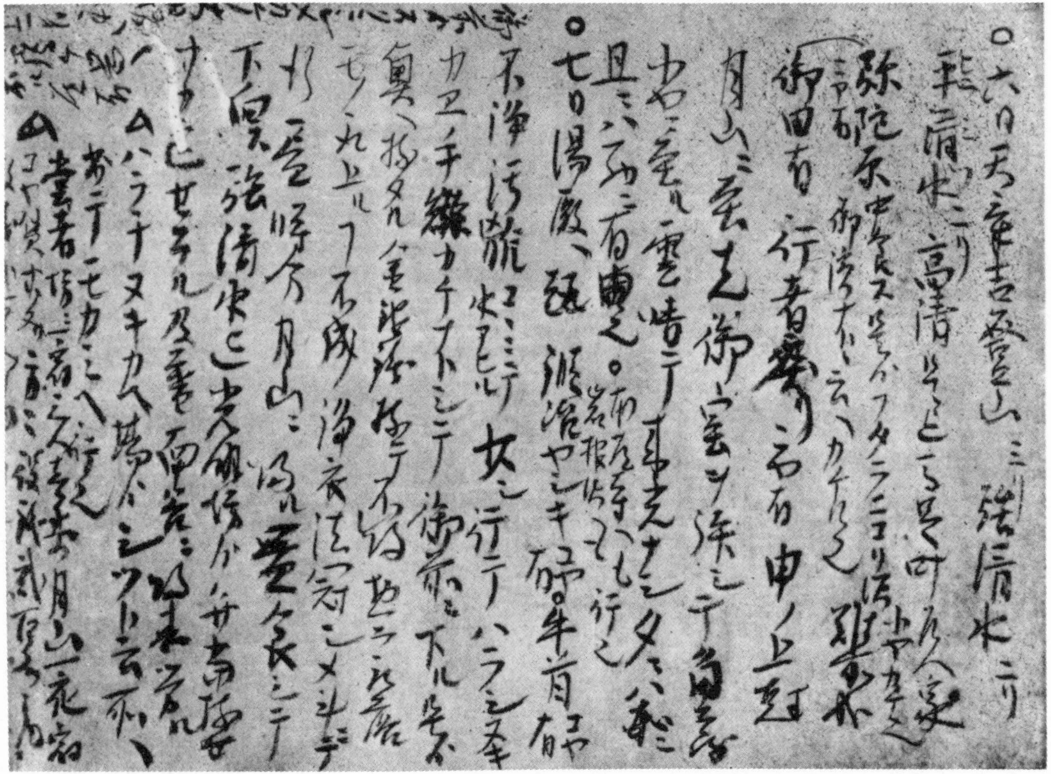

Fig. 21. Sora's diary, Month VI, 6 and 7. Like Bashō, he records the visit to Gassan and Yudono in detail.

is an impression of pain, and the effect is that of a beautiful woman whose heart is sorely troubled.

> Lovely Kisa Bay
> rain-dimmed like Xi Shi in tears
> silk trees nod in bloom.[34]

A peace offering from a defeated Chinese king to his victor, Xi Shi had a beauty thought greatest in tears. It vanquished the victor, who ignored duties as a ruler for her. That is comparison for a place of poetic name, Kisagata. And there rain defines and resolves the tensions between beauty and tears, the erotic and the political, excitement and the sleepily nodding trees. In all this the Chinese allusion has a new function. Rather than initiate what becomes decisively Japanese, as is Bashō's general practice, or serve as axis like Du Fu's couplet quoted at Hiraizumi, Xi Shi provides the focal definition of Kisa Bay. Yet that is also another way of saying Matsushima is finer.

The (explicit) comparison of Kisa Bay with Matsushima is but one kind of recollection that would not be possible in an actual haikai sequence. Another example of (implied) comparison shows that the haikai model is used by Bashō rather than he by it. Two hokku are involved, the first and the last in the journey proper.[35] At his first stop out of Edo, Senju, Bashō had written:

Yuku haru ya	*The departing of spring*
tori naki uo no	the birds cry out regret and fish
me wa namida	have tears in their eyes.

And *The Narrow Road* ends:

Hamaguri no	Like a clam that is torn
Futami ni wakare	flesh from shell at Futami
yuku aki zo.	*the departing of autumn.*

---

34. See Ueda 1991, 257–58. Geological change has altered the once extensive oceanside panorama of Kisa Bay more extensively than any other major place named in *The Narrow Road.*

35. "The journey proper" acknowledges that the first hokku on Bashō's cottage must be disregarded for the symmetry of the first and last. But Bashō pointedly says that the second, the one involved here, "marked the beginning of the pilgrimage" (*Diaries,* 158), so discounting the earlier one affixed to the pillar of his hut.

The unusual symmetry suggests that Bashō was seeking ways to control an account teeming in detail.

These and other literary qualities can be understood by Bashō's strong insistence on including stanzas on love (koi) in the development section of his haikai.[36] Once that emphasis becomes our concern, we see that, after all (and in addition), the Kisa Bay episode conforms to Bashō's normal pattern of using Chinese elements to lead into Japanese. Love is far from the sole concern from Kisa Bay to Kanazawa, but it is an important one. Only knowledge of haikai practice makes Bashō's artistry understandable.

We may start with the gloomy love of Kisa Bay, that of "a beautiful [Chinese] woman whose heart is sorely troubled" (*Diaries*, 185). Bashō also records that at Kisa Bay, Sora composed a hokku on nesting ospreys as representatives of plighted love (*Diaries*, 186; *Zenkō*, 374–78).

> Waves cannot damage
> what has been pledged to hold fast
> the nest of the ospreys.

This hokku has caused discussion from Bashō's time to the present: it designates no season. The best explanation is provided in *Kyorai's Notes* (*Kyoraishō, Taisei*, 500). Kyorai replies to a question about the absence of a season in a hokku: "The Late Master said, 'Hokku as well [as "ordinary" stanzas, hiraku] are not restricted to the four seasons, for there are admirable hokku featuring not a season but love, travel, places of name, parting, etc.'"[37] The hokku seems to be defiantly about love. Defiant, because involving animals and love fulfillment. About love because of its position and the diction of pledging ("chigiri arite ya").

In the ensuing passage of *The Narrow Road*, Bashō composes two poems on his way south toward the Ichiburi Barrier bound for Kanazawa, Fukui, and finally Ōgaki. One of these hokku is set on the eve of the Tanabata Festival. That involves a legend connected with VII.7.

---

36. See the important discussion, "Koi no Ku" ("Love Stanzas") by Andō 1974, 167–78. Love stanzas often appear in renga linked poetry where, as the counterpart of spring and autumn, they must run at least three stanzas. They almost disappear from sequences by haikai poets of other schools; even in Bashō's practice the run is usually no more than two. See *Taisei*, 625.

37. For amplification of my reasoning, see Andō 1974, 167–85.

Only once a year could the celestial Herd Boy (the star Altair) cross the River of Heaven (the Milky Way) to spend the night with his beloved Weaver Girl (the star Vega). Bashō wrote a hokku (*Diaries*, 186) in a style of straightforward generalization difficult to translate.

> First month of autumn
> the night of its sixth day is not
> like usual nights.

It is not clear to me whether the awareness is that of the waiting woman, of her lover about to journey, of the poet, or of all combined. But in terms of waka love topics, the Kisa Bay description suggests resentful love (uramu koi); the osprey hokku plighted love (chigiru koi); and this Tanabata poem waiting love (matsu koi) with suggestions of consummating love (au koi).

After a stretch of road that Bashō describes as exhausting, the travelers reach the Ichiburi Barrier and engage lodging. As has been said earlier, this episode excited special comment when Sora's *Diary* was recovered.

> I was so tired that I searched out a pillow and lay down as soon as I could. Two young women were talking, however, in the next room but one, toward the front of the building. Mingled with their voices was that of an old man, and the story they told revealed that the women were from Niigata in Echigo Province, and that they were prostitutes.

The next morning the sorrowful young women approach Bashō and Sora for permission to follow them to Ise. Bashō explains that he and Sora wander out of the way as well as in it and that other company would be more suitable. That leads to his hokku on the bush clover and moon, and the comment: "I recited the verses to Sora, who set them down in his diary" (*Diaries*, 187–88; *Zenkō*, 389–95). Of course we know that the episode is fictional, and its version of love is certainly one showing how far haikai change can alter received ideas.

As in the development section of a haikai sequence, so here the sequence of love episodes is of course interspersed with other matters. A crucial example is Sora's falling ill and hurrying ahead for treatment.

Fig. 22. Bashō's visit to Tōsai's hut in Fukui. (From Buson 1973.)

With this, we enter the fast close or kyū stage, the equivalent of the back of the final sheet. But there is a further love episode. At Fukui, Bashō searches out one Tōsai, a lesser samurai and a haikai poet of another school (*Diaries*, 194; *Zenkō*, 438–39). In this episode Bashō uses allusions to the high romance of the Yūgao story of *The Tale of Genji (Genji Monogatari)* for a comic depiction of his encounter with Tōsai's old, shabbily dressed wife. He is no more Radiant Genji than she is the tender Yūgao. This is the grand waka topic of Love (Koi) delightfully undercut by haikai change. (See Buson's depiction, fig. 22.)

The range of tone in these love episodes is quite remarkable, a wonderful illustration of the variety we look for in a linked-poetry sequence. The range of amatory experience is very great: from the history of the frowning Chinese beauty, to the conjugal ospreys, to the eve of the Seventh Night, to the prostitutes at Ichiburi, and at last to the self-styled Old Man's replay of young Genji's first great love. All are askew in one haikai fashion or another. (We should recall that Japanese koi and English love differ in sphere of application, in social and gendered coding, and in the emphasis of koi on a yearning, unrequited passion. In haikai it may include male homosexual attachments.) Yet taken together, their agitation of the development section offers a surprising degree of affirmation of a kind of experience Bashō possesses out of imagination and humanity rather than anything that Sora could record.

Aware that with the Fukui episode we are well into the fast close, we must recall that travel is the consistent subtopic and main subject of *The Narrow Road*. The shortness of the episodes and the distances covered offer a version of a fast close that anyone can understand. Suddenly we have an assembly of named, present people such as we have not encountered since the departure scene.

> Our pace quickened by going on horseback, it was not long before we entered the town of Ōgaki, where Sora had arrived from Ise and where Etsujin had also hurried in by horse. We all gathered at Jokō's house. . . . They looked upon me as if I had come back from the dead, sympathized with me for the hardships of travel, and rejoiced with me that I had come through. The strain of travel still weighed upon me. But because it was already the sixth of the Ninth Month, I resolved to get on to observe the rare ceremonies at the Great Shrines of Ise. And so, boarding a boat yet again—

Fig. 23. Bashō's welcome from disciples at Ōgaki at the end of his long journey. (From Buson 1973.)

> Like a clam that is torn
> flesh from shell at Futami
> the departing of autumn.[38]

So Bashō closes, maintaining to the end the model of a haikai sequence. The following of the model is unique in his several accounts of journeys. No other means could have demonstrated so emphatically that his *Narrow Road through the Provinces* is the journey by a haikai poet. The model is unavailable to Sora, both because it was above his ability and because his role precluded it. Johnson and Boswell had of course never heard of haikai. Because Bashō is a poet of travel as well as a traveling poet, his *Narrow Road* is a work of aestheticized experience, of art lived.

---

38. See Buson's sense of this close in figure 23. It differs somewhat from what I infer from Bashō: e.g., he does not mention receiving any massage. But that is as timelessly Japanese—and different from European preoccupations—as the baths Sora records.

What we consider art truly is art, *pace* our right worshipful friends anesthetized by religion or politics. That granted, we must also see in art arguments from design. Humble Sora has least argument because least design. Johnson's Scotland judged by England is also the world judged by Johnson. Boswell's art of conversation is designed for revelation, at which he succeeds better than he knows. Bashō's haikai and his experience are not only isometric but isobiotic with abundance, even of egoism, even in silence. For each, design argues personality, what we can understand as their psychological and moral character. And what is character in our understanding of them as individuals is ideological in cultural terms.[39] We can seek comparability in these four designs by considering the four accounters of wayfaring in their shared guise as historians.

The Motives and Ends of Four Historians

In his "Life" of Plutarch, John Dryden distinguished among kinds of history: annals or "naked history," "history properly so called," and "biography." All four of our travelers are biographers (and autobiographers).[40] In writing about largely unfamiliar people in mostly unfamiliar places, they are historians traveling into territories largely unknown to them. Both old and new attracted and repelled by turns. In seeking to understand them, we naturally bring our own selves into play.[41] We too have our ideologies, and with them our limits. Many things lie beyond our capacities, and it is common experience to find ourselves missing something important or to discover that we are convinced that we understand what we cannot explain.

Our four historians differ in their ways of presentation and engagement. To borrow Sora's title, he and Boswell write *Zuikō Nikki,* diaries by those accompanying more famous men. And they are distinguished from Bashō and Johnson by their use of daily entries. Almost all else

---

39. I must emphasize that by "ideology" I mean the complex of values, ideas, motives, and interests that animates us all, not only by their own strength but also by their mutual reinforcement and even contradiction. To make adequate sense it must be neutral in the sense of being shared by everyone and not fancied to be the perversity or guilt of others.

40. It is remarkable that autobiography should begin so early in Japan (tenth century rather than seventeenth as in England), that it should take the form of diaries, and that they should be considered literary.

41. Bashō's travel to confirm the known is not inconsistent with "The new is the Flower of haikai" (*Taisei,* 633).

seems to bespeak difference. Boswell is very full, whereas Sora writes
what we may term, paraphrasing Dryden, naked diurnals. At first
glance it might seem that Sora was devoid of motives and ends, but in
fact his motives are strong and the most easily identified.

Sora sought above all to be indispensable to Bashō and thereby to
other members of the school. He alone of the four produced more than
one account, as has been shown earlier in this chapter. A few telling
details can be added. The most important compilations recovered about
1940 are those that provide information that verifies or factually cor-
rects Bashō. These are his diaries for two journeys made with Bashō. In
each case, the first word in the title is his own name. He is an authority.

While his authority reflects Bashō's, he is not wholly self-effacing.
The manifesto, "Sora," verifies what is important to the Bashō school
and its leader. The fare may be humble, but what would not readers of
many literatures give to have a Sora to their Dante or Shakespeare? A
major value of his contribution can be formulated in terms like the
classic ones of Bertrand H. Bronson: "Boswell's Johnson," "Johnson's
Johnson," and so on. A "Sora's Johnson" or "Sora's Boswell" would go
far toward settling some disputes. Unfortunately, Sora's Sora has no
great interest.

In other words, the results differ greatly in his and Boswell's application of the principle that nothing germane should be left omitted.
Sora wished to be known as one who accompanied Bashō. His proof
was provision of assured knowledge. We must not ignore the question
of whom he wished to assure. Obviously himself, and almost as obviously Bashō, who no doubt found some use for all Sora's records in
revising *The Narrow Road*. No doubt he sought a wider readership,
including members of the Bashō school and posterity, but only as
defined in a special fashion to those who mattered in the school and
among posterity. In fact, he probably sought to supply all he possibly
could for a restricted group. As has been said earlier, Japanese literary
history abounds with examples of secret teachings. It is not easy to
identify a Western counterpart of an author ambitious to be known and
prized by a few. Alchemists and spies would qualify, but for other
reasons.

Sora has a further and perhaps ultimate end that gives definition to
features of Bashō's *Narrow Road* itself. That end is most simply termed
the glory of the Bashō school. This aim is most apparent in his "Haikai
Register of *The Narrow Road through the Provinces*" ("*Oku no Hosomichi*

Haikai Kakitome)." Here are the hai (haikai sequences) and ku (hokku) noted in his diary as composed on the journey. Often one of Bashō's hokku would provide the basis for a haikai sitting (za). The composing would be a kind of reward for those who entertained Bashō and Sora as well as a demonstration of the vitality of the school even in remote areas. It was also a source for possible selection and republication in later official publications like *The Monkey's Straw Raincoat Collection* (*Sarumino Shū*).[42]

Sora's claim as a historian was strengthened by two further compilations he included, titles that we now see to be more important than we had thought earlier. The first of those is "Reminder Notes of Famous Places in *The Narrow Road through the Provinces*" ("*Oku no Hosomichi Meishō Bibōroku*"). If the waka and renga poets had their compilations of places of poetic name, here is one for haikai. And the other, which may have seemed almost totally irrelevant, is "A Compilation of Names of Divinities according to the *Engi Shiki*" ("*Engi Shiki* Jimmyō Chōshōroku"). By going back to one of the three regnal eras of Daigo (r. 897–930), Sora showed his recognition of Bashō's opposition to the military government under which they lived. The inclusion of those largely local Shinto divinities also suggests that by worshiping at shrines, writing poems about places, and even simply showing reverent interest, Bashō (and Sora) acquired a spiritual aura for themselves and perhaps a conviction of a degree of personal freedom.

Sora has, after all, a claim to be the historian of the Bashō school (Shōfū) between 1689 and 1692. His attempts to glorify Bashō were ignored by the arbiters of taste in the age. But his ends were shared by Bashō himself and followers of the Old Master in many provinces, as well as in urban Kyoto, Osaka, Nagoya, and Edo. It was not Sora's fault that his records for promoting the school have become instead historical accounts. To the extent, and it is not small, that those records enable us to understand Bashō and his work, Sora's motives were satisfied, his ends met. And the fact that he added various compilations to his telegraphic *Nikki* shows that he was much more intellectually, historically aware than that journal suggests.

Had those records not survived, Sora would not be known. The other three travelers differ from him in being very familiar from other

---

42. In fact, *Sarumino Shū* includes a number of hokku composed by Bashō (and Sora) on the journey: nos. 97, 106, 132, 133, 138, 149, (193), 215, 221, 236 as well as from other occasions. See Miner and Odagiri 1982.

writings. Yet there is also this distinction. *The Narrow Road* occupies so important, so central, a place in Bashō's writing that if it did not exist, his stature would be appreciably diminished. The same is not true of Johnson and Boswell, both of whom are better known from more important achievements. Yet even a reader well familiar with their other work will find much in Johnson's *Journey* and Boswell's *Tour* to hold interest. And if there is no striking, otherwise unknown revelation, there are still new things to be learned from their writings.

This can be suggested by the focus of Johnson on the pastoral, the mountains, depopulation, and the desolate. By refusing comment on Edinburgh and Glasgow as superfluous and by emphasizing the Highlands, Johnson created—or delimited—a world, "The Western Islands of Scotland," that he set out to explore mentally, as he and Boswell had done by boat, horse, and on foot. That world of remote isles was to no small degree a polar opposite to what defined English experience to him: London. As his journey began through small towns north of Edinburgh toward St. Andrews, Johnson set down a short seventh paragraph in his *Journey:* "Though we were yet in the most populous part of Scotland, and at so small a distance from the capital, we met few passengers" (2).

Later, making way from Inverness to Fort Augustus, Johnson calmly regards the countryside:

> Most of this day's journey was very pleasant. . . . On the left were high and steep rocks shaded with birch, the hardy native of the North, and covered with fern or heath. On the right the limpid waters of *Lough Ness* were beating their bank, and waving their surface by a gentle agitation. Beyond them were rocks sometimes covered with verdure, and sometimes towering in horrid nakedness. Now and then we espied a little corn-field, which served to impress more strongly the general barrenness. (22)

"Through the dreariness of solitude" (27) well describes the setting of his travels. Matters did not improve, at least to Johnson's mind. He continued dutifully (not that there seems to have been an alternative), and near the end of his account he attributes to Boswell what were no doubt his own responses: they pass scenes "of such gloomy desolation" that Boswell admitted the sense of vacancy and danger (128). Boswell does not mention it. Of course there were people to meet, whether through Boswell's own offices, the reputation of his father, or the claim that Johnson's fame would excite. Johnson's prudence led him to omit a number of experiences that Boswell's far more detailed account show annoyed him. And from his *Journey* itself, we see that he felt it incumbent upon him to acknowledge hospitality with expressions of gratitude and praise. Much of his sense of what may be termed the Scots in place in 1773 must be found, therefore, largely in his generalizations and his observations on unnamed people. Here are representative excerpts from a sustained passage in his long essay inserted into "Ostig in Sky":

> The habitations of men in the *Hebrides* may be distinguished into huts and houses. By a *house*, I mean a building with one story over another; by a *hut*, a dwelling with only one floor. . . .
>
> Of the houses little can be said. They are small, and . . . the rooms are very heterogeneously filled. With want of cleanliness it were ingratitude to reproach them. The servants having been bred upon the naked earth, think every floor clean, and the quick succession of guests, perhaps not over-elegant, does not allow much time for adjusting their apartments.
>
> Huts are of many gradations: from murky dens, to commodious dwellings. . . .
>
> In pastoral countries the condition of the lowest rank of people is sufficiently wretched. . . . where flocks and corn [grain] are the only wealth, there are always more hands than work, and of that work there is little in which skill and dexterity can be much distinguished. He therefore who is born poor never can be rich. The son merely occupies the place of the father, and life knows nothing of progression or advancement.
>
> The petty tenants, and labouring peasants, live in miserable cabins, which afford them little more than shelter from the storms. The Boor [peasant] of *Norway* is said to make all his own utensils. In the *Hebrides*, whatever might be their ingenuity, the want of wood leaves them no materials. They are probably content with such accommodations as stones of different forms and sizes can afford them. (*Journey*, 83–84)

This may seem to verge on a Hobbesian state of nature. (See fig. 8.) We must recall that deep and powerful sympathy for the poor which is among Johnson's noblest moral principles. He had gone to Scotland with a long-standing desire to compare present with earlier social conditions, but for all Boswell's Scottish romance, Johnson found not so much remnants of feudalism as a society agonizing in change (Wain 1974, 303–4). To him, the ideological and historical issues turn on questions whether this social misery has been an enduring condition of life outside the two major cities of Scotland, whether it is a decline from better times, and whether there is some way out of it. He seems to answer yes to each of these questions.

> As there subsists no longer in the Islands much of that peculiar and discriminative form of life, of which the idea had delighted our imagination, we were willing to listen to such accounts of past times as would be given us. But we soon found what memorials were to be expected from an illiterate people, whose whole time is a series of distress; where every morning is labouring with expedients for the evening; and where all mental pains or pleasure arose from the dread of winter, the expectation of spring, the caprices of their Chiefs, and the motions of the neighbouring clans; where there was neither shame from ignorance, nor pride in knowledge; neither curiosity to inquire, nor vanity to communicate. (92)

The plain sense of that paragraph, especially in all but its middle section, is not readily grasped. I believe that this unusual situation implies something of an ideological crux for Johnson. He responds with full fellow-feeling to the poverty and other human misery he observes. Yet he is also confused as to its nature and possible remedies.

One of the causes is religious, a zeal that has destroyed what was once rich. Or so Johnson passionately holds. This theme is announced very early, in the second chapter, where Johnson handsomely acknowledges "the elegance of lettered hospitality" extended him and his friend on the evening of their arrival in St. Andrews. (See figs. 7 and 9.) However:

> In the morning we arose to perambulate a city, which only history shews to have once flourished, and surveyed the ruins of ancient magnificence, of which even the ruins cannot long be visible, unless some care be taken to preserve them; and where is the pleasure of preserving such mournful memorials? They have been

till very lately so much neglected, that every man carried away the stones who fancied that he wanted them.

The cathedral . . . was demolished, as is well known, in the tumult and violence of Knox's reformation. (3)

He is consistently harsher on what might be termed the Calvinist or Presbyterian Reformation in Scotland than on what he repeatedly terms "Romish."[43] On this reading of history, there had been a strong, sweet Scotland until that "tumult and violence" undid it.

But Johnson is well aware that much time had passed and many things had happened since Knox. Religious zeal and destruction may lay low a cathedral, but the widespread human misery requires attention to other causes as well. His explanation takes him into matters where he treads as softly as possible.

One of the principal ones is "the '45," the attempt by Prince Charles Edward (grandson of James II of England) to gain England by raising a Scottish army. The vain hopes ended with crushing defeat by England at the Battle of Culloden in 1746, followed by the disarming of the Scots with other measures, and most importantly to Johnson, what he regards as the economic consequences. Johnson's rather abstract narrative is also extremely concise and clear, as that earlier paragraph was not:

The inhabitants [of "the Western Islands"] were for a long time perhaps not unhappy; but their content was a muddy mixture of pride and ignorance, an indifference for pleasures which they did not know, a blind veneration for their chiefs, and a strong conviction of their own importance.

Their pride has been crushed by the heavy hand of a vindictive conqueror, whose severities have been followed by laws, which, though they cannot be called cruel, have produced much discontent, because they operate on the surface of life, and make every eye bear witness to subjection. To be compelled to a new dress has always been found painful. (*Journey*, 73–74)[44]

---

43. There is scholarly debate whether Johnson can be accurately described as a nonjuror and a Jacobite. The evidence is unclear to me.

44. Johnson alludes here to a provision in the Disarming Act of 1746 prohibiting the use of Highland dress.

The social consequences are great: "Their chiefs now deprived of
their jurisdiction, have already lost much of their influence; and as they
gradually degenerate from patriarchal rulers to rapacious landlords,
they will divest themselves of the little that remains" (74). As rents are
raised exorbitantly, use of the land becomes profitless to many tenants.
The consequence—emigration, depopulation—is one Johnson greatly
regrets and often writes of in his *Journey*. With whatever confirmation
firsthand experience of Scotland brought, much of his discussion bears
the marks of having been thought out long before this journey. Certainly he had grappled with these issues over many years as social
problems in England itself. He saw the issues in terms of the powerful
ideological factors of social justice, economics, religion, and politics,
and it is no wonder that he expressed this or that side of a question
depending on certain crucial variables.

Two important variables must be emphasized. Because of his idea
of conversation as "talking for victory," he might take almost any side
of a complex issue, something not true to any great extent of his writings. Another variable involves his historical sensitivity: what may benefit a society at one stage may be a detriment at another.

The issues were often defined in eighteenth-century England as
those of luxury, made unavoidable by debates from the age of Queen
Anne, especially by Bernard Mandeville's paradoxical formulation of
"private vices, public benefits." Against that hardheaded cynicism,
there was the much more optimistic view of benevolence associated
with the third Earl of Shaftesbury, author of *Characteristics*. Trade was a
crucial example for all sides, as were the exercise of charity, issues of
handling poverty, and the debates over the dangers of depopulation.
Johnson rejected Mandeville's cynical paradox but could not avoid the
issue. He was too pessimistic to accept Shaftesbury's bland assurance,
although he practiced charity himself in his private life. In the main, he
strongly opposed the view that luxury was a benign economic force (his
century's version of trickle-down theory), as can be seen in his periodical writings.[45] Since he was not about to simplify in any party-line

---

45. The stress on what Johnson wrote is necessary, because brief quotations of
conversations in Boswell's life have been adduced to argue that Johnson was an advocate
of luxury (Sekora 1977, 103, 110, 113). The full contexts show Johnson talking for victory
and by no means consistent. What he *wrote* is therefore decisive. See *Rambler* nos. 131, 165,
202; *Idler* 73 (Miner 1958). Also his *Dictionary* definitions of *luxury* may be compared with
those of *trade* and *commerce*.

fashion the issues of trade, his assessments of it varied. It is notable that he remains silent about his friend Goldsmith's isolation of rural enclosure as a source of social disaster. The lines he added to *The Deserted Village* identify another malign force. To Goldsmith's moral—"that states of native strength possess'd / Though very poor, may still be very blessed"—Johnson adds what may seem a non sequitur, although it offers his characteristic definitive moral generalization, which is what Goldsmith sought. We are, then, also to learn

> That trade's proud empire hastes to swift decay,
> As ocean sweeps the labour'd mole away;
> While self-dependent power can time defy,
> As rocks resist the billows and the sky. (427–30)

Although both the Neostoicism and the imagery can be traced back through seventeenth-century interpretations of Horace, the issues were very complex in their English version (Miner 1959). All the more, their application to Scotland was no simple task.

Thoughts of remedy are restricted by the very Johnsonian reflection that "No scheme of policy has, in any country, yet brought the rich and poor on equal terms into courts of judicature" (77). There is also a remarkable two-sentence (or two-period) declaration Ciceronian in its balance until it halts in a bleak Tacitean echo.

> To hinder insurrection, by driving away the people, and to govern peaceably, by having no subjects, is an expedient that argues no great profundity of politicks. To soften the obdurate, to convince the mistaken, to mollify the resentful, are worthy of a statesman; but it affords a legislator little self-applause to consider, that where there was formerly an insurrection, there is now a wilderness. (80)[46]

What remedy can be sought?

We are concerned with what have been called Johnson's "alternations of hope and fear" for the future of Scotland (Lascelless 1971,

---

46. My Roman comparisons are justified by the references to Roman history in the following two paragraphs and by the echo of the grim aphorism of Tacitus: "they make a wilderness and call it peace." Johnson seems to imply that one island, Skye, was not depopulated (130).

xxvii). These revolved in various guises in Johnson's mind: religion to politics, politics to demographic and economic problems, and thence to the possibility of remedy in what he sometimes terms trade and sometimes commerce. Boswell reports Johnson's *conversational* strictures against trade:

> 'Trade is like gaming. If a whole company are gamesters, it must cease, for there is nothing to be won. When all nations are traders, there is nothing to be gained by trade. And it will stop soonest where it is brought to the greatest perfection. Then, only proprietors of land will be great men.' (*Tour*, 193)

This rather foolish comparison testifies either to some degree of division in Johnson's mind or to that urge to talk for victory.

Whatever the defects of commerce considered in the abstract (or argued in conversation), Johnson was of a different mind in *writing* about impoverished Scotland. Highlanders may make good soldiers.

> Having little work to do, they are not willing, nor perhaps able to endure long continuance of manual labour, and are therefore considered as habitually idle.
>
> Having never been supplied with those accommodations, which life extensively diversified with trades affords, they supply their wants by very insufficient shifts, and endure many inconveniences, which a little attention would easily relieve. (*Journey*, 69)

His assessment of Scotland's present state as he saw it finely balances optimism with pessimism:

> Their ignorance grows every day less, but their knowledge is yet of little other use than to shew them their wants. They are now in the period of education, and feel the uneasiness of discipline, without yet perceiving the benefits of instruction. (74)

Against that must be set a quite different assessment that is equally Johnsonian in tone:

> That their poverty is gradually abated, cannot be mentioned among the unpleasing consequences of subjection [by England af-

ter "the '45"]. They are now acquainted with money, and the possibility of gain will by degrees make them industrious. Such is the
effect of the late regulations, that a longer journey than to the
Highlands must be taken by him whose curiosity pants for savage
virtues and barbarian grandeur. (46)

Although one might disagree about this or that (and the final
clause has often been quoted out of context), Johnson seems extraordinarily clearheaded about Scottish problems. He is not the first or the
last person, however, to find that a sober prescription of remedies of
human problems so calls on divergent values and beliefs that a solution
proves elusive and one's very approach bears contradictions. For all the
firm, and some might say dogmatic, views he took with him and his
mighty walking-stick to Scotland, he seems to have been genuinely
upset by a largely deforested landscape and places without people. We
should not wonder, after all, that his account is organized by place
rather than date, or that named places should often be interpreted in
terms of the nameless ones who dwell there.

With the exception of the humility topos in its final clause,
Johnson's last paragraph of his *Journey* seems to be as honest and genuine a summary as *any* author is capable of. Its balanced cadences no
doubt provide almost fugal canons to a modern ear, but the ideas so
poised are none the less convincing for being so finely weighed. It is
unlikely that any of us could assess so well a neighboring country from
a visit of a hundred days.

Such are the things which this journey has given me an opportunity of seeing, and such are the reflections which that sight has
raised. Having passed my time almost wholly in cities, I may have
been surprised by modes of life and appearances of nature, that are
familiar to men of wider survey and more varied conversation.
Novelty and ignorance must always be reciprocal, and I cannot but
be conscious that my thoughts on national manners, are the
thoughts of one who has seen but little. (137)

A very different historical sense animates the eager, nervous
Boswell. He is unlikely to have assumed with his friend from London
any reciprocity between novelty and ignorance. If he shared nothing
else with Milton, it was desire for a "new aquist." It is not difficult to

imagine him waking in the morning and, if he had not drunk too much the night before, telling himself, "This is October 4. I must go at once to see what the day promises for my diary and remember to ask Mr. Johnson . . ." His curiosity is persistent, his interest in others constant, and his perplexity about himself so well founded that it is difficult to identify in him the originating consistencies of mind and character that make our other travelers recognizable. At this distance, we would not wish him to be anything other than his protean self. But at any distance, he is a human entity courting all-too-simple or all-too-confusing summary.

His driven inquisitiveness makes him the ideological telos of his *Tour,* and yet his account creates Johnson as the chief object of display and the areas visited in Scotland the efficient cause. Moreover, like Sora, he finds time—or at least dates—a necessity to his definition of his understanding, which, unlike Sora's, is bountifully literary. To Sora, the days are not Bashō's travelers of the centuries but a means of isolating and preserving facts. To Johnson, the journey is a succession of named places securely connectable by means of his own settled convictions.[47] To Boswell, time is a continuously experienced syntax with "Mr. Johnson" the subject, a place for the adverb, quotation the conspicuous element, and *said* the verb declaring Boswell's presence as narrator and impresario in that wonderfully odd "co-partnery."

Close readers of Boswell's "syntax" conclude that it is a special medium for an exceptional author. He possesses unusual intelligence of a kind at once ceaselessly active and yet curiously passive or impressionable. Taking on the color of his environment, he seems to change, to reveal surprising new features of personality and yet, for all that mercurial flux, neither to change nor to grow. It is extremely difficult therefore to isolate kinds of thought that make up his ideology. In lieu of an ability like his to bring people to life, the approach here will be to discuss his method first, his characterization of others next, and his versions of himself last.

---

47. There are many reasons to know that the self-sufficient, secure Johnson that Boswell depicts did not truly exist. There are also passages showing that Boswell appreciated that and allowed for contradictions in his older friend. But these are matters either off stage or necessary for Boswell to minimize if he is to understand himself and present Johnson to the public.

It will be recalled that the version dealt with here is neither the version first published nor simply raw materials.[48] In fact, what he produced on the way seems to have been far less developed than one had thought—which is another way of saying that the continuousness and the liveliness of his journal are, to a surprising extent, the product of an elastically later art. There is that erroneous impression of mine that dialogue predominates. There really is far less than my mind is convinced there is. From what others write and say it seems that my erroneous impression is shared.

As we have seen earlier, Boswell's *Tour* has a title making clear that it has three subjects: the Hebrides and Scotland more generally, Johnson, and himself. Of these three, Johnson is central, and Boswell's version of his friend is so distinctive that we ought to recall his well known claim made for special suitability to write his *Life* of Johnson: "In the progress of time, when my mind was, as it were, strongly impregnated with the Johnsonian aether, I could, with much more facility and exactness, carry in my memory and commit to paper the exuberant Variety of his wisdom and wit" (Clingham 1992, 1765). Although he does once report (*Tour*, 135) being six days behind in what we may call the first stage of forming a narration from notes, it is not clear what the version was.

Boswell must have been a more exact and prodigiously quick writer than we easily conceive. With his violent prejudice against the Presbyterian clergy, Johnson could declare (215) of one example: "'There is Macaulay—the most ignorant booby and the grossest bastard.' (Coll says Mr. Johnson said Macaulay was as obstinate as a mule and as ignorant as bull, but I do not recollect this.)" Since Boswell's version was apparently approved by Johnson, it must be right. Boswell's boast is in fact to be "most scrupulously exact" (245). His most serious question about his method is one of scale: "Perhaps I put down too many things in this Journal" (165). The world has not thought so, although Malone piloted Boswell's vessel through safer channels by cutting passages like that on Macaulay.

Boswell does not rely solely on a memory impregnated by the Johnsonian ether. He includes letters and other documentary evidence that testifies to his historical claim. He also does not rely on chronology.

---

48. On Boswell's methods, his series of versions, and the role of Edmond Malone, see *Tour*, preface, vii–xi, 345 n. 1, and 357–58 n. 2.

His acknowledgment of the fact is embedded in a passage of considerable interest. He writes first of Johnson and himself; later he introduces
his Bohemian servant, Joseph Ritter.

> We had long talked of "roving among the Hebrides." It was curious
> to repeat the words previously used, and which had impressed our
> imaginations by frequent use; and then to feel how the immediate
> impression from actually roving differed from the one in fancy, or
> agreed with it. It will be curious too, to perceive how the impres-
> sion made by reading this my Journal some years after our roving
> will affect the mind, when compared with the recollection of what
> was felt at the time. Mr. Johnson said I should read my Journal
> about every three years. Joseph made a very good observation
> [about the effect of subsequent readings of the journal]. "Your jour-
> ney," said he, "will always be more agreeable to you."
>   I often do not observe chronology, for fear of losing a thing by
> waiting till I can put it in its exact place. (328–29)

Boswell and Johnson are not the first, or last, to observe the pleasures of
later reading of experiences recorded at the time. It is all the more
curious that Johnson's, Joseph's, and even his own appear to come to
him as a surprise. The implication is that he had a different motivation.
    I can only think that end was to arrest the flow of experience in
order to set it down, to keep a journal in order to make clear, *almost at the
very time of happening,* what it was that had been said and done. The
truly grave danger, which he expresses as a "fear," is that of "losing a
thing" by the effort to ensure that the event is tied to its *time* of occurrence. Boswell knew intuitively and showed actively what has been
repeatedly stressed here: the descending order of importance in the
three constituents of narrative, people, places, and times. He did not so
much know as require the names of the first two to assure himself of his
own presence. He also found the great usefulness of banking, as it were,
a good sum of Johnson's pronouncements and characteristic gestures to
give interest to future moments otherwise lacking in claim. One sentence says it well: "Let me now go back and glean Johnsoniana" (307).
    After Johnson, the people who touch Boswell most deeply are of
course his family, which is to say his wife and his father. A wiser head
than mine—or James Boswell's—is required to understand just what

Boswell felt concerning them.[49] But it is clear that he knew what he ought to feel, and there are intermittent references to "my dear wife" until he and Johnson approach Auchinleck, when his altogether justified apprehensions of an explosion between his strongly opinionated friend and father put other thoughts and names from his mind. While still in the Hebrides, he sets down a truly extraordinary passage on a gloomy October day after a night of poor sleep in very poor quarters. Joseph enters his bedroom and draws the curtains.

> I would have risen, but was afraid to put my hand anywhere in the dark, for fear of spiders, or some uncleanly circumstance of sloth. I was not well at all, but I got up, sat down to my Journal, and soon was better. . . . I wrote to my dear wife. It was a relief to me to think that she would hear of me, though I could not hear of her till I got to Inveraray. I also wrote to my father. I told him that . . . I had been gloomy from having dreamt that I had lost him. I hoped in God he was well, and longed much to see him.

One can only speculate what thoughts went through the mind of the elder Boswell on reading of such a dream, a hope, and longing. Boswell goes on:

> It gives me pain to consider that there is much doubt if he has now that warm affection for me he once had, and which I have for him

and so on in like piteously pious vein (303–4).

What has been said, and is so evidently true for Boswell on Johnson, is true also for him on others: "Writing Johnson's story is also a means of writing Boswell's own" (Clingham 1992, 1766). In fact, although it is difficult to think of another biographer as skilled as Boswell, it is yet more difficult to think of another biographical travel account that is so thoroughly, continuously, and yet as it were accidentally autobiographical. Early in his *Journal* Boswell puts the matter in reverse terms: "I beg it may be understood that I insert my own letters, as I relate my own sayings, rather as keys to what is valuable belonging to others than for their own sake" (6). Four pages later, he has that sen-

---

49. Boswell did all he could to prevent trouble between his father and Johnson, but there was one quarrel culminating in "a retort [by Johnson], which I forbear to mention." And this is in our pre-Malone version (*Tour*, 376).

tence beginning a paragraph on himself, "I am, I flatter myself, completely a citizen of the world."[50] That is less a key to himself than is that
encomium on himself he inserts some pages later (32–33).

Is it not astonishingly difficult—and is the difficulty not truly
significant—to discover in Boswell's copious writings an ironic
passage?

Guile is another, almost childish matter, so transparent is it. One
might say that Boswell is self-deceived, but it is yet more likely that he
regarded himself with unending interest, feeling at every moment that
he was, or earnestly wished to be, sincere. Still, he suffered (and perhaps occasionally enjoyed) bewilderment over what and who he was. If
to know oneself is highest wisdom, Boswell cannot be faulted for failure
to try. But all the resources failed, and they were the resources of a
highly gifted person.

His most promising resource was his ability to capture the personalities of others—in hopes of defining thereby his own. Had he been
successful in this most difficult of ideological explorations, the success
would have carried over from sessions of talk with Johnson and others
to sessions alone. Incidents referred to earlier show that it is extraordinarily brave of Boswell to risk describing scenes by himself. The risk
is worth every moment for the reader, and one can only hope that his
reading and preaching in the ruins of Iona gave him later satisfaction.
The very mystery of his personality—the source of his profoundest
bafflement—is what makes him so fascinating. In other words we may
say that the center of his ideology is a need to define a person, to learn
what "my wife" or "Mr. Johnson" means. What is it that a given person's name signifies? And what in particular is meant by his altogether
natural use of the first-person singular?

By now it can be no cause for surprise that we learn more about his
understanding of others when he reveals himself. We see this in the
passage next quoted. It begins with the names of those others in a given
context that Boswell sought to know. There is a kind of charity in his
honoring of the differing individualities of others. As the passage continues, and as Boswell is led to part from company, the simplifications
and subtractions of the world and people about him lead inevitably to a

---

50. P. 10. Boswell's remark is less self-flattery than self-deception. Using French
models, a tradition going back to Plato, and the device of an oriental philosopher, Goldsmith had created for his periodical, *The Citizen of the World*, an observer detached from
the scene commented on. Boswell disengaged is not Boswell at all.

loneness in which he can only encounter himself. Fascinating enough, although at such moments we are most fully convinced that we understand him best, we are most acutely aware that we do not know whether he understood himself.

It was Sunday, 17 October 1773. Our travelers are to be found at Inchkenneth with the family of Sir Allan Maclean, and in the evening there was Anglican worship.

> Miss Maclean read the evening service with a beautiful decency. We read the responses and other parts that congregations read. . . . Mr. Johnson pointed out to her some prayer, which she read. After all, she and her sister sung the Hymn on the Nativity of our Saviour. It was the 19th Sunday after Trinity. I shall ever remember it. . . . I was truly pious.
>
> I walked out in the dark to the cross, knelt before it, and holding it with both my hands, I prayed with strong devotion, while I had before me the image of that on which my Saviour died for the sins of the world. . . . I felt a kind of pleasing awful [awed] confusion. I was for going into the chapel; but a tremor seized me for ghosts, and I hastened back to the house. It was exceeding dark, and in my timorous hurry I stepped suddenly into a hollow place, and strained a sinew on my right foot. It was painful a while; but rubbing it with rum and vinegar cured it by next day at breakfast. (317)

"In the dark to the cross . . . that on which my Saviour died . . . ghosts . . . rum and vinegar." That is true Boswell, only Boswell, and as close to complete Boswell as we are likely to get.

The printed version of this incident appeared without all following in the new paragraph ("I walked out into the dark . . ."). That sanitizes Boswell, making him harder yet to understand. It also deprives him of much of that rare satisfaction he provides us: the conviction that we understand a complex personality better than its possessor did. By definition, none of us is able to say whether or not we have come upon an allegory of ourselves.

Sora's ambitions for his accounts of travel with Bashō achieve a degree of completeness not attained by the other three writers we are considering. Although that completeness serves his purposes, it is more an obstacle than an aid to literary art. Johnson could have said far more from that extraordinary memory, but it was less his indolence than his sense of purpose achieved that led him to his last word, "Finis." Boswell's end, to understand himself in understanding others, was curiously realized—if but for the reader—in its very frustration. His journal of the journey he shared with Johnson teems with information whose abundance testifies to a fulfilled design beginning and ending in Edinburgh. That design is complete in a strange closure. To paraphrase the title of the last chapter of Johnson's *Rasselas*, Boswell has perfectly realized "The End, in Which the Ends Are Not Won." He might as well go to catch a falling star as to find a single self.

Bashō's *Narrow Road* is the shortest and the most successful in numerous ways, including realization of the ends of his traveling through remote back country. Yet in spite of living on another five years, presumably following his habitual compulsion to revise, he seems to have felt the work unfinished, and it was published only posthumously. What he would have revised further, cut, or added may be left to each of us to guess. Would it be more fictionalizing? Closer adherence to the design of a poetic sequence? Yet more skillfully crafted prose? More social criticism, or more covering of his tracks? Certainty does not exist in those and some other matters connected with his *Narrow Road*. And yet his ends are the most fully realized.

One of the great reasons for Bashō's success is his inheritance of a poetics of place and an aesthetics of travel. The places visited and the travel to them could even be fitted into the counterpart of a linked-poetry sequence. Various kinds of aestheticizing enabled him to make factuality into high art, even when it accommodated, or yielded to, fiction—even indeed when it dwelt on the lowest or most prosaic matters. One may say, in short, that if there is an art of naming, he is its master.

In the remainder of this discussion of our travelers, my own end will be elucidation of the three major tensions, perhaps negations or poisings, that inform *The Narrow Road* along with the means by which Bashō resolved what often seem divergences, shifts, or things hidden from mortal sight.

We must begin farther back, with renewed attention to what travel meant to Bashō. He knew the conventions that have been discussed (e.g., never to the capital), and he was also familiar with a major version, or definition, of it in Japanese literature from earliest times, through poetry, narrative, and drama, and into modern literature. This version is the michiyuki. The *michi* is the same word as in *Oku no Hosomichi*, "the narrow *road* through the provinces." The *yuki* is (in this combination) a nominalized form of the verb *yuku*, meaning "go." The road-going involves various people but shares definition by specified place-names. Organized as it is by the succession of places visited, Johnson's *Journey* is more obviously a michiyuki than are Sora's diary (his *Nikki*) or Boswell's *Tour*, which are ordered by date. Of course that is what the titles chosen suggest.

Bashō's title significantly differs, as we now realize. So indeed does his account, although that makes more explicit use of named places than of named times. The thickly strewn names include places not visited but bypassed: for example, Kasajima (*Diaries*, 168–69; *Zenkō*, 216). We also recall that the names include those that Bashō takes literally, as in the following: "Today we passed the most trying part of our north-country journey, going through dangerous places with such horrible names as Abandoned Parents, Abandoned Children, Excluded Dog, and Rejected Horse" (*Diaries*, 187; *Zenkō*, 389). In the michiyuki shortly after the opening of a nō, the names may be equally evocative but beautiful in association or sound. We need to inquire into this aspect of *The Narrow Road*, because although it contains many brief michiyuki, as the passage just quoted shows, it is also a michiyuki as a whole.

The obvious issue is what a michiyuki conveys, and to decide that for Bashō two explanations are necessary, even if they seem contradictory. According to one explanation, a fundamental Japanese concept of temporal life (and in particular of movement through it) is a spatial crossing what might be termed the threshold from life to death.[51] Evidence for this explanation dates from earliest literature down to (and beyond) lovers' going to double suicides in the plays of Bashō's contemporary, Chikamatsu Monzaemon (1653–1724). For that matter, one need only read again the opening of *The Narrow Road*. A second explanation is less obvious because it lacks a counterpart in our literature. This view holds that places—or, more properly the divinities of places—impart spiritual power to the visitor. Behind this view—which is reflected, for example, in the michiyuki of nō—there is a Shinto, animist belief in a spiritual presence to every location. It also matters that Japanese held to a near heresy in the broad application of the Buddha's vow to make enlightenment available to all sentient crea-

---

51. See the persuasive study by Nakanishi Susumu in Miner 1985, 106–29.

tures. The extreme view is expressed in the declaration, "The plants, the trees, and the earth itself will all attain Buddhahood." Assumptions of this kind lie behind the frequent visits to Yoshino by Jitō (r. 690–97) to ensure her longevity and physical well-being. They also account for the Hananomoto renga poets composing linked poetry (and of people still carrying on) under cherry trees in bloom. It accounts for visits (mōde) to shrine or temple.[52] It is no wonder that Sora set forth his list of divinities or that so much of *The Narrow Road* is devoted to visiting holy sites.

The figurative or extended meanings of *michi* (or "road") include conceptions of virtue, of vocation, and of religious or philosophical "ways." So the character for *michi* read in Sinified fashion as -tō or -dō gives us Shintō (the way of the divinities), butsudō (the way of the buddhas), and so forth.[53] In our present context, however, the further associations of *yuku* are more important. They include departure, naturally enough, and death. It will be recalled that Bashō's first hokku on the road begins with a line on spring's departure ("Yuku haru ya") and his final hokku ends with an exclamatory line on fall's departure ("yuku aki zo"). Then there is Sora's hokku written on departing from Bashō to get medical treatment:

Yukiyukite	Going, going on
taurete fusu to mo	even to collapse and death
hagi no hara	in a bush clover field

By itself, the second line means something closer to "even to collapse and lying," but the stress of the repeated "going" conveys the sense of death. This would be just an interesting touch or a mere coincidence, perhaps, but in fact what Sora wrote has been doctored, and most likely by Bashō. Both in Sora's "Haikai Register" published in his *Nikki* and in the hokku section of the premier Bashō school haikai collection,

---

52. Most of this detail I have taken in one fashion or another from Konishi Jin'ichi, whether in conversation or writings. As for writings, see Konishi 1984, 338–40 on Jitō; and index, s.v., "kotodama" on word magic. And in Konishi 1991, see 425–26 on "Beneath the Cherry Trees" (Hananomoto) renga. Given human nature, none of this is inconsistent with getting drunk under falling cherry petals or showing off a beautiful kimono on the visit to shrine or temple.

53. On michi as virtue or as religious in meaning, see any Japanese dictionary. On michi as vocation, see Konishi 1991, who regards the conception as the major ideological element in medieval Japanese literature. Of course the literal sense is present throughout the journey of *The Narrow Road*, as in the foul roads near Kasajima or that Echigo road with the hazardous names (*Diaries*, 168–69, 186–87; *Zenkō*, 216, 380, and 389).

Sarumino Shū, Sora's first line reads differently: "Izuku ni ka," resulting in something like

> Where will it be
> that though I collapse I shall lie
> in a bush clover field.

Bashō clearly emphasizes in verse the mortal possibilities of the michiyuki. His prose varies more in tone. After some further consideration of the neglected comedy of *The Narrow Road,* it will be the turn of another, graver ideological feature, the political.

Haikai itself bore associations of the comic from its introduction as a category for some poems in the *Kokinshū.*[54] Sometimes Bashō's comedy is directed at others, as when at the Temple Zenshōji he shows the young monks clamoring for him to write them hokku. He knows Zen temple customs, and he protests—albeit in a hokku—that he has already done his service in sweeping some of the temple ground (*Diaries,* 192; *Zenkō,* 427). Sometimes the comedy is more wholly directed at himself. At Asakayama, for example, he depicts himself as one fixated on seeing a kind of iris (hanakatsumi or katsumi) generally called blue flags by gardeners: so around he goes, from marsh to person—"Blue flags? Where are the blue flags?"—until he discovers it is sunset (*Diaries,* 166; *Zenkō,* 195).

Among the lengthier comic scenes is that one in Fukui mentioned earlier (*Diaries,* 194; *Zenkō,* 438–39). It is carefully built up to resemble the initial episode in the first great love of the Radiant Genji, the youngish woman known as Yūgao ("evening face," a gourd flower). In search of a samurai poet, Tōsai, Bashō's inquiries take him to

> a shabby little structure but delightfully overgrown with moon-
> flowers and gourd vines, its entrance all but hidden by a profusion
> of cockscomb and broom trees. I said to myself, "This *has* to be the
> place." I knocked at the entrance, and there appeared a woman of
> the most ragged appearance. "Where do you come from, Your

---

54. Kuriyama 1963, 12–18; see *Kokinshū* Scroll 19. Bashō's haikai developed from not only standard, serious (ushin) renga but also nonstandard, playful (mushin) renga; anyone who has attempted to compose in Japanese both renga and haikai knows what a straitened, narrow path Bashō-style haikai traversed. Bashō's balance, or tension, is exceedingly difficult to sustain. Critical focus on one quality (the comic, the religious, etc.) distorts, conceals Bashō's tonal variety, and neglects his political criticism.

Reverence?" she asked. "My husband has gone to the place of Mr. What-ever-it-was nearby. If you want to speak with him, you had best inquire there." Her manner suggested that she was Tōsai's wife.

Thinking that such beauty in an unpromising place was like some tale of old . . . (*Diaries*, 194; *Zenkō*, 438-44)

The gourd vines growing about a building as dilapidated as Yūgao's are in fact yūgao vines, and "some tale of old" is an echo from the chapter.[55] There is other allusive detail. The broom trees (to use the translators' term), refer to "Hahakigi," the title of the second chapter of *The Tale of Genji*, in which young men gather on a rainy night to discuss the various kinds of women with whom one may have amorous relation. In this delightful, affectionate parody, we have, instead of Radiant Genji, the self-styled Old Man; instead of the tenderly amorous Yūgao, Tōsai's shabbily dressed wife who, far from inviting him in with a poem and a gourd flower, sends him off to her husband elsewhere in the neighborhood (albeit with a polite verb used for those of highest rank in *The Tale of Genji*). The light comic tone is wonderfully sustained by just the right amount of the ludicrous.

Among the many differences between Bashō and Boswell there is one bearing on the use of dialogue. In Boswell, those spoken passages seem the most natural. In Bashō, however, they are frequently a sign of something unusual and often of comedy, whether with the prostitutes at Ichiburi Barrier, the blue flags at Asaka Hill, or the old wife of Tōsai in Fukui. Dialogue (but not quotation of writing) is also often a sign that Bashō is fictionalizing.

The result is multiple significance, as in the first passage of dialogue in *The Narrow Road*, in which that innkeeper at Nikkō has the kindness to inform our travelers that he is an avatar of the Buddha. "I am Buddha Gozaemon," he says. "People call me so, because I am honest down to the last item. Will you not spend a night on your travels at my inn?" (*Diaries*, 159; *Zenkō*, 110). As we saw in an earlier chapter, Bashō here divides into two days what happened as one, to avoid persecution. His point is that Gozaemon is as much—that is not at all—

---

55. Among other echoes, there is, "In what year was it that he came to visit me in Edo?" The Japanese of the opening clause, "Izure no toshi ni ka," differs but by a similar word from the opening phrase of *The Tale of Genji*, "Izure no ôontoki ni ka" ("In what reign was it?").

an avatar (gongen) as is the official gongensama enshrined at Nikkō: Tokugawa Ieyasu, founder of the Edo regime.

The necessarily veiled criticism of the repressive regime can be found again in the Hiraizumi episode and elsewhere in the Bashō oeuvre. But for an example very different in tone from the bright sun of Nikkō summer, there is a passage whose context we have considered only in part, a passage sandwiching a hokku nobody seems to remember with one everybody seems to know.

It will be recalled that after what he terms the most trying day of travel, Bashō arrives at Ichiburi Barrier, done in by exertion, heat, and wet weather. As usual when he feels under strain, he falls ill. At this point we get a curious mélange, only part of which need claim our present attention:

> my illness comes on again and I leave things unrecorded.
>
> > First month of autumn—
> > this eve of the Seventh-Night Festival
> > is not like other nights.
> >
> > The raging ocean—
> > streaming over to Sado Island,
> > the River of Heaven.

Then, with another haikai gap like that between the two hokku:

> Today we traverse Disowned Parents, Disowned Children, Excluded Dog, Rejected Horse—one of the most trying parts of our north country journey, and searching out a pillow to lie down as soon as I could . . . (Diaries, 186–87; Zenkō, 381, 389)

Bashō suffered from both stomach cramps and hemorrhoids. We do not know which afflicted him in that distant back country. For that matter, it is not altogether certain that he fell ill, since Sora's relatively ample entries for the sixth and seventh in his Nikki do not mention it. He also does not mention those highly peculiar place-names.

Sora does show, however, that the two seemingly ill-assorted hokku were in fact written at different times ("Haikai kakitome," Nikki, 113, 116), one in a hokku writing session, the other in a haikai session (49–50). Of course Bashō does say explicitly that he is leaving things out. But he is also implying certain things, and it is up to us to try to fathom what to ask about, what to suppose.

For the first hokku, the surest thing is a concern with the Tanabata Festival. That, it will be recalled, was the legend that on VII.7 the stellar Herd Boy crossed the River of Heaven (Amanogawa, the Milky Way) for his sole annual night with his beloved Weaver Girl. Bashō's first hokku concerns the festival; in *The Monkey's Straw Raincoat Collection*, it is followed by a second (poem 200):

> Do not peep through
> the silk tree's embracing leaves—
> the stars' lights merge.

The poem is vexed as to interpretation, but one thing at least is clear: this is not the Sado Island hokku that follows in *The Narrow Road*. In his travel account, no prose separates the two hokku, and the reader is required to infer that time passes. How much is uncertain. Sora's "Haikai kakitome" specifies that the *other* second hokku (just given) was composed on the topic "Tanabata," in that being unlike its predecessor, which was written on the eve rather than the night of the festival.

In this typical Bashōvian complex of prose and verse in literary layering or reusing, two images stand out, two images crystallized in, but not confined to, the hokku on Sado. (See too Ueda 1991, 260.) Those images are also conceptual terms of great importance. One is of roughness: the raging ocean, "*Araumi ya*," marked off from the rest by the cutting word (kireji), "ya." The other is that of light in the Milky Way or River of Heaven, "Amanogawa," pouring in its myriad stars from where Bashō stands near Niigata to Sado Island ("Sado ni yokotō"). I believe that these two imagistic and conceptual clusters connect this section to the Nikkō one—and for that matter with the Temple of Light hokku concluding the Hiraizumi passage. At Nikkō, the roughness was explicitly in the Chinese characters that once designated the place (Nikō or Futaara, "double rough") and the brightness in the Chinese characters most familiar (Nikkō, "sun's radiance"). The latter is explicit in the prose context, the former—as criticism of the bakufu—is implicit almost to the point of evasion. As a linked-poetry master, Bashō would be acutely aware of the repetition of his roughness and radiance, and his gesture is unmistakable, if not as obvious as some others in his writing.[56] He can only be obliquely criticizing the bakufu government for ill governing. If there is any doubt about his implications, they should be removed by another prose context he composed for the Sado hokku.

The Sado Island stanza was printed twice separately with practically identical prose prefaces.[57] They focus on Sado Island rather than the festival as the center of the experience:

> Certainly this island has been bounteous in gold, and from the past to the present its name has had a fine ring; but to its bounds people convicted of the gravest crimes of state have been confined, and since the name of the island is itself a misery, it gives a chill feeling, and just then when the evening moon is about to set, the surface of the sea is uncannily dark, and while one can peek through a gap in the clouds towering like mountains, in one's ears is the depressing sound of the waves:

> > The raging ocean—
> > streaming over to Sado Island
> > the River of Heaven.

Those of us who have found only majesty and beauty in this hokku have read it like a haiku, barren of context. Deprivation is what the poem conveys in context, deprivation on a cosmic as well as human scale. As for those banished there, the list includes the founder of Nichiren Buddhism, Nichiren himself, along with Abdicated Juntoku, the poetically and politically ambitious Kyōgoku Tamekanu, and that greatest figure in nō, Zeami. All were sent to their misery by bakufu earlier than the Tokugawa. In these contexts, Bashō's ensuing prose is altogether appropriate, even if it seems on first encounter that he must have made up place-names like Disowned Parents—and that perhaps he has implied by the Sado hokku more about Thwarted Lovers and yet more about Banished Sufferers.

---

56. For example, in a duo with Enomoto Kikaku (1661–1707), Bashō joins in substantially repeating the first two in the last two stanzas. See "Poetry Is What I Sell" ("Shi Akindo no Maki") in Miner and Odagiri 1982, 49, 63.

57. See *Taisei*, 352–53. Another separate prose context written for a hokku composed at Shinobuzuri has a clause bearing on this study: "I devote myself to meditations on the *famous places* in Michinoku" ("Michinoku no *nadokoronadokoro* kokoro o omoikomete"), ibid., p. 345 (stress added).

Sora's failure to mention the four places with the grim names requires explanation. We might think that Bashō has made them up. In
fact, all four have been shown to be real places on the travelers' route
southwest down the Sea of Japan coast toward Niigata. The names
appear to derive from the dangerously brief time to run safely between
successive engulfing waves crashing on the particularly rocky shore. A
moment too late and one is done for, parent or child, dog or horse. In the
context of the preceding hokku on a tumultuous sea and miserable exile
on Sado, however, the place-names take on more literal and indeed
larger significance. That is partly because Bashō reorders the succession
of villages from the actual sequence down the coast, which was Rejected Horse, Ejected Dog, Disowned Parents, Disowned Children. His
order suits Neoconfucian or, more generally, East Asian senses of descending series. From the stars of the Seventh Night Festival we move
along that dangerous, miserable coast to what is in effect Drowned
Exile. We may prefer the simplest explanation: Sora does not mention
them, because he and his Old Master did not actually travel through
them. Bashō does, because they were near their route south and too
appropriate in their literalized meanings to ignore.

The image of our human estate does not carry much hope at this
stage of *The Narrow Road*. To a degree unapproached by Johnson and
Boswell, or Sora, misery joins past and present, the heavens and the
earth, the sea and the land, the human and the animal. Many readers
will choose to recall at this point that in his prose-poem opening Bashō
had mentioned that not a few people had met death in travel. The
passage we have been considering is deliberately lower in tone. It also
reveals the crucial roles played by place. Bashō might have written of
other villages passed, and he might have recalled the okesa dance on
Sado. Places dictate names, and names places.

His choices work to other ends. Going places is defined by choice
in naming places. The implications of that for Bashō's art vary, but as
our example shows, they can be profound. In discussing the Sado
hokku (without going on to the place-names), Konishi Jin'ichi
concludes:

> The effect of ceaseless interchange between a romantic aura and
> grim gloom imparts a surpassing irony. An unthought of reversal
> of circumstances—a reversal that we sense to be not simply
> reversal—compels us to experience very strongly the inner ele-

ments pressed toward expression. This technique is born from relating stanzas in haikai sequences, and the elements set to life by
this Sado hokku are undeniably out of the ordinary. With "The
raging ocean . . ." Bashō at last ranks as the equal of Du Fu.[58]

It might be said that Bashō has set misery into a compensating
aesthetic of understanding: to understand may be to accept, especially
to a Buddhist. The acceptance is of misery, however, and in the doubled
rough of this dark stage of his account the stream of light over the
raging sea serves to reveal this world's dark place.

One further ideological element in Bashō's thought remains to be
considered. It is expressed by his paired terms, famous in Japanese
scholarship, fueki and ryūkō. According to Kyorai, Bashō introduced
this teaching about the time of *The Narrow Road* journey.[59] The usual
explanation from Bashō's disciples and from modern critics involves
ryūkō as alternation or change in successive styles practiced and incul-
cated by Bashō: from his early practice agreeable with that of the Danrin
school, thence to the sabi style for which he is most famous, and finally
to his late "light" (karumi) style. In this interpretation, fueki refers, by
contrast, to the unchanging essence of his career, through all his styles.
That interpretation is not so much wrong as superficial in the light of an
alternative explanation that is more complex, comprehensive, and
metaphysical.[60]

One of the difficulties is that much of what Bashō learned of philosophy apparently came from oral sources, and certainly much of his
thought was communicated so. From various reports, however, it is
clear that certain terms recur. The terms (including ryūkō and fueki)
coincide with those used in certain popularizings of that brand of Neoconfucianism known in Japan as Shushigaku. That is, although fueki
and ryūkō can be traced to Chinese thinkers of the Han and Tang
dynasties, in their usage and in their context of other terms they derive
from the teaching of the Song Neoconfucianist thinker Zhu Xi (1139–

58. Konishi 1986, 331. My interpretation of the Sado hokku has been substantially
anticipated on very different thematic grounds by Konishi, 325–31, and the wonderful
comparison with Du Fu would not have occurred to me.

59. See *Kyorai's Notes* (*Kyorai Shō*), *Taisei*, 508, top column. His discussion continues
to the next page. As we shall see, there is other evidence to confirm Kyorai's dating.

60. My account is founded on Konishi 1986, 363–77 and Kuriyama 1981, 61–72,
supplemented by correspondence and conversation with Konishi. It is no simple matter,
and I reserve some features of it for the next chapter.

1200), a philosopher in high repute in the early Edo period. (There is a paradox here: in opposing official bakufu ideology, Bashō draws on one of its principle ideological sources.) An earlier contemporary, Hayashi Razan (1583–1657), offered explanations of "Shushigaku" philosophy in a number of his works, including his popular *Santaishi.*

In the *Narrow Road* Bashō mentions that on 1689.VI.3 at Mount Haguro he and Sora met Zushi (or Kondō) Zakichi. Although it is not his habit to say so in as many words, such provincial poets often entertained and accompanied them. In his *Nikki* entry for VI.3, Sora mentions their arrival at Zakichi's residence and on the fourth composing haikai. The sequence is given in his "Haikai Kakitome," where it is dated 1689.VI.4, as Bashō also dates it, giving his hokku.[61] Zakichi accompanied Bashō and Sora until they left Tsurugaoka by boat down the Mogami River, as Sora records for VI.10 (*Nikki,* 49) and as Bashō mentions without a date (*Diaries,* 183–84; *Zenkō,* 332–55). In other words, Bashō knew his host and companion well, so that Zakichi's philosophical compilation, "Seven Days of Oral Instruction," is as reliable a guide as could be hoped for and shows that in the summer of 1689 Bashō had discussed ideas that Kyorai heard only that winter.

Among the concepts discussed with Zakichi was that of ryūkō, in distinct versions: the ordinary one of fashion or popular change and the transcendent one we seek. In his *Sanzōshi,* Hattori Dohō reports Bashō explaining ryūkō in similar terms and also adding the crucial parallel term, fueki, along with a kind of tertium quid, makoto. For the moment I leave these crucial terms untranslated and unexplained while rendering other parts of Dohō's account.

> In the Master's art, there is a fueki of ten thousand generations. At a given time there is change [henka]. When these two are fully realized, their basis is single. That singleness is the makoto of high art. Not to know fueki is not to know jitsu. Fueki does not pertain to new or old, and in spite of change-ryūkō, its form well appears in makoto. . . . Also, things undergoing a thousand, ten thousand changes are the kotowari [or ri] of nature. (*Taisei,* 631)

---

61. The haikai is a kasen hachigin (thirty-six stanzas, eight poets.) After Bashō's hokku, Zakichi (under his haikai pen name, Rogan) followed with the waki and Sora with the daisan (2d and 3d stanzas).

Terms like fueki, ryūkō, makoto, ri, ki [as in kimochi], shi'i (usual modern meaning "self-will"), dō (michi), dōri (modern "just reason, reality"), and zōka (modern meaning: creation, nature) appearing in Bashō's discussion are precisely those of the Neoconfucianism explained by Razan and others. It is now necessary to try to offer definitions that will not do too great injustice to Bashō's thought.

The three crucial terms and their relation can readily be set forth. (I have tried to honor my sources, but the translations are mine.)

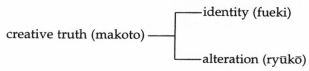

creative truth (makoto) ⎯⎯⎯⎯ identity (fueki) / alteration (ryūkō)

The terms most closely related to makoto as creative *truth* are ri (kotowari), or reason, and dōri, or just reason. The terms most closely related to makoto as *creative* truth are zōka or natural creativity and ki or inspiriting (both the Japanese and English have breath as a root meaning). Without the creative force, the truth would not come into being as a functioning entity. Fueki or identity and ryūkō or alteration are the two manifested sides or functional aspects of makoto or creative truth.

It very much appears that, about the time of his journey on the narrow road, Bashō felt a need to sort out his ideas, to order his thoughts, to produce a unified theory of his poetic practice. The first expression of that need can be found in that famous passage of a year or two before *The Narrow Road*: "The true way [in the next sentence fūga, high art] is a single thing in the waka of Saigyō, the renga of Sōgi, the painting of Sesshū, and the tea of Rikyū."[62] Can one doubt that we are invited to extend the series, adding "as also in the haikai of Bashō?"

Given the social and artistic hierarchies of seventeenth-century Japan, the combination of Bashō's precarious claims, his personal character, and his ambitions necessitated an ideology the most developed, or at least the most complex, of our four travelers. As has been suggested, at this distance one cannot help but see a degree of contradiction between his bitter criticism of the Edo regime, which based its legitimacy chiefly on Zhu Xi's Neoconfucianism, and his own use of the same resources to give validity as well as unity to his concep-

---

62. *Taisei,* 301. The term "zōka" also makes its appearance in the next sentence, so strengthening the argument.

tion of his own art. Such contradictions are not difficult to discover in other writers, however. Humble Sora undertook to justify the effort that went into *The Narrow Road*. Johnson's thoughts on religion and trade conflict at many points. And much of Boswell's appeal derives precisely from the inability we share with him to know just what his motives are. But there is a special reason to close this chapter with Bashō. His conception of the complementarity of identity (fueki) and alteration (ryūkō), and even more his idea of their generation by creative truth, will serve to give us a final view and, I hope, fuller understanding of the significance of nominal reference for literary purposes.

Chapter 5

Giving and Recalling Names

we have discovered that names have by nature a truth, and that not
everyone knows how to give a thing a name.

—Plato.

They made names and poetry.

—Randolph Henry Ash.

How, one may ask, do the Tiwi constantly manage to fabricate new
names in these circumstances?

—Claude Lévi-Strauss.

when the truth is at last revealed to them they cannot entirely dismantle all fiction from it.

—Rose Tremain.

Issues of Utility

"If it be a question of words and names" (Acts 18:15), there are sure to
be problems with the answer and, with luck, some opportunities in the
problems. We have been concerned with four versions of words and
names of people, places, and times. The names of people have been
chiefly those of Bashō and Sora, Johnson and Boswell; the names of
places have included Matsushima and Inverness, Skye and Fukui; the
names of times have ranged from breakfast and noon to the Seventh
Night and the centuries. The differences are not only of people, places,
and times. The names given differ in being proper or common nouns
(Bashō, his centuries), in being Japanese or Scottish (Matsushima and
Skye), and in being fictional or factual (Seventh Night, noon). Some of
us have seen a number of the Japanese and Scottish places, and anyone
reading this will know of breakfast and noon. It seems all very simple.
But all who ponder that question of words and names find puzzles in

the issues and bafflement over the difficulty of accounting for what seems, without reflection, so simple to understand. But reflect, consider we must, if only to sort out issues and criteria determining what it is useful to consider.

Most of us are optimistic enough to hold that some solutions are better than others. But sometimes problems are more valuable than the solutions offered and, as an example, I shall recur to my errancy concerning collections (discussed in the first chapter). Some solutions are Strong Assertions essential to progress but progressively less useful on iteration by others (e.g., Miyoshi 1974). That is because the Strong Assertion testifies to the existence of a serious issue, whereas loss of the problematic is a gelding or spaying of what was vital. It is particularly true in the humanities that no problem is quite so serious as the absence of problems. A corollary holds that some problems really are more useful than others. It is possible that somebody might say that the named people, places, and times we have been considering are all "textual effects," that Bashō and Johnson are effects of language and no more.[1] If that is a problem, it is not a useful one. One may recall Socrates: "these are not reasons but only ingenious excuses for having no reasons concerning the truth of words."[2] The sayer is subject to the logical rule that what is postulated of the species is true of its exemplars: if the textualist axiom were true, each pronouncement could be made— not by a "somebody" real—but by "textual effects," and the like. Naive realism is wisdom itself by comparison with such sophisticated nonsense. A less than humdrum version will concern us shortly.

Matters of naming are fraught with difficulty, but whether they be taken as philosophical problems or as the practice of a Boswell, they make little sense without assuming some version of realism, of reference, and of intention involving people in places and times. To assume a real world is to take on problems of how well what is known by us bears on the way things truly are, a question none of us can answer except by assuming what seems useful and observing what others seem to assume.

---

1. The view that authors are such effects seems to be the point of Morris 1986. Morris writes, for example, that Ono no Komachi "has been for eleven hundred years an effect produced by a handful of ninth-century waka texts" (672). I hope that this statement by a very serious, thoughtful person means only that we know little of her life, and that the critic I admire on other grounds is not himself an effect produced, etc.

2. *Cratylus*, 426; Jowett 1892, 1:371. The first epigraph is from the same source, 1:332.

It certainly is possible, for all we know, that what we know of our real world is erroneous. If the errors are slight and what we know of the reality we presume is generally right, we shall be able in time to make necessary corrections. If the error is radical and total, we shall never be able to know it. We shall save ourselves, and others, a deal of trouble by not moping over a state we have no way of knowing to be wrong. It might be argued that people and time exist as we know them but that places do not. The utility of the assumption is not clear, however, since we are unable to conceive of someone existing on a New Year's Day nowhere. Meaningful problems require the existence, rather than the nonexistence, of something. Our daily lives do show how easily we can confuse the identities of two people, get lost in an unfamiliar place, or mistake the time. Yet it is evident that such error no more proves nonexistence than honesty guarantees one's being correct.

It is embarrassing to insist that no special credit can be expected for allowing that the world exists. Yet it is more accurate to say that our knowledge enables, and constrains, us to know as we are able to know. It is this Standard Human Assumption that enables us to ask the questions and debate the issues that in fact we ask and debate. There are degrees of what is termed philosophical skepticism: by Cicero's time, the Academy had taken up a skeptical approach tolerating other views. Extreme skepticism like that of Carneades in the earlier (or third) Academy was more dogmatic. (Dogmatic skeptics are no rarer than my-perquisites-first radicals.) Yet it often is not far removed from certain kinds of idealism, as fortuitously shown by the presence of Berkeley as well as Hume among the contemporaries of Johnson and Boswell.

As a contrast to realism, skepticism, and idealism, there is orthodox Mahayana Buddhism. Excerpts from one of the few available clear discussions of this matter show that there are real alternatives to our familiar modern Western formulations, of problems and solutions alike. (Ellipses are mostly of non-English words.)

> The Mahāyāna [philosophers] . . . viewed Dependent Origination . . . as their ultimate Emptiness . . . The Void is not an entity apart from this world but the same reality as phenomenal appearance: the world of transmigration . . . when properly understood is itself Nirvāna. Viewed as arising interdependently, all persons and things are Void, empty of all persisting, static form; but the provisional reality (ke) of this same world is also a truth not to be denied.

Hence the famous statement in the . . . [*Heart Sutra*]: "Form is no
other than Emptiness, Emptiness no other than Form." . . . This
central concept . . . uses negative terminology to indicate that the
Absolute is ultimately devoid, empty, of all determinate characteristics. But Buddhist philosophers have always been careful to
warn critics that its negative language does not argue for nihilism,
for the denial of existence; rather, it uses a via negativa to lead us to
the positive Ground of all things.[3]

It may be added that poets used as figural images the sky for the Void
(the Chinese characters being the same), the moon for enlightenment.
And that the Japanese court had an annual observance pertinent to this
study: the butsumyōe, or recitation of the names, in relation to depictions, of some three thousand Buddhas and bodhisattvas. It is a long,
steep via negativa with many turns. Earnest inquirers may console
themselves with the plenitude of useful problems.

Of them, only a few that are pertinent to the present investigations
will be mentioned. One we shall get to is possible difference between
fictional and other names. One we shall consider before that is how the
same name can designate the "same thing" changed over time. But we
may begin with one raised by our intercultural perspective rather than
by philosophical or onomastic considerations: the differing relation (if
difference can be presumed) between the naming of a self and a person.

Who Died in Osaka in 1694?

The Old Man we have followed on "the narrow road through the provinces" did not return to Edo for another two years (1691) after closing
his account with a line of verse exclaiming, "the departing of autumn!"
After three more years, and on V.11, he set out for what he had been
planning for two years as his longest journey: west and south to the
second largest of the Japanese islands, Kyushu. The idea was to journey
through "the western provinces and rest his legs in Nagasaki [Kyorai's
birthplace], watch the overseas ships come and go, and hear the speech
of people who sounded different" (Andō 1974, 54–55). After a short
stay in the general capital area, he went to Osaka to visit, it seems, one
of the rising stars of his school, Shadō. He got no farther by that early
winter season, the Tenth Month of 1694. Late in the preceding month he

---

3. Robert Morrell in Miner, Odagiri, and Morrell 1985, 286.

had been confined to bed by illness, and when illness came on him again at Shadō's residence, it was soon clear that the road ahead led only to another world. He composed his last known hokku:

> Stricken in travel
> and across wasted fields dreams
> chase about in vain whirl.

On X.10 the ever-loyal Kyorai arrived from Kyoto. The most gifted member of the school, Kikaku, arrived on the eleventh. By about four the next afternoon, the old poet had died. Four years earlier he had written an almost allegorical forecast about a migrating bird.

> The stricken goose
> falls through the cold of night
> a traveler's sleep.

(On these hokku, see also Ueda 1991, 413–14, 300–301). Who was it that died there and then in Osaka?

One version of the "Stricken in travel" hokku names as its author "Okina" ("old man"), a self-designation accepted by his followers and used by Sora in his *Nikki*. There are no birth or death records for a person so named. As a child of a minor samurai family, he was given a young boy's name. On dying, he acquired a posthumous Buddhist name. But in our sense of real names and of a physician's statement, the person declared dead on that winter afternoon in Osaka was (family name first) Matsuo Munefusa. Not one Japanese in ten thousand knows the given name.

For that matter, it is next to impossible to find that name in a normal sentence. As a proper name, it may well be one of Saul Kripke's "rigid" designators. But the utility of what is not used cannot be general. A common explanation for this by no means uncommon situation in Japan during the Edo period (and other periods, including modern times as well) is that Japanese have an attenuated, weak, fragmentary sense of self developed from attention to certain kinds of evidence. As a Strong Assertion, it is typically begun with attention to language, to the Japanese language most specially, and to the language of the "modern Japanese novel" in particular, and to the "I-novel" or shishōsetsu above all.[4] (It is sometimes retro-related to kinds of premodern fiction and to "lyric," i.e., Japanese poetry.) The term shishōsetsu is said to derive from the German ich-Roman, and the thing itself has been defined variously by Japanese. It is a kind of prose narrative that seems to entail autobiographical fact, often including details that can be shown to be lifted from diaries and letters or that can be verified from other sources. Leaving the correspondence between fact and fiction for a later point in this discussion, anybody familiar (as Bashō certainly was) with classical Japanese "diaries of the road" (or of the house, for that matter) will not be surprised that an article like the shishōsetsu should exist. The surprise lies not in the nature of the problem but in the nature of some solutions.

The solution that will be referred to may lead us into the area of cultural essentialism and relativism where, it will be recalled from chapter 1, my little vessel hit a rock. But we begin with the issue of the Japanese sense of selfhood. "The Japanese," we are told, "have been less convinced of (we might even say have been uninterested in) the self's tangibility or value" (Fowler 1988, 13). The explanation offered is that the Japanese are unlike the Rousseaus and Romantics in the West, who however much they "questioned the individual's place in society . . . never sought refuge in depictions of private life for their own sakes." As a result, "the literary naturalism imported by Japanese writers yielded, inevitably, nothing more than technically brilliant depictions of the writers themselves living in studied isolation" (54).

Fowler pursues his argument on the wide front of modern literary narrative in Japan by raising and answering a question at the beginning of his second chapter.

Why the preponderance of first-person narration in modern Japanese *shōsetsu?* We are led by the insights gained in Chapter 1 to conclude that it is due paradoxically to a lack of a sense of self—

---

4. The Strong Assertion is best considered in terms of Miyoshi 1974. See Chapter 1, "The New Language" (pp. 3–37, which includes discussion of the writer Futabatei Shimei) and what is probably the most explicit formulation of the core ideas, the discussion of Natsume Sōseki (pp. 79–82). The force and tone of the argument are best conveyed by Miyoshi himself speaking before others (as I can attest). It is not surprising therefore that the thesis of langauge and attenuated sense of self should be presented by one of Miyoshi's students, Edward Fowler (Fowler 1988), and that he should follow Miyoshi's spirit carefully by considering the language/self issue in respect to the so-called "I-novel" (shishōsetsu or watakushishōsetsu).

and to the concomitant lack of an isolable, autonomous "other."
(28)

What then of the divinity of modern Japanese prose narrative (shōsetsu no kami), Shiga Naoya (1883–1971), and his famous shishōsetsu in that extraordinary lucid style? "Shiga," we are told, "even by signing the texts he writes, paradoxically confirmed his absence from them" (51).

Miyoshi's own version is broader and stronger, as one or two lengthy quotations must suffice to show.

> Japanese society does not, in short, promote the necessary condition for growth of the novelistic imagination: the egalitarian sensibility that sees a unique human personality in powerful statesman and day-laborer alike. Instead, people are regarded according to their assigned social slots. . . .
>
> The novel, on the other hand, in order to explore the inverted universe that an individual consciousness is, always pulls toward freeing people from their role characteristics, and it is against such energy that Japanese society works so relentlessly with its tribalism and ceremonialism. . . .
>
> The notion of the inner self, whether that of the author or his character[s], throws a more serious impediment in the way of the novel's development in Japan. Japanese writers are essentially lonely souls who in their inward search for the core of existence often identify themselves with a Dostoyevsky or a Rilke. And yet in finally facing themselves, they discover a strange emptiness. (Miyoshi 1984:80–81)

These ideas are not distorted by Fowler, who writes in his introduction, "The *shishōsetsu* is often formally unsatisfying, then, because it does not follow the narrative conventions that have governed western fiction" (Fowler 1988, xx). If that were not bad enough, "it is" still "not to say that western fiction lacks parallels to the *shishōsetsu*" (xvi).

If this logic is accepted, we have a premise of an unusual language (Japanese), another premise somehow related of a highly attenuated sense of self, and a conclusion of an "emptiness" from which western languages, senses of self, and novels are not only free but superior and, in their superiority, are able to do also what the empty Japanese counterpart cannot. Since it would be difficult to reach this conclusion on reading *The Tale of Genji,* either something happened to the Japanese langauge and self on their way to modernity or the description is faulty.

Since I believe that the description is wrong but that Miyoshi's Strong Assertion has yet good reasons for us to consider it at this length, it is necessary first to account for its value, then to identify where it goes wrong, and finally to offer an explanation that uses its virtues without leading to a dead end. The value of the interpretation is that it accounts for our sense that there is a difference between the experience of reading, say, *The Narrow Road* in Japanese and reading it in English. Since those are obviously languages, the difference must involve the languages. The problem is partly the conception of language that recently dominated our literary criticism. That can be set aside for another time. (Those, however, who wish to explore the matter in respect to the shishōsetsu may consult Reed, 1985.) We shall be better off with the issue Miyoshi identified—that of selfhood.

If we retreat a step or two, it becomes clear that we are considering ways of defining, and naming as one means of defining, human identity. If this were the place for extended discussion, certain topics would require study—Japanese attitudes toward reclusion, crowds, and suicide, for example. For briefer consideration, which will cover our travelers in Scotland as well, human identity can be distinguished in two versions: selfhood and personhood. The identity of a self is exclusive, inner directed; it is founded on that memory of distinctive continuing existence which constitutes private life as each of us knows it from awareness of the pain of injury or the joy in the company of certain people. By distinction, the identity of a person is specified and recognized by a name. We seldom name ourselves. We routinely name others. We do have a name and may give it to others, as Japanese do constantly with their name cards and by other means such as are involved in introductions and similar situations familiar to our social life. Naming establishes one's place in a society of other persons with their names, including the social roles and purposes that go with them by relation to other persons (with their selves).

That being the obvious case, it follows that Japanese selves are like non-Japanese selves—except as these selves are impinged upon by that further dimension of human identity, their persons. Japanese awareness of personhood, not of selfhood, is the crucial factor. No personal nouns or other names are necessary to give an acute sense of self. A standard Japanese expression, Ureshii wa, can only be that of a woman declaring her happy selfhood, just as a comparable expression, Iran zo, can only be that of a man's self declaring his distaste. The predication in "I'm so happy!" or "I don't want it!" is that of and about a self, with no need of an English pronoun.

The declaration to others and the gender roles are social, however, as are the choices of levels of politeness, humbleness, and so on. Because it is the nature of Japanese social life, it is the nature of the language as used that definitions of relation, status, and occasion are crucial. Every Japanese finds it constantly necessary to define or adjust personhood with each daily social encounter. The acknowledged identifications of others do not require even personal nouns or names in the sense that they emerge in translation: "eldest sister," "Mr. carpenter," "honored two people" (a waitress's announcement to another waitress that a pair of people have entered the door), "honorable section chief," and so forth. Moreover, in ways that all but totally defy translation and defeat explanation, the choice of language expresses deference or superiority, honor or contempt. The shishōsetsu may indeed not be an "I-novel," but it offers a chance precisely to emphasize selfhood over personhood, and in doing so is apt to seem much more authentic than a mastery of consummate depiction of others. In brief, I believe that a particularly *strong* Japanese sense of selfhood responds to an equally unusually strong sense of personhood and that the complementarity is what supplies a crucial dynamic to Japanese views of that larger entity, human identity—whether in the modern novel, in older poetry, or in the office.

That conclusion itself requires adjustment. As we have seen in earlier chapters, we must be alert to emphasis on points of attention as well as points of view. Boswell requires attention to other persons to define his own person as a desperate means to understand his self. Between Shirakawa Barrier and Matsushima, Bashō dwells to an extraordinary degree on reduction of the personhood that belongs to others as well as to himself, but on the increase of his selfhood in relation to what may be termed the equivalent of personhood for place. In all this, it is quite true that Scottish Boswell differs from Japanese Bashō. But he differs from English Johnson as well, just as Bashō differs from his fellow Japanese, Sora.

None of this is particularly wise or rich in solution of grand problems. It is not recondite, but familiar. It also carries conviction, and it leaves problems of naming easier to understand if not necessarily to solve.

We may now return to consideration of what names may imply. Japanese are unusually active in devising multiple names or appellations for the same man or woman. Names like Bashō and Okina are obviously of dividual *persons,* or they would not be so divided. The *individual* who died in Osaka was a self as opposed to a person. The Japanese language is extraordinarily rich in words designating selves, precisely because the sense of self is so strong. That strength derives from the burden of constant adjustment of one's personhood in relating to other selves-persons.

The importance of selfhood is of course not confined to Japanese and other East Asians. And actual linguistic usage may seem quite confusing: as observed before, Japanese is very rich in the personal nouns that are counterpart to our pronouns, but they are used as little as possible. A common substitution for one of the first-"person" singular nouns is "jibun," meaning "(my)self"; as for the second or third "person" one may say "gojibun," so adding an honorific; or for emphasis on a *particular* third "person," "honnin," meaning the central individual person, the one involved.

The death of that self in Osaka was also the death of a multiple and polyonomous *person.* The demise put an end to the various persons, to the various literary and social avatars of the *self,* and to that self as well. "Bashō" and the like were no longer persons who could act or speak. Other persons, who might have referred, as Sora did in his *Nikki,* to "Okina," would now find equivalents of "the Master" or "the Former Master" to be more practical. Such matters are not unknown, if less common in degree, in our own experience.[5]

Reflecting social and cultural assumptions as they do, human naming practices vary enormously: "Some societies jealously watch over their names and make them last practically for ever, others squander them and destroy them at the end of every individual existence" (Lévi-Strauss 1966, 199). In addition, the "Tiwi system of naming" is one "intermediate between these two forms." At the time of the study, there were about eleven hundred Tiwi, each with three names, and none of

---

5. A late UCLA colleague, Alfred Longueil, was the sole person who addressed me in the old-fashioned proper succession of names: Mr. Miner, Miner, and Earl. The three persons named were, I presume, one self.

the thirty-three hundred denominations the same. To rehearse only a few of their rules governing naming:

> Every time a woman remarries, her husband gives new names not just to his predecessor's children but to all the children his wife has borne throughout her life whoever was their father. As the Tiwi practice a form of polygymy chiefly favoring old men, a man has little hope of marriage before the age of thirty-five and women pass from husband to husband. This is due to the difference in age between husband and wife which makes it very likely that a husband will die before his wife. No one can therefore boast a definitive name until his mother's death. (199–200)

The system is cumbrous but logical:

> relations and positions are here put on the same footing. In addition, the abolition of a relation involves in each case that of the proper names which were a function of it either socially (names bestowed by the deceased) or linguistically (words which resemble the deceased's names). And every creation of a new relation starts a process of renaming within the domain of the relation. (200)

Numerous other details, including various easements, are involved. And they show, as evidence from other sources would also, that our understanding of human naming must presume great variety of practice. It is as impossible as unnecessary to mention any large portion of them here. But a few are worth specifying.

1. Names are designations of individuals within a group according to the values and customs of the group.
2. A given self will likely have several designations of the personhoods assigned to the particular selfhood.
3. Although the designations are "rigid" and clear within the naming community, they may not be so outside.
4. Changes in names may involve loss and substitution, addition of the new, adoption of those of a group joined, granting of nicknames (Tom, Dick, and Harry—which also possess a further meaning in combination), and surnames in the old sense: Aristides *the Just*, Scipio *Africanus Major*, etc.

Bashō's "Hokku Composed during Illness" ("Byōchūgin") can be looked at again.

Tabi ni yande	Stricken in travel
yume wa kareno o	and across wasted fields dreams
kakemeguru	chase about in vain whirl.

None of the three nouns (tabi-travel; yume-dreams; no-fields) is a personal noun, although everyone presumes an implied first person: *my* dreams. Although a death may put an end to the functions of names in one sense, any account of it must include a self. And doing that requires specification of one or more persons of that self. For example, "Abraham Lincoln, while president of the United States, died of gunshot by John Wilkes Booth." Abraham Lincoln himself died from being shot in Ford's theater, but other selves have succeeded to the personhood of "president of the United States." Although the self dies, it may "live on" in conjunction with and designated by specific historical personhood. A self died there in Osaka, as a self and a self-undesignated person foretold in the hokku. But Bashō remains.

Identity and Alteration

"Bashō remains." To make sense, the words must mean that somebody or something we can refer to by that name has continuing historical existence. As we have just seen, *Bashō* is but one of many names designating the personhood—the poetic personhood, it may be added—related to a mortal selfhood. Occasionally we have made use of translations of other names (e.g., "the Master") more or less synonymously with *Bashō*. That is of course how he is known today, although there were periods in his lifetime before he had, or used, that pen name. There were times when he visited his brother in Iga province when he would not be called by a pen name. And there were times when there were alternatives like *Okina*. Without including all the names of "Bashō," we may order a number of them in a sequence reflecting their chronological appearance in his work.

Unlike (Iwanami, Kawai) Sora and (Enomoto, Takarai) Kikaku, he had but one family surname, Matsuo, so reducing our survey to a given name and pen names—to what for painters are often called "styles" (*gō*; and for a haikai poet, *haigō*). So the following will suffice.

Munefusa	His given name as a grown male
Tōsei	Pen name under which he received recognition as a leading haikai poet in Edo (Hakusendō and Furabō are among others)
Bashō	Later pen name by which he is known today; taken from his Bashō An or Banana Plant Hermitage in the Fukugawa area of Edo
Ha-se-[w]o	Unmarked syllabary version of *Bashō,* used particularly to sign copies of his poems and pictures
Okina	Old Man, used increasingly in the 1680s and 1690s; "old" really has positive associations, being the *Lao* in Lao-tzu, sometimes used for others (Lao Du [Fu]; and in China still in use by wives as an intimate form with a shortened version of their husbands' given names)
Senshi, Shi	The (former) Master; posthumous respectful denomination

The six designations follow chronological order but overlap in time and usage. Some (e.g., Shi) were bestowed by others, some (e.g., Bashō) were self-chosen. All in all, both in the conditions mentioned and in the very multiplicity it is not an example such as a philosopher would care to use. But perhaps there is something to be said for the rough plants from the plains of history as a change from the neater hothouse productions of philosophy.

Because those half-dozen names were taken or given at different times, they refer not only to a varying or multiple personhood but to a continuous self that in physical terms matured, grew older, and died at the then reasonably advanced age of fifty. He knew or imagined the debilities of age in the seventeenth century, as is shown by one of his stanzas (the eleventh) from a trio sequence with Kyorai and Bonchō:

> all that I can do
> is suck upon the bones of fish
> and think of old age.[6]

Some earlier Japanese poets lived to eighty and more: the waka poet Fujiwara Shunzei (1114–1204) and the renga poet Sōgi (1421–1502), for

---

6. "Throughout the Town" ("Ichinaka wa no Maki"), usually dated 1690:VI. Miner 1979a, 305. My comments imply no autobiographical reference or self-reference.

example. But even in our time fifty years is ample time not only to reach age but to feel some of its changes.

As we have seen, Bashō himself was concerned with the two principles of identity and alteration as poetic and metaphysical concepts. Most literary critics today (and pretty consistently since the Romantics) approach these matters with an interest in change, in what is new. Hattori Dohō, who is with Kyorai one of the two principal preservers of Bashō's conversation and thought, writes of change as henka and as ryūkō (*Taisei*, 631). Like Bashō, Dohō joins with that change a concept of continuing identity, the stable "fueki of ten thousand generations," something that "does not pertain to the new or old" (ibid.). The position held by Bashō is closer to that of the philosophers than to that of some critics. It is not so much change over time that constitutes the important issue but the maintaining of identity.

Among the philosophers' Standard Examples, that for the issue of identity is the imagined ship, Jason's *Argo*. By the time he arrived home with the golden fleece, every part of the ship had been replaced. Yet it was still the *Argo*. It is easy enough to shift to a human self to discover the relevance of the example to our sense of ourselves as an identity continuous in change. Some have attributed our continuity over time to one's memory of oneself. (To the idealist Bishop Berkeley, it was divine knowledge.) That cannot apply to the *Argo*, unless we shift from memory by and of a human self to a memory by a human self of a ship.

In devising his collocation, identity-alteration (fueki-ryūkō), Bashō's priority accorded to identity seems to imply what any considerer will conclude sooner or later. That is, it is possible to speak of change or alteration only in terms of what retains identity. French politics and Antarctic icebergs are certainly different, and each alters in time. But lacking mutuality as they do, it is illogical to speak, unless by catachresis, of one changing *into the other*.

In other words, Bashō's six and more names may represent changes marking different stages of his life and career. With the final change, death, the end came not only to a legal self-person we may designate Matsuo Munefusa but also to all those other persons now known to one and all by the single personhood of the haikai pen name (haigō), Bashō.

Once we posit a human identity continuous in selfhood, *Bashō* and its alternatives designating various personhoods are attributable to that self. That is a matter of evident and simple fact, although there are also possibilities less evident and far from simple. For an example, we may recall Bashō and Sora's meeting with the penitent prostitutes at Ichiburi. It is a fact that the episode appears in *The Narrow Road*. It is a fact that there were places called Niigata and Ichiburi Barrier. It is a fact that Japanese society included prostitutes. But it is also a fact that the incident is a fiction.

To explore some of these matters a bit farther, we may recall that stanza on a toothless old man's sucking bones. It is the eleventh in the sequence of thirty-six stanzas composed by Bashō with Nozawa Bonchō (d. 1714) and Kyorai, "Throughout the Town" ("Ichinaka wa no Maki"). Bashō's stanza is the eleventh, a joined or successor stanza (tsukeku) following the tenth by Bonchō, and it next becomes a predecessor stanza (maeku) to the twelfth by Kyorai. One of the things we notice is that the differing stanzaic connections produce alterations in our sense of who is who: our "sense," because (as is altogether common) there are no personal nouns, no equivalents of *I* or *he* in the Japanese.

	At Nanao Bay in Noto	
(Bonchō)	the winter cold is hard to bear	(10)
	all that I can do	
	is suck upon the bones of fish	
(Bashō)	and think of old age	(11)

	All that he can do	
	is suck upon the bones of fish	
	thinking of his age	
(Kyorai)	as he lets his mistress's lover	(12)
	through the gate with his key	

The alterations seem to be no greater, and perhaps are less, than those implied by change of names. But here, where we have no persons named, there is nonetheless a kind of alteration differing from those we have been considering. That old man who now sucks fish bones, huddling against the cold, and that old man who then lets in the lover are one in the sense that, although neither *old* man is implied by Bonchō's or by Kyorai's stanzas, they exist by virtue of Bashō's intermediate stanza. But a man who suffers in the cold on a remote peninsula is someone who exists as Bashō's old man solely in conjunction with Bonchō's stanza. And the man who then admits the lover of his mistress in the capital exists as Bashō's old man solely in conjunction with Kyorai's stanza, which Bashō had no way of foretelling. These are also facts about fictional stanzas, since all the stanzas after the first in a linked-poetry sequence are presumed to be fictional. We know that the prostitutes at Ichiburi are fictional because we have Sora's *Nikki*, but without it Japanese would assume (and did assume) that it was factual, like the rest of *The Narrow Road*.

In brief, names (but not only names) present a different set of meanings and therefore of problems when we shift from fact to fiction and ask, in this matter, what is truth?[7]

"What Is Truth?"

We cannot get directly to the creative truth (makoto) that enabled Bashō to unite his principles of identity and alteration. So many issues are urgent that artful dodges like textuality are a waste of time. Bacon's Pontius Pilate asked in jest, "What is truth?" and fled to other business. As Lord Chancellor, Sir Francis surely knew the temptation himself. We observe that most of what follows in that essay, "Of Truth," is about falsehood. A basic implication of that fact is that it is possible to distinguish between the true and the false, providing certain conditions are met. We not only think it a possible, but normally find it a necessary presumption.

It does not follow, however, that what is obviously necessary is equally easy or even possible. Not only are there many things we cannot know for lack of knowledge of how to know them or lack of sufficient evidence, but failures of memory or care forfeit much of what we can know. Right here is where skepticism belongs, at home. It is comic, or pathetic, to observe how handily we scale down what we accept as the degree of necessary evidence when it is inadequate (as with earlier historical periods) or when there is so much that sorting out is onerous (as with recent historical periods). The strongest proof of what is true is commonly our desire to believe it. Other truth candidates seem compromised by the company they keep. When the search for truth grows arduous, what is only probable or possible grows more attractive. As

---

7. It is instructive to imagine the example discussed as an entry in Johnson's *Dictionary:* there would be an interplay between the fact of the designation of meanings, the facts existing in the words defined and the words defining them, and the quotations used for illustration, some of which are factual and some fictional.

one narrator says of her characters: "they do not always wish to know the truth about a thing. And when the truth is at last revealed to them they cannot entirely dismantle all fiction from it" (Tremain 1991, 229). Candide was right not only about gardening but in saying we need not be taught to be ignorant.

Yet the distinctions between fiction, fact, and truth matter. They serve useful, necessary human purposes. As illustration we need only take the names in the preceding paragraph: Bashō, Sir Francis Bacon, Pontius Pilate, Candide. The first three are historical, but in each case the familiar names conceal problems. Those of Bashō have been mentioned, and those of Bacon and Pilate could be. All three are real, factual, true people who existed. Candide is fictional, but what he says about our ignorance requiring no cultivation is as true as Bacon's " 'What is truth?' said jesting Pilate and would not stay for an answer" (see John 18:38).

Necessity makes us urgent logicians. The urgency so intensifies our need to discover order and make sense that we often claim meaning and truth out of need or even desire. There is a ready example: Noam Chomsky's famous sentence devised to be at once entirely grammatical, syntactic, and meaningless.

Colorless green dreams sleep furiously.

Taking up the gauntlet of sense, we boldly construct a paraphrase that makes sense. For example: "As yet featureless but fecund anticipations lie temporarily dormant but ready to rage." Our compulsion to discover sense extends beyond meaning to discovery of the meaning we desire. Howard Hibbett once told me that when, after Mao's death, there were Chinese visitors once again to Harvard, one of them, a pack of cigarettes in hand, pointed to a sign in the Yen-Chin Institute.

> ## NO SMOKING PERMITTED

His question was, "Is smoking also permitted?" Our "rage for order" leads us to seek it, particularly to our advantage. We are also anti-Pilates, insisting on staying for, or with, an answer. And, like Samuel Johnson, we go to our Scotlands prepared with a "book of remarks" that may save time by establishing truth even before we examine the evidence. Of course, like Johnson, we also may act responsibly and "revise" in the light of new evidence.

We often require evidence rather than mere data and logic as adequate means for truth. And our distinction between what is true and what is false resembles our distinction between fact and fiction in having a necessary prior presumption. Whatever else may be said of fact and fiction, each presumes a world in which the doing (factum) of the one and the devising (fictio) of the other can be distinguished. That is, we assume, and others seem to assume also, that the distinctions between fiction, truth, and falsehood are made in a world where they are empirical, useful, and valid. If we are all deluded in such matters, we shall go on acting as if we are not, and the very denier is self-deprived of logic to prove us wrong.

In describing the skeptical claim, the philosophers' Standard Example tells those of us who think we really are doing the laundry, kissing, or word-processing that we may be, after all (before all?) but brains in a vat imagining, with the Psalmist's gentiles, a vain thing. But given our never having seen a brain functioning in a vat, and being of the perhaps not entirely ad hoc opinion that our usual conception may be at least as likely as that odd minimalism, it seems not unreasonable to ask the Compleat Skeptic to prove the proposition, including the existence of brain and vat.[8] Otherwise we may suspect of that vat what Gertrude Stein remarked about another place, there is no there there.

Let it first be proved that the world does *not* exist. Presumably the proof will have to come from someone who is named Not Even Nobody and is nowhere at the nontime.

Languages and experience offer variously useful means to sort out these matters. English has not only those gainsayers, negatives and adversatives, but also those grammatical cousins of fictions, conditionals and subjunctives. We find it comforting to consider that however much effort it is to ascend that "huge hill / Cragged and steep" where Donne's "Truth stands," she exists and we shall reach her at last. We may say with Bashō that "the way of truth is a single thing," at least if we have something corresponding to his religious "way" (michi, dō). In this, we are have no obligation to consider the not true to be a single thing. Fictions, lies, and mistakes are not all the same. We distinguish one from the next by presumptions about motives, intentions. Bacon's claim that "The mixture of a lie doth ever add pleasure" confuses a lie with a fiction. Lies vary from brazen attempts to deceive to Iago-like

---

8. I have wondered, however, whether the philosophers' brain in a vat was Samuel Beckett's starting point for *The Unnameable*.

insinuations, but are always assertions of the truth of what the liar knows to be false. The necessary intention in the act of the predication is deception. Mistakes may yield even more serious results than the casual lie, but the mistaken individual declares what is thought to be true. It will have been noticed that paradoxes and ironies also play their roles.

The history of Western criticism shows that in spite of some disclaimers, critics have consistently held that literature is (as literature) rather more wholly fictional than less. It is difficult for me to assess what such people think when it is pointed out that supposers in other parts of the world may presume very different things. In particular, East Asian critics and readers assume (in the absence of contrary evidence) that literature is factual.[9] Whether arguing from their entertainment of fiction or of fact, many critics (beginning with Aristotle) also enter a higher claim: literature is true.[10] Since names are shared by the factual and the fictional, their nature, their status affords focus to these issues.

The Prevalence—and Basis—of Fiction

Sora's *Nikki* is not a test case. Western critics, who do not couple literature with factuality, would grant that it is factual but question quite properly its literary status. Johnson's *Journey* provides a far more interesting basis for discussion of literary fictionality and factuality. Assuming from its style that it is literary, it seems a dominantly factual record interspersed with opinions, generalizations, polite mollifications, and evasions. Yet it has none or little of Bashō's poetry, exciting variety, or aesthetic of place. It lacks Boswell's care with dialogue, possessing but minimally Boswell's "fictional means to present the historical truth" in scenes that are so skillfully constructed as to seem actual occurrence (Clingham 1992, 1765). If Sora's account is the purest, the most antisep-

---

9. See Miner 1990, index, s.v. "factuality" and "fictionality." And see the example of efforts to redeem the factuality or truth of a poem by Du Fu discussed pp. 108–13. Of course it was recognized that certain stories and all plays betrayed their fictionality. It is curious that Aristotle should discover possibilities for nonfictional elements in drama, and curious also that he should do so in a discussion concerning *names* (*Poetics*, chap. 9).

10. Of course literature is yet more apt to seem true when it is assumed to be factual, as with the emphasis on the ordinary in the "realistic novel." It is also the case that literatures develop—within recognizable limits—conventions and styles, culture by culture and age by age, for what is ordinary or out of the ordinary. Mimesis in the West, and affective-expressive poetics elsewhere, presume the world to be real and in principle knowable.

tically preserved from contamination by doubtful fiction, specious interest, or literariness, Johnson's account is really extraordinarily skillful in making his historical recollections and connections of many kinds (religious and political as well as literary) seem inevitable. Of course there is nothing inevitable about them whatsoever, any more than there is in his choices of what to include and what to leave out.

Without denying the dominant factuality of Johnson's *Journey*, we can witness him making fiction by what may be termed his choices of what to tell and how to tell it. There is a firm eighteenth-century explanation for "ascending discrepancies . . . between world and body, between body and mind, and between mind and spirit"; it is a general "statement about the nature of mind, and about the relations between the realm of intellect and the realm of historical, social, and physical contingency." The explainer is our Boswell in his *Life* of his friend but who, I very much believe, had his mercurial self equally in view:

> Man is, in general, made up of contradictory qualities, and these will ever shew themselves in strange succession, where a consistency in appearance at least, if not in reality, has not been attained by long habits of philosophical discipline. In proportion to the native vigour of the mind, the contradictory qualities will be more prominent, and more difficult to be adjusted.[11]

It is of most significance, however, that the two most interesting and *convincing* accounts are those by Bashō and Boswell. In the periodic golden moments of Bashō's prose, as in the fifty hokku by himself included with verse by others, we recognize that their aesthetic nature has transformed fact. Even if the hokku are factual, they do not come to the table cold like Sora's "There are ku" (i.e., we composed hokku). Nor is Sora's saying "[We] visited Hikaridō" at all the same as Bashō's evocation of the meaning of that name as the Temple of Light to close his monody on the vanished splendors of Hiraizumi. No special skill as a reader is required to make this comparison. Nor is any great critical penetration necessary to see that Bashō irradiates fact with an aesthetic quality only sporadically fictive. But let the confident reader explain how to write like Bashō and the discerning critic distinguish the fact

---

11. First quotations from Clingham 1992, 1768; the long quotation is from Boswell's *Life*, 4:426, quoted by Clingham. Perhaps Boswell seeks to calm his own inner sea with the comfort of a generalization.

from the imagined clause by clause. As Virgil said, there is the work, there the task; and few return.

The operations of fiction may be very subtle: we need only think how long it was assumed that Bashō really did meet young prostitutes at Ichiburi Barrier. Moreover, from Herodotus and Thucydides to our writers and to ourselves, what is factual may be aestheticized or also fictionalized in two ways no less significant for being common. One is to offer what people said. No matter how deeply Boswell breathed that Johnsonian ether, and no matter how genuinely based it is on actual speech noted in some shorthand, his dialogue is a brilliant aesthetic creation. The other aestheticizing of a crucial kind makes events and people plausible by offering what may be termed causal explanation for behavior: in brief, by supplying motivation. This is a major respect in which Johnson's *Journey* has its fictional or, at best, its virtual dimension. It is fascinating that the speeches in Thucydides (and Boswell) have led to accusations of fabrication and fiction, whereas the critics have swallowed whole the motivations he (like Johnson) assigns historical figures he never met.

The situation may not be as stark as that of the story of Metternich's response to Castlereagh's suicide: "I wonder what he meant by that." But it is usually more complex, as when Boswell behaves in ways that his explanations fall far short of accounting for—with the effect of suggesting or even dramatizing to us the hidden motivation: a human being's desperate attempt to understand himself and his need to choose from among conflicting senses of oughts and desires. We may recall his pain at Johnson's cruel joke to have him castrated, his embracing an outside cross on a dark night, and his oral performance among the ruins at Iona. Or we may consider this succinct statement of Boswell's purpose: "to create an alternative authority to that of his father, the legal-authoritarian establishment of Scotland and England, and the implacable theological claims of a Calvinist deity" (Clingham 1992, 1767).

Although a poet and writing in a tradition of poetic diaries, Sora had a rare genius for excluding the aesthetic from extended writing, where, whether literary or historical, it is all but inevitably to be found. But for further discrimination we need to recognize that neither the general rule of factual writing's containing nonfactual elements nor his exception to it apply to the larger class to which literature belongs, the aesthetic. In fact all kinds of aesthetic expression except literature are as it were wholly apart from both fictionality and factuality. It defies effort, or sense, to propose that a fugue or a formal garden is fictional or factual, true or false, much less that it lies. The same holds for the Eiffel Tower and the Tokyo Tower. No matter how beautiful a fugal canon, a vase, or a tower, all are radically distant not only from fact and truth, but as also from fiction and lies.[12]

Of course there may be facts or lies postulated *about* nonverbal artistic creations and presentations. For example, there may be in a museum a piece of Korean celadon ware labeled a Silla dynasty ewer. Investigation may show that although the dynastic ascription is correct, the function ascribed is mistaken. Or it may be true that it is a ewer, but that it was made in the Yi dynasty. Either way, the facts or mistakes (or lies) *about* the jar have no connection with the cognitive status *of* the vessel. The jar is not in itself a fact or a fiction, and there is no point to considering its truth status.

The addition of language alters the case. A librettoless string quartet resembles the Silla vase; an opera (even if sung in a language unknown to a listener) will be taken to be fictional.

To be articulated and to be communicable, fact and truth must be linguistically expressible. All fiction and some facts may, however, be construed to belong on a spectrum of expressions taken to be *dominantly* neither true nor false, neither not true nor not false, what I would term the virtual.[13] The most memorable expression of this potential quality of literature is by a contemporary of Bashō and Sora, the dramatist Chikamatsu Monzaemon (1653–1724). Here is what he is reliably reported to have said, very much at length, as befits one of the world's most important characterizations of art:

> Art is that which occupies the narrow margin between the true and the false. . . . It deals with the false and yet is not false; it deals with the true and yet is not true; our pleasure is located between the two. A relevant incident: there was a certain lady serving at the palace who developed a passionate relation with a certain lord. Her chamber was in the depths of a splendid room, and since he was unable to enter it [probably because it belonged to a higher-born lady whom she attended], she had only a glimpse of him from time to

---

12. Pantomime and miming dance provide marginal instances.

13. See Miner 1990, 44–47; also index, s.v. "virtual (aesthetic) truth status" and "truth statuses, literary." It should be observed that the virtual includes nonliterary entities as well: e.g., subjunctive predications and legal fictions. From the latter, *fictio* in Roman law, we derive our *fiction*.

time through a gap in the blinds. So great was her yearning for him that she had a wooden image of him carved. The countenance and features differed from those of usual images in its accuracy to a cat's whisker. The coloring of the complexion was indescribably exact, each hair was in place, the ears and nose and the teeth in their very number were faultlessly made. Such was the work that if you placed the man and the image side by side the only distinction was which had a soul. But when she regarded it closely, the sight of a living person exactly imitated so chilled the lady's ardor that she felt distaste at once. In spite of herself, she found that her love was gone, and so unpleasant was it to have the model by her side that before long she got rid of it. As this shows, if we represent a living thing exactly as it is, for example even [the legendary Chinese beauty] Yang Guefei herself, there would be something arousing disgust. For this reason, in any artistic depiction, whether the likeness be drawn or carved in wood, along with close resemblance of the shape there will be some deviance, and after all that is why people like it. It is the same for the design of a play—within recognizable likeness there will be points of deviance . . . and since this is after all the nature of art, it is what constitutes the pleasure people take in it.[14]

Among the things that might be remarked about this locus classicus is that the limited but uncommitted participation of the virtual (that neither true nor false) with truth and falsehood may explain why East Asians prefer to characterize literature as fact, and Europeans to do so as fiction. As we have seen, nonverbal arts are not describable as fictional (or nonfictional); and literature shows that, in verbally expressed art, the virtual can accommodate both fact and fiction. On the other hand, it is all but impossible to write connectedly at length without having recourse to fiction or other guises of the aesthetic such as the imaginary (Iser 1993). We would deceive ourselves if we believed that we could exclude those elements from factual telling. So much is evident.

---

14. Miner 1990, 45 (revised). For "deviance" we may read "conventions" or "coding." It is truly remarkable how Chikamatsu reverses not only Aristotle on the pleasure of depiction even of cadavers but also the Pygmalion story. For extended discussion, see Miner 1983.

There is a further simple and serious issue: the logical priority of fact or the fictional/imaginary. Once the question is asked, the answer comes quickly: fact is prior. Every predication—the ceaselessly iterated task of language—that is fictional or imaginary depends on a basis in fact. There is a famous five-word proposition: "All happy families are alike." Surely "It is a truth universally acknowledged" that the aphoristic nature of the sentence suggests fiction, and no proof is required for the intuition that there is very much else that is "made up" or "imagined" in that lengthy novel, *Anna Karenina*. But Tolstoy's fictional sentence can make no sense without the assumption of the factual existence of happiness and families, Russia, his age, his culture, his language, social organization, the Napoleonic war, and so on. As evidence, one need only consider how easily it (and most other fictional sentences) could be part of nonfictional talk or writing.

It should be evident that the prior existence of fact is necessary to the existence of fiction as well as the imaginary. If not, Vaihinger's extensive study, *The Philosophy of "As If"*, should make it clear, since he deals with science and logic more than with literature.[15] Bentham also makes the point in his *Theory of Fictions:*

> Every fictitious entity bears some relation to some real entity, and can no otherwise be understood than in so far as that relation is perceived—a conception of that relation is obtained.[16]

In other words, not only are fiction and the larger category of the (verbally expressed) virtual dependent on fact; they depend on it to make sense, to exist. As one philosopher has put it, "that which can cause anything, even illusion, must be a reality" (Mill 1976, 5; "What Is Poetry?"). Without presumption of reality and of truth status, the aesthetic, imaginary, or fictional use of language is strictly meaningless. Without presumption of fact, linguistic meaningfulness is impossible.

---

15. Vaihinger 1924, excellent as it is, bears certain problems. For example, he meaninglessly categorizes social fictions (greetings when meeting somebody, "dears" and "sincerelys" in letters) as "*Poetic* fiction" (83). He also fails to see that a fictional linguistic expression is to be shared, whereas in arts not involving verbal means, fictionality is a meaningless concept. Nonetheless, this book is most helpfully suggestive.

16. Ogden 1932, 12. Ogden's introduction is very nearly as long as Bentham's treatise (152 to 156 pp.). Vaihinger is useful in making clear that the relation of a fiction to what it presumes is not representation, not mimesis, not "copies of reality" (1924, 16); he is also neither a naive realist nor skeptic. For a detailed discussion of the virtues and limitations of Bentham, Vaihinger, and Ogden, see Iser 1993, chaps. 1 and 3.

That these matters are true does not in itself prove that a poem has truth status or a sentence has meaning. But it is a basis, a start.

If any doubt remains, we can consider the wonderland in which Alice finds herself. (Readers desiring a quick review may consider whether Alice's *wonderland* is a name? a proper noun? If Alice has no patronym or other surname, is she less real than if, on three occasions, she were named Alice Liddell? As a fiction, can she have an identifiable self? What is the effect on the narrative of abandoning names of places and times? Or of "Lewis Carroll"'s being a pen name?) We constantly recognize the margin between basis in real fact (human personality, place, time, spoken words, actions, motives clear and obscure, etc.) and violation of fact. Rudely put, if the presumption of fact did not exist, we could not presume this fiction. That is in no small part because we are able by the presumption to judge the momentary suspension of fact in the presumed exact likeness of Tweedledum and Tweedledee. It is telling that the priority of fact and our compulsion to make sense has led a number of people to boast success in showing that "Jabberwocky" makes proper English sense. (There are several translations into German alone.)

To make sense is, however, still not necessarily to acquire a truth status. As we all know, our *poetry* derives through Latin from the Greek verb for "to make," *poiein* or *poein*. And a fiction is something made or fabricated, with *fiction* derived from Latin *fingere*, that is, "to make up" or "to devise" (as opposed to *facere*, "to make"—although that could also be used for poetry). The *fictio* of Roman law, the origin of our *fiction*, was typically a devising of a legal person such as the Roman Senate (or General Motors), which could be assigned powers otherwise those, or like those, of real persons. Yet being made up, devised, is not restricted to fictions. History and other sustained, integral uses of language are also makings up, devisings: because statement of fact equally requires linguistic action.

We do, however, use *fact* in another sense, that of the Latin *res naturae*: the state of things, reality, actuality, truth. In that sense, *fact* (*facts, factuality*) designates the given as opposed to the made.

To these distinctions we must add another that is obscured by our word *history*, which we use in two distinct senses. One sense involves fact or factuality in the meaning just given and may be termed history as event. The second sense designates writing or talk about history as event and may be termed history as account (Miner 1984). Almost all examples of the second and all with *history* in a title are histories as accounts based more fully on prior accounts than directly on history as events. A novelist is much more apt to draw directly on history as event in creating characters from people known than is a historian. And as was hinted at in respect to Thucydides, a historian will fictionalize, and precisely in such matters as motivation that impart to the persons treated the greatest conviction of reality. The complex "dialectic" of fact and fiction and other elements in historical writing has been described in great detail (Ricoeur 1955–58), and in brief as "the actual refiguration of time, now become human time through the interweaving of history and fiction" (3:180).

An illustration from a fictional story, George Eliot's "Janet's Repentance" (in *Scenes of Clerical Life*) will suggest refigurations and interweavings of a complementary kind. Eliot based on real people and events this story of a highly abusive husband, Robert Dempster, and of his wife, Janet, who becomes an alcoholic to numb her suffering. He is injured and dies from an accident caused by wild and indeed alcoholic driving of his gig (Eliot 1973, chaps. 21–24). The accident has been well prepared for, but it cannot escape a sense of authorial convenience, of fictionality. In fact the accident did happen to the original of Dempster (chap. 11), and once Eliot's story became known, people who knew the original individuals devised identifications as if it were a roman à clef. By contrast, everyone seems to agree on the conviction carried by certain wholly fictionalized chapters like the first, which features Dempster in a rowdy pub argument.

Eliot went on to write freer fictions, but just as "Janet's Repentance" could not exist without pubs, lawyers, orchards, and churches, a *Felix Holt* could not exist without politics and much else that we have been considering in four travel accounts as persons, places, times, and their names. Deprived of those things, no story or history could be written.

Given these considerations, the decision whether a given literary expression is factual or nonfactual is literally not simple: it incorporates *both* fact and nonfact. Also, as we have seen, it is obvious that fiction—the fashioned, the feigned, the imaginary—depends on fact.

If this be doubted, one need only seek to imagine a play, a novel, a haiku for that matter from which every factual element of the human, the locospatial, and the temporal has been excluded. The result would be unintelligibility, something considerably less than dadaism, less even than a language one cannot understand. And yet it is also true that the bare factuality of the human, the locospatial, and the temporal do not satisfy us, especially when the satisfaction we seek derives from what can be expressed in natural languages. (The joys discoverable in artificial languages like algebra are "another story.")

It further follows that for the literary version of the aesthetic a fact-fiction distinction is inadequate. That is not solely because a literary narrative employs both elements. It is rather because the qualities and conventions by which the literary is distinguished are—culture by culture, age by age, and sometimes individual by individual—an interfusion of fact, fiction, the imaginary, and the conventional. The virtual is related but not restricted to or coextensive with the last three. Because the aesthetic presumes and has basis in fact, fact can be derived from the aesthetic, whatever its nature and degree of fact, its nature and degree of the fictive or the imaginary, its conventional coding. We can and do distinguish, for example, fact from fiction or convention. But we distinguish them as elements that we decode (interpret, make sense of, understand) from whatever aesthetic or historical coding (conventions) they possess.

With these postulates, we are able to find great heuristic value in Bashō's complex postulation about his haikai art. To assist recall, here is that simplified, combined English-Japanese graph of his thesis.

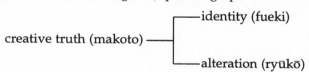

Without what may be termed a phenomenal world, without flux, without novelty, without ryūkō, there would only be stasis, fixity, sameness.[17] Yet without the assumptions of steadfastness, without assurance that the nature of things and the conditions of being hold to themselves, without fueki, there would be only anarchy, confusion, and meaninglessness. These complementary qualities do not suffice in themselves, however. Whether one is concerned with the metaphysics of ontology (or to advert to German, the Bauformen, Grundlagen, and Wissenschaft of both Sein and Wesen) or whether one is concerned with

---

17. Jean H. Hagstrum remarks how like this seems to Johnson's conception of the discordia concors constituting wit. See also Hagstrum 1967, chap. 8. One need not be Boswell to savor the idea of a Neoconfucian Johnson.

the creation of artistic expression, a creative principle, a providential fiat, a power to bring into being is required. Bashō believed, as other poets have and yet do, that the creative result is truth. His belief or conviction is not proof, and without some kind of probative force, some kind of adherence to an acceptable truth standard, there are insufficient grounds for any philosopher I know of to say his belief is true.

We have been given a very convenient summary for the "three main criteria for judging scientific propositions" (Fokkema 1989). These are

1. "correspondence with the empirical facts it [a proposition] purports to describe";
2. "agreement with theories held to be correct . . . coherence";
3. validity "on the basis of argument among a particular community of scholars . . . consensus." (123)

These are as unexceptionable as such brief compass allows, although many of us would wish to add logical consistency, "inner coherence," to the proposition, and although some people may need to be reminded that "scientific" here is used in the European sense of Wissenschaft. Using these criteria, it will be found difficult to characterize historical writing, but not literature, as true.

That and other like efforts may be spared here. It is enough to remark that the issue of what is required for a belief to be true does vary from Wissenschaft to Wissenschaft. It would take a fancy syllogism, a great deal of repeatability of experiment, and a sleepy reader to get seven hundred lines of trochaic tetrameter to be considered a sonnet. It would also take effort to find greater truth in a letter by me on growing older than in Shakespeare's "That time of year thou may'st in me behold." For that matter, the nimblest philosophers have severe problems with the status of names in literature, a topic that now concerns us for a last time.

Naming

In "Speaking of Nothing," Keith S. Donnellan distinguishes three nullities involving names, one of which—"discourse about fiction"—he purposefully excludes.[18] His reasons are blessedly clear:

18. This is a republication of a 1974 essay, given as chap. 9 in Schwartz 1977; here p. 218.

Under "discourse about fiction" I mean to include those occasions on which it is a presupposition of the discourse that fictional, mythological, legendary (and so forth) persons, places, or things are under discussion. I believe, for example, that said with the right intention, the following sentences would express true propositions: "The Green Hornet's car was called 'Black Beauty,'" "Snow White lived with seven dwarves," and "To reach the underworld, one must first cross the river Styx." (By the "right intention" I mean that the speaker wishes to be taken as talking about fiction, mythology, or legend.) At the same time I also believe it is true that neither the Green Hornet, his car, Snow White, nor the River Styx exists or ever has existed. These two beliefs, however, are entirely consistent. And therein lies the puzzle: how can there be true propositions that apparently involve predicating properties of what does not exist? (1977, 218–19)

And, as he adds in a note, "The denial of Snow White's existence, it should be noted, is in discourse about actuality, while the statement that she enraptured a prince is in discourse about fiction" (219 n. 9).

R. J. Nelson takes a similar position, albeit one that is less clear in expression and more complex in its formulation. We may begin where he sounds most like Donnellan:

What is to be learned from Brentano is that reference is indeed intentional and, if he is right, is not explainable in purely physical terms. He gives us a dilemma: either reference is unanalyzably object directed (as are beliefs, hopes etc.) or there can be no semantics and, in general, no psychology. Beliefs, expectations etc. as well as referring [sic], which may be "about" [what Donnellan terms fictions] Titania or Pegasus, are prima-facie nonphysical if by "physical" we mean to imply complete relations and structures of minds and objects. (Nelson 1992, 35)

Nelson has already insisted, however, upon another distinction involving "Naming and Reference: The Link of Word to Object" (the title of his book). That is "The difference between the reference or application of a word and its meaning or sense," which, as he adds, is subject to great dispute. But we can see at once that the two do not coincide. As he explains, "For instance 'mermaid' *means* half fish, half girl, but does not apply [refer] to anything, i.e., there are no mermaids." But more is involved. "Conversely, a term could mean one thing and refer to many. For instance, in 'I am reading this sentence,' 'I' has a fixed meaning but a different referent for each reader—one for you . . . and another for me." The next words are: "Just what the difference is for proper names is not clear" (4).

There is a certain confusing asymmetry in the two propositions with their examples.

A. *Mermaids* has meaning but has no reference.
B. *I* has meaning and has multiple reference.

What of that which has no meaning but has reference? And what of that which has no reference but has (singular or multiple) meaning? Nelson's approach is to drop concern with meaning and consider reference. He goes on to identify referential terms: proper names and descriptions, indefinite pronouns (his example is *some*), personal pronouns and demonstratives (7). He divides "logical names" into singular terms (proper names, definite descriptions, definite pronouns, and what he terms indexicals); and with them he puts general terms, predicates. Before long he arrives at a series of severe difficulties, which I shall number only to set them apart.

1. "Assuming we really had a characterization of the role of singular versus general terms that was non-committal on reference . . . we could be on our way. But we do not have one. . . . As things stand, a name is not a name unless it refers. This is intolerable for science and everyday talk as well as for theology and fiction." (12)
2. "A name is a name owing to its linguistic role. Yet can one explain role without tacit appeal to a referent? The fact is, there are names having no referent. This is one of the chief puzzles about reference." (22)
3. One solution might be to define *use* as a criterion in terms of "psychology and cognitive science. Nonbearing names simply would not be used in making statements, but only for fictions or for noncommittal descriptions." However, "The trouble is that relegating questions of reference, truth, and so forth to use obscures the role of the agent-user as constitutive of primary refer-

ence. To retain the agent is of course precisely to block the move to abstraction. The proposal to abstract from use and consign questions of assertability to psychology of language use obscures the nature of the anatomy of reference."[19]

Clearly, description and analysis of naming are very difficult tasks. If there is any criticism to be made of the philosophers' discussions of naming in aesthetic matters, as I believe there is, it should be prefaced by two remarks. The first is a matter about which many literary critics (particularly "theorists") have gone particularly wrong. Philosophers are altogether convincing in holding that naming is a species of reference and that, as such, it is an intentional act. The so-called baptismal naming already discussed should make that evident. The second matter is less immediately decisive. But clearly nominal reference, naming, implies if it does not absolutely require, philosophical realism. That stipulation or presumption excels others in parsimony of explanation and (most of us think, as perhaps all of us act) at least equal in adequacy. Nominalists do appear from time to time in philosophical discussions (e.g., Nelson 1992, 19–20), but they are rare. These two matters are valuable, not because they simplify other considerations (they don't), but because they offer some clarity within their purviews.

We must now turn to other matters in which the philosophers have been of less help. To begin with, they (although certainly not only they) have confused matters by tacitly identifying literary naming with the whole reach of aesthetic naming. We may offer a description or predication of a certain object as our *Silla dynasty celadon ewer,* and that predication is considered by philosophers dealing with naming. *An eighteenth-century symphony* would be another such, as would *a twentieth-century oil painting.* But those descriptions are not nominal references with the stricter indexical quality of *the "Jupiter" Symphony (of Mozart)* and *the "Guernica" (of Picasso).* Without these indexical descriptions or titles, the more general descriptions lack particular reference, and whatever meaning they have is rather of a class than of an individual. And since the class titles may be used for different examples, the indexical properties of the names of aesthetic examples are limited. In other words, to

---

19. Nelson 1992, 22–23. My quotations are from his introduction. His chapters take up the issues raised here by my selection along with others. It is both a strength and weakness of his excellent account that it is so wide ranging, including, for example, numbers.

the extent that a given literary example is purely aesthetic, or to the extent that we consider solely its aesthetic character, our powers of nominal reference are limited.

Philosophers have shown other grounds for understanding that nominal reference varies in strictness and comprehensiveness. Single proper nouns permit greatest "rigidity." Names of plural proper nouns are less rigid, as are nonrestricted singular proper nouns (*a* Canadian), and so on to singular common nouns and plural common nouns. (One's stand—or agility—can be tested by where and why one would place numbers on this scale.) Some philosophical discussions of names are restricted to single proper nouns. The point of mentioning this is to emphasize that the distinctions hold no less in literary usage: compare James's novel, *The American*, with Gershwin's musical composition, *An American in Paris*, or—in their differing formulations—Shakespeare's *Tragedy of Hamlet, Prince of Denmark* with Faulkner's novel, *The Hamlet*. The title of the play is obviously more wholly indexical.

Another area requiring clarity is that of fictions. As we have seen, there is no useful sense to calling a vase or tune fictional. What is yet more to the point, literature may be dominantly factual: witness Bashō, Boswell, and Johnson. (Although Sora is all but wholly factual, it is not possible to give evidence of his *Nikki*'s being aesthetic, literary.) I really do not think that this fact carries the weight that philosophers assign to the distinction between fictional and nonfictional names, but it is a reminder that they, too, need help in logical sorting.

It is certainly true that many literary names are fictional, as (for the most part) are the individual persons, places, times, and other things that fictional names designate. But there are major exceptions. Spenser's Gloriana is fictional but designates the factual Elizabeth I. His Arthur is fictional, seems to have designated Leicester, and then to have had his fictional status insisted on, to give Spenser some defense as court politics changed. In the Stuart period, allusion and religious typology were used to identify a king like Charles I with the biblical King David. David was a principal "type" of Jesus Christ, so retrospectively bestowing on Charles a quasi divinity.[20] Charles I, David, and Jesus are all historical figures. In Tremaine's *Restoration* Charles II is a historical figure, whereas almost all other personal "names" or characters are fictional. It would also be a great mistake to believe, however, that

---

20. See Thomas Stanley's *Psalterium Carolinum* for the Charles-David identification, and see various masques, poems, and *Eikon Basilike* for the Christo-typical.

because they are historical our knowledge of them fully excludes aesthetic or fictional features. Yes, the England of Dickens's novels may be fictionalized, but it would also be a great mistake to believe that because it is fictionalized it lacks factual features. As I have found necessary to emphasize, in narrative and in dramatic plots, persons are clearly of greatest importance, next places, and thirdly times (which is not to say that place and time are unimportant). Often time is less fictionalized than place, and place than persons—an emphasis we observe grow stronger from Dickens's *Pickwick Papers* on.

There are even harder issues. Set in quattrocento Florence, George Eliot's *Romola* includes factual, historical characters including Savonarola and Poliziano. Does anyone take them to be individuals as substantial—as true—as the entirely fictional Romola? Factuality is no more a sine qua non of literary truth than is fictionality for literary status.

Or again, one of the epigraphs to this chapter is taken from the following passage of *The Garden of Proserpina* by Randolph Henry Ash:

> The first men named this place and named the world.
> They made the words for it: garden and tree
> Dragon and snake or woman, grass and gold
> And apples. They made names and poetry.
> The things *were* what they named them. Next
> They mixed the names and made a metaphor
> Or truth, or visible truth, apples of gold.

Of course this is from A. S. Byatt's *Possession*. Ash is a Victorian poet (modeled on Robert Browning?), a fictional character whose elusive history is sought out by the fictional hero, heroine, and another literary researcher. Ash is, so to speak, more fictional than the novel's fictional hero, Roland. Then, a few pages later, as Roland reads from Ash, a historical figure is introduced.

> He heard Ash's voice, certainly his voice, his own unmistakable voice, and he heard the language moving around, weaving its own patterns, beyond the reach of any single human, writer or reader. He heard Vico saying that the first men were poets and the first words were names that also were things, and he heard his own strange, necessary meaningless *lists* . . . and saw what they were.

If the fictional Ash has put into verse the historical Vico's ideas (rather than the Genesis account of naming in Eden), the fictional hero next learns something similar from the fictional Ash:

> What Ash said—not to him specifically, there was no privileged communication, though it was he who happened to be there, at that time, to understand it—was that the lists were the important thing, the words that named things, the language of poetry. (Byatt 1990, 504, 512, 513)

From among a number of difficult issues in this, one may ask whether the main fictional prose narrative is not, rather surprisingly, seemingly less factual than the second-remove fictional verse account? Whether the factual Vico does not seem more fictional than Ash and the hero? So it seems to me, although the grounds for decision are not easily specified. In any event, I do feel sure that the account of creation and Edenic naming in *Paradise Lost* 7–8 seems less fictional than does the account in *Possession,* although Milton's version also has its surrogate narrators, no less than the angel Raphael and then Adam himself on his chat with God about Eve's creation. Also, Milton's Raphael seems more factual than does Byatt's Vico. Finally, these beliefs or understandings seem to contradict one's sense of how things ought to be.

There are probably several ways of explaining this somewhat surprising set of conclusions about features of *Paradise Lost.* Mine will be to recur to Bashō's concepts. Using them, we may judge Milton's account to have greater force than George Eliot's in its creative truth (makoto), because the complex of matters is so much more important to him and his age, something further manifested by the relatively greater importance of identity (fueki) over alteration (ryūkō) in his writing. Much the same can be said for the greater force of Boswell's near frenzy in scenes where he is alone by comparison with Johnson's depiction of himself *solus.* Of course, students of Johnson are well aware that his personal character led him to keep from the light much that Boswell felt compelled to put in the view of others as well as of himself.

Four such different people inevitably took to their common experience of back-country travel understandings of themselves that help account for differences in their understanding of their travels with another person. Had they told about exploring Edo and London, or had the Japanese and English exchanged their centuries, the results would certainly differ. Had the Japanese visited Scotland, or the reverse—but we need not stretch the subjunctive point. It will be enough to draw toward conclusion this discussion of nominal reference by our four authors of travel. We can arrange them confidently on a scale of increasing fictionality: Sora, Johnson, Boswell, and Bashō. Yet even Bashō's *Narrow Road* is dominantly factual. Moreover, what (by comparison to the other three) is most aesthetically heightened in his account— namely, place—also is at once factual and central without being "restricted" by mere fact or "distorted" by mere fiction. Why should a location of two hundred or so islands just off a coast not have the pines that grow in that sandy soil, and why should it not then be named Matsushima, Islands of Pines? Observing poverty, deforestation, and underpopulation in Scotland, why should Johnson not synthesize these facts into a factual whole that yet derives much of its force from the fictional energies of his desire for causal connections and motives that are not demonstrably factual?

There really is no necessary or absolute opposition in literature between fact and fiction. That is partly because fiction is dependent on fact and partly because literature, being verbal in medium and a variety of human expression, is propositional. Fact and fiction sometimes do work oppositionally in literature, but there is no necessary ground for conflict. In fact, the extremely various balancings, the exchanges between fact and fiction—the "interinanimation" (Donne's word) of Bashō's "identity" and "alteration"—is of such variety and changeability that explanation of one alone is extremely difficult. One can indeed seek to honor these pluralities of factualty and fictionality, but it is not simple to do so without losing one's reader's and one's own way—or patience.[21]

The simplest approach would seem to be offering a series of six categories in schematic form. In view of the discussion of them earlier in this chapter identification will be more expeditious, and clearer, than extended discussion. The brief descriptions are of course meant to postulate the necessary rather than the adequate. It will be observed that a given expression will belong to more than one category.

---

21. What does it mean that we so assiduously avoid raising "the truth status" of literature? Hospers 1948 retains its valor and its status as a lonely classic, and Valdés 1992 adds an interpretive dimension. Some brief consideration of what I prefer to think of as truth statuses (i.e., the plural) will appear shortly.

The true. That which is logically or probatively coherent itself and
  probatively consonant in predications with what is predicated
The factual. That which has been done or is
The propositional. That which offers predication by someone about
  someone or something
The fictional. That which has been made up, devised to resemble or
  be in lieu of the factual (but which need not be aesthetic); by
  extension inclusive of the imaginary
The virtual. That which is neither true nor false; not restricted to the
  fictional, as nonliterary arts and some literary features show
The aesthetic. That which, by convention, acquires its status apart
  from, while yet incorporating in varying degree, the other
  categories mentioned here, and for expressive ends

Among the other things that may or ought to be said, there are
three clusters of issues that repay attention. The first will be phrased as
two versions of a question addressed to anyone concerned with the
status of literature. It must be presumed that we seek to know and say
things that are meaningful, things that are true, about literature. Presuming those wishes, how can we do so if literature is devoid of meanings? Presuming our desire to know and postulate truth, not only about
but in literature, how can we do so if literature is devoid of truth? These
questions of course apply to any other kind of knowledge as well.

The second matter involves a few of the relations and discrimina-
tions that can and, for various uses ought, to be made of the six categories given above. One set involves the propositional. Clearly, the propositional involves language and therefore does not (without taking
"language" metaphorically) include the nonverbal aesthetic kinds. The
propositional does include: (1) the fictional elements in literature; (2) the
factual elements in literature; (3) the factual elements in nonliterary
expression. By distinction, the factual includes: (4) facts *about* even the
virtual (e.g., the picture in question is an oil painting of a Madonna and
child by Giotto); (5) facts *of* apply to 2 and 3 (e.g., our travelers did what
they report where and when they say) but not to 1. In actual literary
practices, or examples, there is constant fluctuation and adjustment of
the factual and fictional (and otherwise virtual). As a result, these elements may enforce each other or exist in a tension of opposition. Since
the conventions by which literature is distinguished (the verbal, prosody, etc.) vary from one culture or age to another, expectations and

tastes also vary, with practice sometimes varying from what it is presumed to be. In other words, our distinctions like those preceding are
those of coexisting, albeit differentiating, cognitive elements.

The third set of issues will return us before long to our travelers.
Since knowledge is describable at least as that which can be remembered and expressed, the kinds of knowledge are not only coexistent
but susceptible to differentiation in their relations with each other.[22] A
central distinction is that between the adaptive and adaptable nature of
kinds of knowledge. Some kinds—logic and mathematics, for
example—are highly adaptable by other kinds of knowledge but relatively very little adaptive of them. Other kinds—literature and history,
for example—are highly adaptive of other kinds of knowledge but
relatively very little adaptable by them. This being the case, literature is
as it were highly hospitable to other kinds of knowledge, including the
values attributed to them.

It should cause no surprise, therefore, that Napoleon and other
historical characters can exist with fictional ones in a Russian or a
French novel. Nor should it startle the most timid that Aristotle should
have discussed this issue under the head of names (*Poetics,* 9). The
assumptions that literature is characteristically factual or that it is
characteristically fictional are equally culturally related and equally
partial. These matters are particularly highlighted by literary use of
names.

Boswell's two most important names in the *Journal* are very obviously Samuel Johnson and James Boswell. Their names accordingly
appear on his title page. There is another person whose importance
receives the curious testimony of being referred to by a name that is a
predicate instead of a proper noun. It is odd that he should uniformly
write "my dear wife" rather than "Margaret," "my dear wife, Margaret," some nickname of endearment, or simply "M." The fact that he
chooses—for a journal—the form he does suggests that he wishes to
find a way to name minimally while gesturing to do so maximally.
(Why he should do so is of course another matter.) There are also special
names in his narrationis personae, those on the letters he appends at the
end of his account. They are appropriate documentary evidence. They
also have the attraction of bearing his name at their beginning and that
of a well-known, well-placed individual at the end. Let these small

---

22. On the issues dealt with here, see Miner 1979b.

tokens testify to the care that has gone into Boswell's larger constructions.

Johnson's organization by chapters with place-names focuses his account on Scotland rather than on individuals. In dealing with individuals, he does use names. And when he does, it is with a formal politeness that must have relieved Boswell's anxieties. Johnson is almost exaggeratedly scrupulous in avoiding names in his English and Scottish comparisons. There are some exceptions, mostly at the beginning and implied here and there in his long essay made part of "Ostig in Sky," but his care suggests that, like Boswell (and in spite of what he says), he had from the outset the intention to publish an account of what he found. As usual in his writing (intimate forms like prayers apart), Johnson absorbs his own name and person into the functions of narrator, commentator, and judge.

Sora's personal names are far more thickly sown than Bashō's *Narrow Road* would lead one to expect. (This leads to the relatively greater importance of Bashō's place-names.) But one brief passage has been held in reserve for this last mention of Bashō's companion. It is the conclusion to his entry for IV.1. (I have indicated a <place-name> whose pronunciation is unclear.) "That night in <Kami Hachiishi> in Nikkō [?we engaged—two characters illegible] lodging at the place of one Gozaemon" (Sora 1943, 5). That is the full factual basis of Bashō's report of encounter with an innkeeper who speaks to the travelers, "They call me Buddha Gozaemon." If the innkeeper had named himself as Bashō says, its extraordinary nature would have led Sora to record the fact: we realize that Bashō is fictionalizing in a way extending the factual beyond fact. It is significant that he should have felt that such a fiction was necessary, along with a manipulation of dates, to provide adequate cover for bitter comment on the Tokugawa military government or bakufu. The comic insertion of a fictional name enables him to satirize what he does not name!

The Sado passage is yet more indirect. Those strange place-names (literalized "Abandoned Parents," etc.) and his own unidentified but clear unhappiness enable him again to criticize the Tokugawa regime without the danger in use of names belonging to it. The places named are also on the opposite coast from Edo. By contrast, there is the delicious literary humor in the implied names of the Fukui episode. For, as we have seen, Bashō's allusions cast himself as Radiant Genji and the shabbily dressed old woman of the run-down residence as the youthful Yūgao.

The most conspicuous features of Bashō's naming involve, however, other people and other places. "People of the past" (kojin) are evoked as focuses of meaning and values, and of them it is of course the two who died five centuries before who matter most. Repeated allusions and other evocations of that earlier poet and traveler, Monk Saigyō, intermittently remind the reader of the understanding and even enlightenment that poetic travel might bring (or prevent). The heroic, tragic figures of Yoshitsune and his associates appear repeatedly, coming to that grand climax at Hiraizumi.[23]

Quite properly for a traveling poet, it is his handling of place-names that most clearly reveals his artistic command. As people and time almost seem to disappear in the account of his travel from Shirakawa Barrier to Matsushima, he offers in their place exactly that, place, and indeed he names places of poetic name (nadokoro, meisho). It is not an exaggeration to say that his handling of place-names implies intent to celebrate as places of poetic name many not hitherto granted that status. As Saigyō and other waka poets had done, and as Sōgi and other renga poets had done, Bashō may be said to have transferred the places he visited from geographical to poetic realities. The most obvious symptom of that is his recurrent literalizing into description of the meanings of names. Although traces of such literalizing can be found in earlier Japanese literature, his frequent recurrence to it in passages ranging from the sublime to the scatological make his poetics of place unique in a literature rich in such resources and very different from anything to be found in the other three writers. That transformation is possible only in a literature possessing an aesthetic of place-names. And only Bashō could thereby be able to devise his prose account as a prose version of a poetic form, modeling as he does his *Narrow Road* on a linked-poetry sequence.

In his *Naming and Reference: The Link of Word to Object*, R. J. Nelson describes "naming and reference" as "something so distinctly human"

---

23. Perhaps Bashō's antibakufu aim in using Yoshitsune led him to diminish the roles of two people closer to that doomed figure than were any others whose names he introduced. Yoshitsune's loyal retainer, Benkei, is glanced at in the episode concerning the family of Vice Governor Satō (*Diaries*, 167; *Zenkō*, 205), but not at Hiraizumi. His accomplished concubine, Shizuka Gozen, is not mentioned at all.

as almost to defy "deciding what sort of puzzle it is." It is more extensive even than "ontology," and both that extent and that importance lead him to ask with a wry blankness, "Where would one put 'naming' in a college curriculum?" (Nelson 1992, 26). He implies that it is the business of philosophers and cognitive psychologists—along with unspecified others.

All our evidence leads, however, to the conclusion that naming is a species of reference. As we have been seeing, reference presumes an agent referring, some object physical or conceptual referred to, a spatiotemporal place for the act to be made, and the so to speak indirect object, the person for whom the reference is made. Naming is far from being the sole kind of reference. We would need to include as well allusion and quotation, numbering and other kinds of mensuration, directions, and certain forms of deixis. In the idealized model of the hemispheric lateralizing of our brains, the linguistic dimensions of reference are chiefly represented in the left cerebral hemisphere, and the others in the right (Miner 1976). There is a mass of nerve lines or commissures, the corpus callosum, that enables the lateralized sides to function together. Unlike measurements, naming may involve nearly the total brain, including areas representing memory and affective functions.

As this account of four versions of travel in remote parts of two nations shows, naming involves yet more than an individual's cortical and subcortical activity. If, in literature, nominal reference concerned only naming and referring, it would be important to us. But literary naming involves more than the relation of our words to the objects important to us. It concerns past and present human efforts to understand what it is we may identify by name as ourselves, others, and features of the world we share—the names of humble detail and of high purpose. To those people we must add the troublesome as well as the exalted scenes of our lives. There are also the times of our three-score years and ten, both in their sustained order and their ecstatic moments. We recall Bashō's telling us at the outset of his *Narrow Road* that the days and months are the travelers of the centuries over ways often straitened. Like him, we are loosened clouds in a sky that is both our passage and our end. Naming is not so much a matter of a college curriculum as, for each of us, a means of presenting our curriculum vitae.

Appendixes

Places and Dates of the Two Journeys

It is difficult to come by conveniently set forth, clear dates of places visited on the two journeys (particularly Bashō and Sora's), and for good reason. In each pair each writer uses his own system, and yet we must rely on them. Neither Bashō nor Johnson is generous with dates. For these and other reasons, some things simply cannot be known. What follows treats first the Japanese, and then the English journey.

So vague is Bashō about dates that modern editors divide his *Narrow Road through the Provinces* (*Oku no Hosomichi*) by places the poet mentions. Sora's *Nikki,* which is organized by dates, is clear and reliable in itself. But because matching Sora's with Bashō's account is sometimes difficult, and because Sora's illness took him from Bashō's side during a major portion of the end of the journey, some dates simply are unclear. The dates given below for the Japanese travelers are, then, Sora's as interpreted by three chief, but not wholly concordant, sources (supplemented by Andō 1974): *Zenkō,* Bashō 1959, and Sugiura 1968. (For a different set of dates, whose basis is unclear, see Ogata and Morikawa 1989.)

The dates given refer to a month and day in 1689 when the two travelers (excluding Sora after his departure) were in the place, whether as day of arrival, as one of more than one day, or as day of departure. When, in these terms, the dates are clear or nearly so, they are simply entered below. Where they are probable, dates are entered after a question mark. Where they are uncertain, only a question mark is entered. Even with these qualifications, uncertainties remain.

The dates set forth below are given both in terms of the calendar in use at the time and by modern Western equivalents. That calendar was a year of twelve months of thirty days each, corrected from the 360-day year to the solar realities of years of 365–66 days by various intercalary expansions and occasional shrinkings by use of a "small month" (shō no tsuki) of 29 days. In Japan, there was an intercalary Month I in 1689, and the Month III was a "small" one. The former has no application, since the travelers did not set out until III. As just shown, months are here designated for the premodern Japanese calendar by large roman numerals (I–XII). In the Japanese pattern of dating years by their number in a regnal era, 1689—the year of Bashō's account—is, as he mentions, Genroku 2.

The places mentioned have been divided by headings specifying segments. These suggest portions that reflect most critics' sense of major units and of places of relatively greater (or lesser) importance.

It should be emphasized that the initial and closing dates are especially uncertain. Rather than rehearse various theories, it is simpler to say that we do not know when or how long Bashō was at Sampū's cottage or when he left for Senju. Perhaps that is because we cannot be certain when Sora joined him. After Sora departs to seek medical treatment ca. VIII.5 (18 September), Bashō's dates again grow uncertain. It is unclear just when he arrived to be greeted by his waiting disciples in Ōgaki and how long he stayed there. From Ōgaki he made his way to Nagashima on the Pacific shore. On IX.8 (20 October), again with Sora's company, he set forth by boat for his native province of Iga, whence he gradually made his way to the area of the capital, Kyoto. In fact, his journey recorded in *The Narrow Road* was but the first half year of a two and a half year period of poetic travel—and absence from Edo.

Bashō and Sora's 1689 Journey

Place, etc.	*Date (Premodern and Modern)*	
Prefatory		
Sampū's Cottage	III.20	May 9
To the Nikkō area		
Senju	27	16
Sōka	28	17
Muro no Yashima	29	18
Nikkō	IV.1	19
To Shirakawa no Seki		
Nasu	2	20
Kurobane	3	21
Unganji	5	23
Sesshōseki	19	June 6

Ashino no Sato	20	7
Shirakawa no Seki	21	8
To Sendai and Matsushima		
Sukagawa	22	9
Asakayama	V.1	17
Shinobu Mojizuri	2	18
The Satō's Memorial	2	18
Iizuka	3	19
Date no Ōkido	3	19
Kasajima	4	20
Takekuma no Matsu	4	20
Sendai	4	20
Tsubo no Ishibumi	8	24
Sue no Matsuyama	9	25
Shiogama	9	25
Matsushima	9	25
To Hiraizumi and West across the Mountains:		
Ryūshakuji, Gassan		
Hiraizumi and Hikaridō	13	29
Iwade, Shitomae no Seki	14	30
Obanazawa	17	July 3
Temple Ryūshakuji	27	13
Mogamigawa	VI.2	18
Haguroyama	3	19
Gassan, Yudono	6	22
The Kisagata Area		
Tsurugaoka, Sakata	10	26
Kisagata	15	31
Southwest to Ichiburi no Seki		
Echigo Road	25	Aug. 9
Niigata	VII.2	16
Ichiburi no Seki	12	26
Kanazawa and Beyond		
Kanazawa	15	29
Komatsu	24	Sept. 7
Nata	27	10
(Yamanaka—not on the map	?	?)
South to Fukui, Ōgaki		
Stricken Sora Parts	VIII.5	18

Temples Daishōji, Zenshōji	?8	?21
Yoshizaki, Shiogoshi	?	?
Maruoka (or Matsuoka)	?10	?23
Fukui	?12	?25
Tsuruga	14	27
Beach Iro no Hama	16	29
Ōgaki	?IX.3	?Oct. 15
Nagashima to Embark for Ise	8	20

Johnson and Boswell's 1773 Journey

Note: Places are given in Johnson's spelling with usual versions in parenthesis.

The much less difficult problem of dates in 1773 for the travelers in Scotland involves almost solely matching Johnson's places (which serve as his entry or chapter titles) with the appropriate dates from the much more expansive account by Boswell (whose entries are by dates). Since England had changed in 1752 to the New Style or Gregorian calendar, Boswell's dating is the same as ours.

Here, too, segments have been marked to give a sense of the stages of the journey.

Introductory	
Boswell pp. 3–11	
Johnson p. 3 (one paragraph)	
Johnson arrives in Edinburgh	Aug. 14
North to St. Andrews, Aberdeen	
Depart Edinburgh, arrive St. Andrews	18
Aberbrothick (Arbroath)	20
Montrose	20–21
Aberdeen	21–23
To Inverness, the Highlands	
Slains Castle	24–25
Banff	25
Elgin	26
Fores (Forres), Caldor (Cawdor), Ft. George	26–28
Inverness	28–30
Lough (Loch) Ness	30

Fall of Fiers		30
Fort Augustus		30
Anoch		31
Glensheals (Glen Shiel)	Sept.	1
Ratiken (Mam Rattacham), Glenelg		1
Isle of Sky (Skye)		
Armidel (Armadale)		2
Coriatachan (Coirechatachan)		?
Raasay		8
Dunvegan		13–21
Ulnish (Ullinish)		21–23
Talisher		23–25
Ostig		?30
Armidel (Armadale)	Oct.	1–3
Other Isles		
Col (Coll)		3–11
Grissipol (Grissipoll) on Coll		12–14
Castle of Col(l)		?13–14
Mull		14–16
Ulva		16
Inch Kenneth (Inchkenneth, incl. Iona)		17–19
Back to Mainland, Auchinleck, Edinburgh		
(From this point places are derived from		
Boswell as much as from Johnson)		
Cross to the Scottish Main Land		22
Glen Croe		?
Loch Lomond		26
Glasgow		28–29
Auchinleck	Nov.	1
Edinburgh		9–22

Patterns of Renga and Haikai Sequences for Bashō's *Oku no Hosomichi*

Haikai in Japanese Literary History

By the twelfth century Japanese poets were composing renga linked poems, as a game or as a relaxation from formal composition of waka (poems in pure, un-Sinified Japanese). Play gradually turned to earnest, producing a serious, decorous, standard (ushin) renga. Thereafter a need was felt for another playful, less decorous, or nonstandard (mushin) renga. From elements of these two kinds and other sources poets gradually defined a new kind designated haikai (no) renga. *Haikai* connotes a degree of playfulness, humor, irregularity—in short a lower decorum typified by the social rank of poets and audience, by lower subjects, and by lower and Sinified words. In Bashō's lifetime (1644–94), there were three main schools of haikai. The Teimon, established by Matsunaga Teitoku (1571–1653), was the oldest. The Danrin, founded by Nishiyama Sōin (1605–82), emerged next. The Shōfū, or Bashō school, was the last to be founded and lost its vitality upon Bashō's death. In fact, success came with difficulty in his style, which precariously balanced deep seriousness with a comic art.

Principal Features of Haikai Practices and Forms

Knowledge of certain features of linked poetry is necessary to understand *The Narrow Road*. There are few shortcuts in explaining or understanding these matters. It will be understandable if some readers are bewildered. Others may be skeptical about the existence or presence of certain features. That is also understandable. But the more one knows about these matters, the more thoroughly they can be found to pervade standard renga, haikai, and nō. Their absence from Western poetry is hardly a defect in Japanese.

Sora's *Nikki* records poetic composition on the journey, distinguishing between hai or full haikai sequences and ku or hokku. Hokku are the grandparents of modern haiku (a word that did not exist until the eighteenth century), but in theory or aspiration they were what their name means, "beginning stanzas." In practice they were often very similar to haiku. Since Bashō did not know the word *haiku,* and since he prided himself for mastery of sequences more than for opening stanzas, only *hokku* is proper for his "opening stanzas." He includes in *The Narrow Road* fifty of his hokku along with those by Sora and others, waka by various poets, and quotation or echoes of Chinese poetry. Sora's *Nikki* included a supplement giving the haikai sequences composed using Bashō's hokku.

Four stanzas in a renga or haikai sequence have names:

Hokku	First stanza
Waki	Second stanza
Daisan	Third stanza
Ageku	Final stanza

The hokku and other odd-numbered stanzas consist of three lines in five, seven, and five syllables. The waki and other even-numbered stanzas consist of two lines in seven syllables. The shortest possible sequence was therefore referred to as hokku-waki. Hokku-ageku may seem more logical, but the name used suggests that a proper sequence really ought to be longer. Those familiar with the tanka form of waka will recognize that a hokku-waki was the same in lines and other prosodic features. In earlier times it is basically impossible to distinguish between waka capped poems (two lines in sevens added by a second person to a first person's three lines in five, seven, five syllables—or the reverse) and hokku-waki. To add a perhaps clarifying distinction to the confusing terminology, the early version of hokku-waki is called short renga (tanrenga) in distinction from long renga (chōrenga). Long renga is also termed chain or linked renga (kusari renga), because of the rule that a given stanza relates semantically only to its predecessor—and therefore is related to by its successor.

Sequences might be composed by various numbers of people. Three or four are most common in Bashō's best-known examples. But there are a number of examples of composition with just one partner and of composition with much larger groups. Solo composition of sequences was frequent in Danrin haikai especially, but no example survives from Bashō himself.

The standard or most typical sequence for linked poetry—at least by poets outside the Bashō school—is that in one hundred stanzas (hyakuin). Bashō preferred sequences of thirty-six stanzas (kasen), although he composed in longer units both earlier and later in his career. These and other lengths may be set down in order of decreasing length:

100	Hyakuin
50	Gojūin
44	Yoyoshi
36	Kasen
18	Hankasen
8	Sho-omote (as if first 8 of 100)
2	Hokku-Waki

In addition, there were one-thousand-stanza (senku) and ten-thousand-stanza (manku) stanza sequences made up of hundred-stanza sequences, but Bashō wrote none. There was also the unspecified number, iisute.

Although Bashō composed in all the listed lengths, the kasen and the hyakuin are unquestionably the most important in his practice and for understanding *The Narrow Road*. It is particularly necessary to understand how the stanzas were written and grouped. Sheets of paper were folded across, with the seam on the top, and stanzas were written on the exposed front and back sides. The one-hundred-stanza hyakuin required four sheets, and the thirty-six-stanza kasen required two to obtain the requisite number of stanzas and for other important reasons, as we shall see in a moment.

Hyakuin Form: 100 Stanzas

First sheet
    Front   1–8   (eight stanzas)
    Back   9–22 (fourteen stanzas)
Second sheet
    Front   23–36 (fourteen stanzas)
    Back   37–50 (fourteen stanzas)
Third sheet
    Front   51–64 (fourteen stanzas)

Back	65–78	(fourteen stanzas)
Fourth sheet		
Front	79–92	(fourteen stanzas)
Back	93–100	(eight stanzas)

Kasen Form: 36 Stanzas

First sheet		
Front	1–6	(six stanzas)
Back	7–18	(twelve stanzas)
Second sheet		
Front	19–30	(twelve stanzas)
Back	31–36	(six stanzas)

Some Canons of Haikai

In linked poetry, renga and haikai alike, each *side* should have one stanza on the moon (= Moon) and each *sheet* one on unspecified blossoms (= Flower; but the meaning is cherry blossoms). The last Moon (fourth sheet, back) is almost invariably omitted. Although there are often supernumerary Moons or Flowers, there was an appointed place for each required Moon and Flower. In a hundred-stanza sequence, the place for a Moon on the front side of a sheet is the penultimate stanza (e.g., seventh of eight of the front of the first sheet of a hyakuin) and the place for the Flower is the penultimate stanza of the back side (21), with the Moon demoted, as it were, to three stanzas earlier (18). In practice, there are often great departures, especially in haikai, although the rule for the last Flower's appearance in the penultimate stanza of the whole is more insistently observed in haikai than in renga. It will help now to set these matters in outline form. First, the pattern for a hyakuin.

1–22	First Sheet		
	1–8	Front.	Moon 7.
	9–22	Back.	Moon 18. Flower 21.
23–50	Second Sheet.		
	23–36	Front.	Moon 35
	37–50	Back.	Moon 46. Flower 49.
51–78	Third Sheet.		
	51–64	Front.	Moon 63.

	65–78 Back.	Moon 74. Flower 77.
79–100	Fourth Sheet.	
	79–92 Front.	Moon 91.
	93–100 Back.	Moon omitted. Flower 99.

And now for a kasen.

1–18	First Sheet.	
	1–6 Front.	Moon 5.
	7–18 Back.	Moon 15. Flower 17.
19–36	Second Sheet.	
	19–30 Front.	Moon 29.
	31–36 Back.	Moon omitted. Flower 35.

To give form, coherence, and meaning to stanzas composed in quick alternation by a number of poets, extremely elaborate canons were instituted. As the preceding diagrams show, each of the sides (except the last) was to have a Moon stanza and each of the sheets a Flower or Blossom stanza. Each had its appointed place, the honoring or violation of which provides one source of interest. A Moon designates autumn unless otherwise qualified: e.g., the summer moon, natsu no tsuki. To qualify as a Moon stanza, the word *tsuki* must be used in its sense of "moon" and not of "month." A Flower always designates spring. By this time it invariably means cherry blossoms, but the mention of that or any other particular flower is not a Flower stanza, which requires solely "hana" ("flower").

Each stanza has a topic, which is either one of the four seasons or miscellaneous (zō). There are numerous subtopics: evanescence (mujō), love (koi), travel (tabi), and so on. Thus, to the extent that *The Narrow Road through the Provinces* is to be read as a prose-and-verse version of a haikai sequence, we can identify the topic of each episode and, what is no less significant than obvious, must understand that travel is a subtopic throughout.

Three other, less obvious matters are of very much greater, in fact of crucial, importance to understanding Bashō's art in *The Narrow Road*. Two of them involve the central Japanese aesthetic principle that beauty requires asymmetry, some examples of which have already been given (e.g., no last Moon). In a linked-poetry sequence, successive individual stanzas must vary in impressiveness. Uniformity is distasteful; plain or low stanzas heighten the beauty of impressive stanzas as well as imparting attractive vitality to the sequence as an artistic unit. This rule or aesthetic principle accounts for the extraordinary drop in tone from the episode at Hiraizumi to that at Shitomae no Seki, and the great rise from a dangerous stretch of road with repellent place-names to the comic romance of Fukui. The second manifestation of asymmetry in linked poetry involves the degree of closeness or, as Bashō put it, of heaviness in the relation of a stanza to its predecessor. It is not surprising that certain features of uniformity or closeness mark the portion from Shirakawa no Seki to Matsushima, as discussed in chapter 3. The shifting degree of connectedness found almost everywhere else is a prominent feature once one is alerted to it.

The third and most challenging application of the linked poetry form involves its rhythmic features. Renga adapted from court music a three-stage rhythm that it bequeathed to nō as well as haikai. Explanation requires recollection of the fronts and backs of the two sheets for a thirty-six-stanza kasen and of the four sheets for a hundred-stanza hyakuin. Each linked sequence has three formal parts: a jo, or introduction; a ha, or development ("breakage"); and a kyū, or fast close. (A three-movement sonata provides an analogy, except that in linked poetry the second movement is agitated rather than slow.) The introduction consists of the front of the first sheet; the fast close consists of the back of the final sheet. All between is development.

	Kasen (36 stanzas)	*Hyakuin (100 stanzas)*
Jo: Introduction	1–6	1–8
Ha: Development	7–30	9–92
Kyū: Fast close	31–36	93–100

The Modeling of *Oku no Hosomichi* on Haikai Sequences

As the discussion in chapter 4 suggests, it is now widely accepted that Bashō patterns his narrative on this jo-ha-kyū rhythm. When Sora's *Diary* was recovered in the 1940s, there was initial shock to discover that Bashō had made up the episode of meeting with penitent prostitutes at Ichiburi no Seki. It is now appreciated why Bashō should want such an episode. Unlike masters in the other schools of haikai, he continued to insist on the importance of love as a subject and as a means of agitating or destabilizing in the second stage of the introduction-development–fast close rhythm.

There are limits to the possible application of that rhythm and the haikai model more generally to *The Narrow Road*. A haikai sequence was factual only in its first stanza, which necessarily made use of the circumstances of place and time where the poets found themselves. All subsequent stanzas are fictional. Although there are fictional touches here and there, and although Bashō is a master of omission by selection, what he does include in his narrative is very largely factual and verifiable from Sora's *Diary*. For more extensive discussion of these canons and details, see the full account in Konishi 1971 or the briefer one in English, Miner 1979b.

Yet it is the degree of application of haikai canons rather than their limits that must strike every reader comparing Bashō's account not only with Johnson's and Boswell's but also with Sora's. In his opening passage, Bashō quotes a hokku he composed on leaving his Banana Plant Hermitage, or Bashō An, and says that he attached it to a pillar along with the other seven stanzas making up the eight of a front side of the first of four sheets of a hundred-stanza haikai. An increasing number of commentators on *The Narrow Road through the Provinces* had been saying ever more positively that the work fits with the design of a haikai sequence. Andō Tsuguo advanced the analogy into a strong argument that Bashō's work was closely modeled on a hundred-stanza sequence, apparently using Bashō's remark about composing the front of a first sheet to attach to the pillar of his hermitage.

> If we envision *The Narrow Road* in terms of the four sheets of a haikai sequence in emulation of one in a hundred stanzas [hyakuin], the first sheet extends to the passing of Shirakawa, the second to the end of the Hiraizumi episode, the third through Yamanaka hot springs, and the fourth or last sheet from Sora's departure to Bashō's arrival in Ōgaki. (Andō 1974, 181)

The closeness of his comparison is suggested by his remarking that, so divided according to the four sheets of a hyakuin, *The Narrow Road* shows "no great departure" from the established pattern for Moons and Flowers.

If we match Andō's proposed divisions to the forty-one pages of the translation in *Diaries,* we can see what is entailed. The places can be understood in detail by consultation with appendix 1. Moon and Flower stanzas will also be indicated. Compare with the pattern of the hyakuin previously given.

Andō's Division as for a Hyakuin

Sheet 1. Through Shirakawa no Seki. Pages 1–9 (9 pages).
   Moons at pp. 1, 16, 18. Flower at p. 2.
Sheet 2. Through Hiraizumi. Pages 10–21 (11–12 pages).
   Moons at pp. 16, 18. Flower at p. 10.
Sheet 3. Through Yamanaka. Pages 21–35 (14 pages).
   Moons at pp. 26 (twice), 27 (twice), 32. No Flower.
Sheet 4. To End. Pages 36–41 (6–7 pages).
   Moons at 36, 39 (3 times). No Flower.

Judging by the rules of linked poetry, there are twelve Moons and two Flowers. Four of the Moons appear near the end where none is expected, and there is no Flower after the first page for the second sheet. Whether or not this is "no great departure" must be a matter of judgment. The greatest objection to raise against Andō's excellent suggestion is, however, his taking as an equivalent of the fourth sheet so brief a portion of the whole: his sheets are respectively about nine, twelve, fourteen, and six pages, which seems awkward. For page equivalents (from a total of forty) of the eight sides of the four sheets of a hyakuin, we would expect the front of the first sheet and the back of the fourth to be two pages in length, and the other sides six pages each. Andō does not speak of sides but only sheets. Yet his suggested proportioning can be compared with that on which a hyakuin is founded.

Proportioning a Hyakuin to 40 Units (pages)

Standard Proportions	Andō's Proportions
Sheet 1: 8 Stanzas	Sheet 1: 10 stanzas
Front 2, Back 6	
Sheet 2: 12 Stanzas	Sheet 2: 12 stanzas
Front 6, Back 6	
Sheet 3: 12 Stanzas	Sheet 3: 14 stanzas
Front 6, Back 6	
Sheet 4: 8 Stanzas	Sheet 4: 6 stanzas
Front 6, Back 2	

Given the discrepancies, it is conceivable that Andō had in mind not narrative lengths but distances traveled. But if so, that would seem to require explanation. There is a greater problem still in trying to ascertain from his model any sense of the jo-ha-kyū rhythm.

In the spirit of his insight, we can consider an alternative. That is simply using the proportions for a kasen of thirty-six stanzas instead of following a design for a hyakuin. Again, compare with the set form of the kasen, given above.

> Sheet 1. Edo-Hiraizumi. Pp. 1–21. (21 pp.).
>> Front. Edo-Ashino. Pp. 1–8 (7 pp.).
>>> Moon at p. 1. Flower at p. 2.
>> Back. Shirakawa-Hiraizumi. Pp. 8–21 (14 pp.).
>>> Moons at pp. 16, 18. Flower at p. 10.
> Sheet 2. Hiraizumi-End. Pp. 21–41 (20 pp.)
>> Front. Hiraizumi-Yamanaka. Pp. 21–35 (14 pp.).
>>> Moons at 26, 26; 27, 27; 32. No Flower.
>> Back. Sora Departs-End. Pp. 35–41 (6 pp.).
>>> Moons at 36; 39, 39, 39. No Flower.

There are still supernumerary Moons and no Flower at the equivalent of the thirty-fifth stanza. But both sides of the first sheet are close to actual practice. Also, Bashō could hardly introduce a Flower stanza in the autumn season of the back of the second sheet. What is more important, the jo-ha-kyū rhythm is honored far better.

> Jo   Pp. 1–7. Front, first sheet. Edo-Ashino.

> Ha   Pp. 8–21. Back, first sheet. Shirakawa-Hiraizumi.
>   Pp. 21–35. Front, second sheet. Shitomae no Seki-Yamanaka.

> Kyū   Pp. 35–41. Back, second sheet. Sora Departs-End.

The kasen pattern has the great virtue, then, of rendering the jo or introduction and the kyū or fast close into equal length and in just proportion of one-third (one-sixth each) to the two-thirds of the ha or development section between. The kasen pattern has a second virtue in being the design that Bashō actually favored and practiced as a matter of choice.

From this examination, any reader can judge the degree of use Bashō makes of his haikai pattern to order his *Oku no Hosomichi*. Insistence on exact correspondence seems both impossible to sustain and misguided conceptually as what would be of use to Bashō. It seems wiser to consider the usefulness of a kasen as a general rather than exact model for the patterning of the narrative and the jo-ha-kyū rhythm. In addition, nothing else explains so well the fluctuations in tone in his work. That is, extremes like his following the magnificence of Hiraizumi and Hikaridō with the vermin and scatology of Shitomae no Seki correspond to the haikai conceptions and linking of stanzas. As explained in chapter 5, this involves fluctuating use of his episodes: varying topics, subtopics, and motifs; varying impressiveness; and varying degree of closeness of relation between one unit and the next. The topics vary through the three seasons (summer to autumn) of his travels or, lacking a seasonal focus, a stanza a unit is miscellaneous (zō) in topic. Travel is a subtopic throughout, with love, evanescence, and others making their appearance. Among the varying motifs are peaks, watersides, persons, dwellings, night, radiance (sun, moon, stars), and—above all—places of name (nadokoro) with all the rich complexity they bear. On such grounds (and those are really the ones envisioned by Andō) rather than in minute correspondences, Bashō can be held to have modeled *Oku no Hosomichi* on the design of a haikai sequence. And once we agree with recent Japanese critics on that, we understand the terms in which it makes best sense to read what the Old Man so carefully provides for us.

Bibliography

Tokyo is the place of publication unless otherwise specified. For a few entries additional information is supplied. See also Abbreviations, on page xix.

Abe Kimio. 1979. *Shōkō Oku no Hosomichi*. Revised and enlarged by Hisatomi Tetsuo. Meiji Shoin. Excellent review of criticism of *Oku no Hosomichi*, including its haikai design.

Alford, Richard D. 1988. *Naming and Identity: A Cross-Cultural Study of Personal Naming Practices*. New Haven: HRAF.

Andō Tsuguo. 1974. *Bashō, Oku no Hosomichi*. Tankōsha. *Nihon no Tabibito*, 6.

Apollonius of Rhodes. 1959. *The Voyage of Argo*. Trans. E. V. Rieu. Harmondsworth, Middlesex.: Penguin.

Aristotle. 1947. *Introduction to Aristotle*, ed. Richard McKeon. New York: Modern Library. Translation from W. D. Ross's Oxford edition.

Ayer, A. J. 1964. *The Concept of a Person and Other Essays*. London: Macmillan.

Bashō Matsuo. 1959. *Bashō Bunshū*. Ed. Sugiura Shōichirō et al. Iwanami Shoten. *Nihon Koten Bungaku Taikei*, 46.

Baxter, Timothy M. S. 1992. *The Cratylus: Plato's Critique of Naming*. Leiden: E. J. Brill.

Boswell, James. 1948. *Life of Samuel Johnson. L.L.D.* Ed. Chauncey Brewster Tinker. 2 vols. in 1. Oxford: Oxford University Press.

Brodsky-Lacour, Claudia. 1995. "Grounds of Comparison." *World Literature Today* 69:271–74.

Bronson, Bertrand H. 1944. "Johnson and Boswell: Three Essays." *University of California Studies in English* 3:363–476.

Brooke-Rose, Christine. 1958. *A Grammar of Metaphor*. London: Secker and Warburg.

Buson Yosa. 1973. *Oku no Hosomichi Emaki*. Ed. Okada Rihēe. Kyoto: Yutaka Shobō. Buson's famous calligraphic and pictorial version was done in 1779. The portion of the book with pictures is unpaginated.

Byatt, A. S. 1990. *Possession: A Romance*. New York: Vintage Books.

Carroll, John M. 1985. *What's in a Name? An Essay in the Psychology of Reference*. New York: W. H. Freeman.

Chisholm, Roderick M. 1981. *The First Person: An Essay on Reference and Intentionality*. Brighton, Sussex: Harvester.

Cicero, Marcus Tullius. 1971. *The Tusculan Disputations*. Trans. J. E. King. London: Heinemann (Loeb).

Clingham, Greg. 1992. "Boswell's Historiography." *Transactions of the Eighth International Congress on the Enlightenment*. Oxford: Voltaire Foundation.

Cordimer, Charles. 1780. *Antiquities and Scenery of the North of Scotland*. London.

———. 1788. *Remarkable Ruins and Romantic Prospects of North England*. London.

Culler, Jonathan. 1995. "Comparability." *World Literature Today* 69:268–70.

Donnellan, Keith S. 1977. "Speaking of Nothing." In Schwartz 1977, 216–44.

Eliot, George. 1973. "Janet's Repentance," In *Scenes of Clerical Life*, ed. David Lodge. London: Penguin.

Evans, J. M. 1968. *Paradise Lost and the Genesis Tradition*. Oxford: Clarendon.

Ferry, Anne. 1988. *The Art of Naming*. Chicago: University of Chicago Press.

Fisch, Harold. 1967. "Hebraic Style and Motifs in *Paradise Lost*." In *Language and Style in Milton*, ed. Ronald David Emma and John T. Shawcross, 30–64. New York: Frederick Ungar.

Fokkema, Douwe. 1989. "Towards a Methodology in Intercultural Studies." In *Aspects of Comparative Literature: Current Approaches*, ed. Chandra Mohan, 117–30. New Delhi: India Publishers.

Fowler, Edward. 1988. *The Rhetoric of Confession: Shishōsetsu in Early Twentieth-Century Japanese Fiction*. Berkeley and Los Angeles: University of California Press.

Grose, Thomas. 1797. *The Antiquities of Scotland*. London.

Hagstrum, Jean H. 1967. *Samuel Johnson's Literary Criticism*. 2d ed. Chicago: University of Chicago Press.

Hospers, John. 1948. *Meaning and Truth in the Arts*. Chapel Hill: University of North Carolina Press.

Iser, Wolfgang. 1993. *The Fictive and the Imaginary: Charting Literary Anthropology*. Baltimore: Johns Hopkins University Press.

Itō Sei et al. 1968. *Shinchō Nihon Bungaku Shōjiten*. Shinchōsha.

Jacobs, Noah Jonathan. 1969. *Naming-Day in Eden: The Creation and Recreation of Language*. Oxford: Clarendon.

Jowett, Benjamin. 1892. *The Dialogues of Plato*. 5 vols. 3d ed. Oxford: Clarendon.

———. 1900. *Thucydides*. 2 vols. 2d ed. Oxford: Clarendon.

Katagiri Yōichi. 1983. *Utamakura Utakotoba*. Kadokawa Shoten.

Konishi Jin'ichi. 1971. *Sōgi*. Chikuma Shobō.

———. 1984. *A History of Japanese Literature*. Vol. 1. Princeton: Princeton University Press.

———. 1986. *Nihon Bungeishi*. Vol. 4. Kōdansha.

———. 1991. *A History of Japanese Literature*. Vol. 3. Princeton: Princeton University Press.

Kripke, Saul A. 1980. *Naming and Necessity*. Cambridge, Mass.: Harvard University Press. Rev. ed.

Kuriyama Riichi. 1963. *Haikaishi*. Takama Senjo.

———. 1981. *Bashō no Haikai Biron*. Takama Shobō.

Lascelles, Mary, ed. 1971. *A Journey to the Western Islands of Scotland*, by Samuel Johnson. New Haven: Yale University Press.

Leonard, John. 1990. *Naming in Paradise: Milton and the Language of Adam and Eve*. Oxford: Clarendon.

Lévi-Strauss, Claude. 1966. *The Savage Mind.* Chicago: University of Chicago Press.

Melas, Natalie. 1995. "Versions of Incommensurability." *World Literature Today* 69:275–80.

Mill, John Stuart. 1976. *Essays on Poetry.* Ed. C. Parvin Sharples. Columbia: University of South Carolina Press.

Miner, Earl. 1958. "Dr. Johnson, Mandeville, and 'Publick Benefits.'" *Huntington Library Quarterly* 21:159–66.

———. 1959. "The Making of *The Deserted Village.*" *Huntington Library Quarterly* 22:125–41.

———, ed. and trans. 1969. *Japanese Poetic Diaries.* Berkeley and Los Angeles: University of California Press.

———. 1976. "That Literature Is a Kind of Knowledge." *Critical Inquiry* 2:487–518.

———. 1978–79. "The Genesis and Development of Poetic Systems." *Critical Inquiry* 5:339–53, 533–68.

———. 1979a. *Japanese Linked Poetry.* Princeton: Princeton University Press.

———. 1979b. "Some Remarks on the Question of Literary Values." *Southern Review* (Adelaide), 12:45–62.

———. 1983. "The Grounds of Mimetic and Nonmimetic Art: The Western Sister Arts in a Japanese Mirror." In *Articulate Images,* ed. Richard Wendorf, 70–97. Minneapolis: University of Minnesota Press.

———. 1984. "Milton and the Histories." In *Politics of Discourse,* ed. Kevin Sharpe and Steven N. Zwicker, 181–203, 335–38. Berkeley and Los Angeles: University of California Press.

———, ed. 1985. *Principles of Classical Japanese Literature.* Princeton: Princeton University Press.

———. 1987. "Some Theoretical and Methodological Topics for Comparative Literature." *Poetics Today* 8:123–40.

———. 1990. *Comparative Poetics: An Intercultural Essay on Theories of Literature.* Princeton: Princeton University Press.

———. 1991. "On the Genesis and Development of Literary Systems II: The Case of India." *Revue de la Littérature Comparée* 65:143–52.

———. 1992. "Fūryū no Hajime—*Oku no Hosomichi* Nadokoro Samazama." *Mugendai,* no. 92 (1992): 17–23.

———. 1995. "Nadokoro to Shite no Shizen—Shirakawa no Seki kara Matsushima e no Bashō no Tabi." In Mori Haruhide, ed., *Fūkei no Shūjigaku.* Eihōsha.

Miner, Earl and Hiroko Odagiri, trans. and eds. 1982. *The Monkey's Straw Raincoat and Other Poetry of the Bashō School.* Princeton: Princeton University Press.

Miner, Earl, Hiroko Odagiri, and Robert E. Morrell. 1985. *The Princeton Companion to Classical Japanese Literature.* Princeton: Princeton University Press.

Mitchell, W. J. T. 1994. *Picture Theory.* Chicago: University of Chicago Press.

Miyoshi, Masao. 1974. *Accomplices of Silence.* Berkeley and Los Angeles: University of California Press.

Morris, Mark. 1986. "Waka and Form, Waka and History." *Harvard Journal of Asiatic Studies* 46:551–610.

Nakamura Hajime. 1962. *Shin Bukkyō Jiten*. Seishin Shobō.

Nakanishi Susumu. 1978. *Kyō no Seishinshi*. Kōdansha.

Nelson, R. J. 1992. *Naming and Reference: The Link of Word to Object*. London: Routledge.

Ogata, Tsutomu. 1994. *Oku No Hosomichi*. Vol. 5 in the Series of Iwanami Kōza, *Nihon Bungaku to Bukkyō*. Iwanami Shoten.

Ogata Tsutomu and Morikawa Akira, eds. 1989. *Oku no Hosomichi Zufu*. Asahi Shimbun Sha.

Ogden, C. K. 1932. *Bentham's Theory of Fictions*. New York: Harcourt Brace.

Pennant, Thomas. 1774. *A Tour in Scotland and Voyage to the Hebrides*. Chester.

Philippi, Donald L. 1968. *Kojiki*. University of Tokyo Press.

Pottle, Frederick A. 1966. *James Boswell: The Earlier Years 1740–1769*. New York: McGraw Hill.

Quennell, Peter. 1972. *Samuel Johnson, His Friends and Enemies*. London: Weidenfeld and Nicolson.

Reed, Barbara Mito. 1985. "Language, Narrative Structure, and the *Shishōsetsu*." Ph.D. diss., Princeton University.

Ricoeur, Paul. 1955–58. *Time and Narrative*. 3 vols. Trans. Kathleen Blamey and David Pellauer. Chicago: University of Chicago Press. Vol. 3 cited.

Rogers, Pat, ed. 1993. *Johnson and Boswell in Scotland: A Journey to the Hebrides*. New Haven: Yale University Press.

Rowlandson, Thomas. 1786. *The Picturesque Beauties of Boswell*. London.

Schwartz, Stephen P., ed. 1977. *Naming, Necessity, and Natural Kinds*. Ithaca: Cornell University Press. Valuable introduction, pp. 13–41.

Schwarz, David S. 1979. *Naming and Referring: The Semantics and Pragmatics of Singular Terms*. Berlin: de Gruyter.

Sekora, John. 1977. *Luxury: The Concept in Western Thought, Eden to Smollett*. Baltimore: Johns Hopkins University Press.

Sora [surname Iwanami, later Kawai]. 1943. *Sora Oku no Hosomichi Zuikō Nikki . . .*, ed. Yamamoto Yasusaburō. Ogawa Shobō. Besides his title diary of the journey with Bashō, this includes: "*Oku no Hosomichi* Haikai Kakitome" ("Haikai Register of . . ."); "*Oku no Hosomichi* Meishō Bibōroku" ("Reminder Notes of Famous Places in . . ."); "*Engi Shiki* Jimmyō Chōshōroku" ("A Compilation of Names of Divinities according to the *Engi Shiki*"); "Sora Genroku Yonen Kinki Jun'yū Nikki" ("Sora's 1691 Diary of a Tour [with Bashō] of Provinces in the Capital Area"); a variant text of *The Narrow Road;* and *Oku no Hosomichi* no Tenkō to Ryoshuku Ichiranhyō" ("A Simplified Chart of Weather and Lodging in . . ."). Sugiura 1959 reprints all but the last and the 1692 *Nikki*.

Sugiura Shōichirō et al., eds. 1959. *Oku no Hosomichi Hyōshaku*. Tōkyōdō. Note that this differs from Bashō 1959, ed. by the same Sugiura et al.

———. 1968. *Oku no Hosomichi*, by Matsuo Bashō [with Sora, *Zuikō Nikki*, etc.]. Iwanami Bunkō.

Tooker, Elisabeth, ed. 1984. *Naming Systems*. Washington: American Ethnological Society.

Tremain, Rose. 1991. *Restoration: A Novel of Seventeenth-Century England*. Harmondsworth, Middlesex: Penguin.

Ueda, Makoto. 1991. *Bashō and His Interpreters: Selected Hokku with Commentary*. Stanford: Stanford University Press.

Vaihinger, Hans. 1924. *The Philosophy of "As If" (Die Philosophie des Als-Ob)*. Trans. C. K. Ogden. London: Kegan Paul.

Valdés, Mario J. 1992. *World-Making: The Literary Truth-Claim and the Interpretation of Texts*. Toronto: University of Toronto Press.

Wain, John. 1974. *Samuel Johnson*. London: Macmillan.

Waley, Arthur. 1949. *The Analects of Confucius*. London: Allen and Unwin.

Watanabe Minoru, ed. 1976. *Ise Monogatari*. In *Shinchō Nihon Koten Shūsei*. Shinchōsha.

Yamada Yoshio, and Hoshika Muneichi (or Sōichi). 1936. *Renga Hōshiki Kōyō*. Iwanami Shoten.

Yang, Vincent. 1991. "The Concept of Naming in Eastern and Western Poetic Traditions," *Tamkang Review* 21:347–75.

Zelditch, Morris. 1971. "Intelligible Comparisons." In *Comparative Methods in Sociology*, ed. Ivan Vallier. Berkeley and Los Angeles: University of California Press, pp. 267–307.

Index

For the accounts and names of the four main authors, fewer but extended entries are given here in lieu of hundreds of bare numerical references to them.

This book has been composed by
Agnew's Electronic Manuscript Processing Service, Inc.
Printed by Braun-Brumfield, Inc.
Copyedited by Richard Isomaki
Book design by Jillian Downey
Jacket design by Lisa Langhoff
Typography: Palatino
Paper: Glatfelter Natural